"This book is a rare treat. New Testament scholars seldom have their basic underlying assumptions about truth, time and the nature of history subjected to careful scrutiny. Yet their assumptions about these notions profoundly shape everything they purport to describe in the name of 'history'. It is then a special opportunity to have Sam Adams's trained philosophical and theological mind probe the assumptions underlying the work of the most widely read New Testament scholar of our day, N. T. Wright. But the result is something rather more than mere learned description. In the hands of Adams's gentle but firm critique, we are lead to a different interpretative place where those critical assumptions concerning truth, time and history are—at least arguably—aligned more accurately and fruitfully with the notion that ultimately informs all valid Christian scholarship: the disclosure of the nature of God in the person of Jesus Christ. Most New Testament scholars pay lip service to this central notion—to this truth above all truths—but do not really know what to do with it, and so tend to lapse back into shabby old historical habits with all their accompanying distortions and vulnerabilities. In graceful conversation with Wright, Adams shows both theologians and New Testament scholars exactly what to do with it."

Douglas A. Campbell, Duke University

"At the heart of N. T. Wright's massive and influential output there is a set of fundamental and contestable methodological claims about 'worldview', critical realism and the relationship between theology and history. To date these claims have not been subjected to a thoroughgoing analysis and critique. Samuel Adams takes up that daunting and crucial task with great intelligence, maturity and grace in this timely, groundbreaking work on Wright's theological method. The result, however, goes beyond the engagement with Wright. In the end Adams makes his own constructive contribution to theology today by proposing an 'apocalyptic' understanding of the reality of God in history. Followers of Wright will be challenged by this book. Theologians will be reminded that the gospel is not a method, but the power of God in the word of the cross."

Douglas Harink, The King's University, Edmonton, Canada

"What does it mean for theologians and biblical scholars to take seriously the singular apocalypse of Jesus Christ? This question lies at the heart of Samuel Adams's important volume. His wise, generous and learned response moves apocalyptic theology forward in unsettling and significant ways."

Beverly Roberts Gaventa, Baylor University

"N. T. Wright is widely recognized to be the most influential Christian thinker since C. S. Lewis and a leading biblical scholar recently wrote that 'he may well be the most widely read and influential New Testament scholar of all time'! Despite this, there has been limited engagement with his theological methodology and suppositions. This impressive monograph combines academic scholarship of a high order with penetrating theological insight to provide a level of critical engagement with Wright's approach that we have not yet witnessed. Adams draws on the immense strengths in Wright's program while offering critical yet constructive theological engagement of a kind that significantly advances the discussion of his work. As such it is an outstanding theological introduction to what Wright is seeking to accomplish that should also inspire and challenge biblical scholars and theologians to examine the interface between their work and the essential affirmations of the Christian faith. Not only should this book prove invaluable to academics and students alike, but its lucidity and eloquence should also make it accessible to a wider audience. Highly recommended!"

Alan J. Torrance, University of St. Andrews

NEW EXPLORATIONS IN THEOLOGY

THE REALITY OF GOD AND HISTORICAL METHOD

APOCALYPTIC THEOLOGY IN CONVERSATION WITH N. T. WRIGHT

SAMUEL V. ADAMS

IVP Academic
An imprint of InterVarsity Press
Downers Grove, Illinois

InterVarsity Press
P.O. Box 1400, Downers Grove, IL 60515-1426
ivpress.com
email@ivpress.com

InterVarsity Press® is the book-publishing division of InterVarsity Christian Fellowship/USA®, a movement of students and faculty active on campus at hundreds of universities, colleges and schools of nursing in the United States of America, and a member movement of the International Fellowship of Evangelical Students. For information about local and regional activities, visit intervarsity.org.

Scripture quotations, unless otherwise noted, are from the New Revised Standard Version of the Bible, copyright 1989 by the Division of Christian Education of the National Council of the Churches of Christ in the USA. Used by permission. All rights reserved.

Cover design: Cindy Kiple
Interior design: Beth McGill

ISBN 978-0-8308-4914-7 (print)
ISBN 978-0-8308-9950-0 (digital)

Printed in the United States of America ∞

Library of Congress Cataloging-in-Publication Data
Adams, Samuel V., 1972-
 The reality of God and historical method : apocalyptic theology in conversation with N.T. Wright / Samuel V. Adams.
  pages cm.—(New explorations in theology)
 Includes bibliographical references and index.
 ISBN 978-0-8308-4914-7 (pbk. : alk. paper)
 1. End of the world. 2. History—Religious aspects—Christianity. 3. Theology—Methodology.
4. Wright, N. T. (Nicholas Thomas) I. Title.
 BT877.A33 2015
 236—dc23

                                                                                    2015033923

P	23	22	21	20	19	18	17	16	15	14	13	12	11	10	9	8	7	6	5	4	3	2	1
Y	35	34	33	32	31	30	29	28	27	26	25	24	23	22	21	20	19	18	17	16	15

For Andrea,

You're the keeper of the flame

And you burn so bright.

Contents

Acknowledgments   9

Abbreviations   13

Introduction   15

1 History and Theology According to the Historian:
   N. T. Wright's Historical and Theological Method   20
      The Historical Context   22
      From Critique to Construct   33
      Conclusion   63

2 Theology According to the Theologians:
   Critical Realism and the Object of Knowledge in Theology   65
      CRw and the Object of Knowledge   67
      The Condition: Søren Kierkegaard   83
      John 3:1-21   99
      Conclusion   103

3 Apocalyptic, Continuity and Discontinuity:
   Soteriological Implications for a Theology of History   107
      A Rupture in Understanding: A Properly Theological
        Hermeneutic Is Apocalyptic   110
      Apocalyptic and Soteriology: Beginning with the
        New Beginning   126
      Conclusion   140

4 Christology and Creation: Furthering the Apocalyptic Logic   141
      Christology: *Anhypostasia* and *Enhypostasia*   141
      Creation and Apocalyptic   152
      N. T. Wright and Apocalyptic Reconsidered   166
      Conclusion   171

5 History According to the Theologians:

  From a Theology of History to a Theology of Historiography   173

    Toward a Theology of History and Historiography   173

    A Theology of History   183

    Historiography According to Theology: Three Theses   204

    Conclusion   227

6 An Apocalyptic Reappraisal of Apocalyptic   228

    The Controversy   232

    Apocalypses and the Covenant: Reading Irruption

      in the Context of a Long Story   237

    Paul's Epistemology   240

    Apocalypse and the Apocalyptic Logic of the

      Singular Apocalypse   247

    The Apocalypse of Jesus Christ as an Apocalypse   259

    The Question of Israel   261

    Conclusion   269

7 Conclusion   271

Bibliography   275

Author and Subject Index   287

Scripture Index   293

Acknowledgments

IF WITHIN THESE PAGES there is a good argument, theological insight and a faithful treatment of Scripture, it is in large part due to the enormous influence of those teachers from whom I have had the privilege to learn over the last two decades. My doctoral supervisor at the University of St. Andrews, Alan Torrance, has been an enthusiastic and challenging mentor who consistently kept me focused on the question, "Does it matter?" More than an encouragement to relevance, this question was a direct challenge in the tedium of doctoral work to bear faithful witness to the priority of God's gracious act in Jesus Christ. In this and many other ways Alan's clear, sharp intellect and wisdom have been profoundly formative for my own life of teaching and scholarship. And yet, it is his friendship that will remain his greatest gift to me and to my family.

Others who have contributed to my theological development while at St. Andrews and who deserve mention include Trevor Hart and Grant Macaskill. Kendall Soulen and Paul Martens were visiting scholars while I was struggling through early stages of my doctoral work, and each of them in their own way had a transforming effect. Conversations with Douglas Harink were also helpful as I began to look more closely at N. T. Wright's historical and theological method. Prior to St. Andrews, and going back to my undergraduate days at Westmont College, I was deeply influenced by Jonathan R. Wilson, who, with passion and precision, introduced me to the fascinating world of the doctrine of the Trinity. Jonathan was also my systematic theology teacher at Fuller Theological Seminary and has been a wonderful conversation partner ever since. This whole theological journey was begun at Westmont when Michael McClymond introduced me to Kierkegaard's *Fragments*, and provided the opportunity to teach our Modern Christianity class, an event that launched the long and circuitous journey that has now led, among other things, to this book.

Many thanks are also in order to Tom Wright, whose willingness to take seriously my stumbling "apocalyptic" theology in formal seminars or conversations over coffee has been a significant encouragement to this entire project. Prior to publication he has neither read this book nor engaged in a deep way with the unique arguments it advances, a point that must be mentioned at the outset. It is my sincerest hope that he is honored by this engagement, for both his friendship and scholarship have been, and continue to be, gifts that I hold dear.

Family, friends and church have all, in large and small ways, contributed to the completion of this project. My parents, Phil and Dottie Adams, have encouraged me in this direction from the very beginning; there is no greater gift than a home ordered around the reality of God and in which the Christian faith is central and intellectual inquiry and discussion are encouraged. Marion Wells opened doors that seemed impossible to open and has become family in the process. Conversations with Andrew Hay, who sat next to me in the Roundel at St. Mary's, helped to shine much-needed light into the dark Scottish days filled with thesis writing and research. Over the past decade, with a short three-year stopover at the Free Church in St. Andrews, Bend Mennonite Church in Central Oregon has been that Christian community with whom my family has prayed, worshiped, struggled and rejoiced. Their support has been the display of God's abundance in our life.

The completion of my doctoral thesis and now this present book took place during my first two years teaching and directing the new graduate program in social justice at Kilns College in Bend, Oregon. My students have been wonderful conversation partners and, with their astute questions and deep concern for God's justice, a constant reminder to me why a theology in submission to the reality of the living God is so important. My thanks especially go out to my assistant (assistant *to* the director), David Miller, and to my colleagues at Kilns: Ken Wytsma, Melissa McCreery and Mike Caba.

My wife, Andrea, and children, Owen, Everett and Eleni, have been and continue to be the source of greatest joy, keeping my apocalyptic theological musings firmly rooted in the day-to-day holiness of family chaos. Above all, Andrea's faithful friendship, her deep concern for the wholeness of our family and her joy for our life together have been the abundance out of which this work could flow. This book is dedicated to her.

Abbreviations

WORKS BY N. T. WRIGHT

Christian Origins and the Question of God series

The New Testament and the People of God	NTPG
Jesus and the Victory of God	JVG
The Resurrection of the Son of God	RSG
Paul and the Faithfulness of God	PFG

Other frequently cited, edited works

Jesus, Paul and the People of God	JPPG
Jesus and the Restoration of Israel	JRI

Introduction

NOBODY LIKES BOOKS ON METHOD. This is a book on method. As Jeffrey Stout has famously written, "preoccupation with method is like clearing your throat: it can go on for only so long before you lose your audience."[1] It is also true that there are defenders of method. Method is, in one sense, simply a reflection on assumptions; to assume without examination is to be trapped in an unwitting solipsism. No one does theology in a vacuum, and there is no Archimedean perspective from which to lift the weight of the subject matter with the ever-elusive lever of objectivity. Without reflection on method we would all be the masters of our own Procrustean beds. The postmodern situation, whatever it is, is at least an awareness that we all start embedded in contexts and language games that need every once in a while to "be dug out and inspected."[2] To dig out and inspect is also a contextual exercise, and around and around we go. . . . My task in this book on historical and theological method is not to limit myself to methodological questions, but to engage these questions within a constructive theological argument. The central part of this book, then, reads more like the beginnings of a systematic theology; it is systematic to the extent that it argues for a particular, sequential logic as Christian dogmatics are brought into conversation with the question of historical method. This book is also a critique, a critical dialogue with one of today's preeminent

---

[1]Jeffrey Stout, *Ethics After Babel: The Languages of Morals and Their Discontents* (Princeton, NJ: Princeton University Press, 2001), 163.
[2]*NTPG*, 117.

biblical scholars, N. T. Wright. Wright's work on method sets the stage, and his continuing work on the question of God in the New Testament provides the primary dialogical material for my constructive arguments. But more than anything this book is an exercise in thinking beyond the question of God for theology and history to the question of the *reality* of God, and what methodological impositions are necessarily implied for both areas of inquiry.

If Ernst Troeltsch was right in saying that the intellectual revolutions of the sixteenth century introduced a crisis for Christianity of "world-historical dimensions,"[3] and that this crisis made the traditional historical basis of Christianity untenable, then the work of N. T. Wright has been a major force in answering that crisis with the scientific and methodological rigor needed to restore the historical grounding of traditional orthodox Christianity. Troeltsch, of course, was working within the modern problematic created by Lessing's "ugly ditch," the gap between the "contingent truths of history" and the "necessary truths of reason."[4] Ever since Lessing published and commented on Reimarus's treatise, modern religious thinkers have produced a variety of attempts to overcome this gap and provide the believer with the appropriate conception of the relationship between historical events and the experience of faith. Given the total cultural influence of Christianity in Europe, these debates all centered around the historical question of Jesus and the significance his historicity could have for faith. Troeltsch asks the paradigmatic question as it addresses the modern crisis: "Whether we possess enough certain knowledge about him to understand historically the emergence of Christianity, let alone justify attaching religious faith and conviction to the historical fact."[5]

To the first of these concerns, Wright has done a significant amount of work, making strong historical arguments that make sense of the emergence of Christianity as it is inseparably linked to the messianic event that took place around the historic person of Jesus of Nazareth. The first three volumes in his Christian Origins and the Question of God series develop a significant and coherent account of the historical forces that led a first-century Jew to be crucified and for his followers to come to the conclusion that he was indeed

---

[3]Ernst Troeltsch, *Writings on Theology and Religion*, trans. and ed. Robert Morgan and Michael Pye (Louisville: Westminster John Knox, 1990), 185.
[4]Gotthold Ephraim Lessing, *Philosophical and Theological Writings*, trans. and ed. H. B. Nisbet (Cambridge: Cambridge University Press, 2005), 85.
[5]Troeltsch, *Writings on Theology and Religion*, 182.

who he claimed to be. To the second concern Wright also directs his attention, raising the overall question in his series as the very question that, according to Lessing, cannot be asked; that is, he raises the question of God. How can he, and for that matter, anybody, move from the historical questions to the theological question? How does Wright move from historical arguments to theological ones? Are his moves valid? Do they overcome the broad, ugly ditch?

Of course, it can be argued that the modern assumption behind Lessing's gap is simply wrong. There is no gap. This is just how knowledge works. To a large extent this is the sort of move that Wright makes. He rethinks the way we know things historically and theologically so that the gap loses its central force. It remains to be seen if this attempt succeeds. The purpose of this book, then, is to examine the question of God, as Wright appropriately focuses our attention, but to examine it *not* from the historian's side of things but rather from the side of the theologian. Can what theologians say about God make sense of both the historical question and the theological question and articulate them in such a way that does justice to both? At its most basic level, the question I am asking is this: What does the reality of God mean for historical knowledge? This is, after all, what theologians do best: they allow the reality of God to determine their method and attempt to conform their formulations and systems as best as they can to this reality. Of course, it often works the other way around! There is no shortage of theology that has endeavored, wittingly or unwittingly, to conform God to human formulations and limits.[6] Nevertheless, it makes sense to ask the historian who is investigating God, even "the question of God," to do what theologians ought to do, that is, to work out a method that somehow makes room for the reality of the god in question.

To make the central question of this present work hinge upon the reality of God is also to associate it with a particular theological trajectory (if not a definite tradition) that has attempted to accommodate theological work to the priority of the living and active Word of God. This trajectory, roughly sketched and with many missing voices, follows from the Protestant Reformation to Søren Kierkegaard; from Kierkegaard's radical opposition to Christendom it

---

[6]One way this unwittingly happens is through the pronouns we use to refer to God. Our overwhelming use of masculine pronouns in reference to God tends to conform God to cultural norms of masculinity. Nevertheless, my own prose and many of the sources referenced in these pages use this traditional formula and, rather than attempt the awkward reconfiguration of this use through various devices, I have let this use stand. I ask only for the reader's patience in this area.

proceeds to Karl Barth, Dietrich Bonhoeffer and, more recently, to T. F. Torrance. A contemporary appropriation of the basic insights of Kierkegaard, Barth and Bonhoeffer have been brought together with a certain reading of Paul led, in the United States, by J. Louis Martyn, which is now going by the name *apocalyptic theology*.[7] While remaining controversial, this movement is neither "closed" nor definite, so it remains to be seen exactly how its particular contribution will emerge and what difference it will have on the overall theological scene. It is from within this trajectory, roughly termed *apocalyptic*, that the question of the reality of God for historical method that I am addressing will both be articulated and answered. By choosing this trajectory from which to mount a critique of Wright's method, I am simply affirming that it offers a particular tradition of theological questioning that cannot be avoided if the aim of this book's thesis is to be accomplished. In other words, to raise these questions against the background of Wright's historical method is to oblige oneself to engage this apocalyptic trajectory. In this sense, then, this book is an apocalyptic critique of the theological and historical method of the work of N. T. Wright. But it engages in this critique not only in order to bring together two unique perspectives, but also to further both the understanding of the theological implications of Wright's work and the development of this apocalyptic theological trajectory.

The book moves ahead in six chapters. The first is an overview and description of Wright's historical and theological method as they both are grounded in his critical realist epistemology. The second chapter argues for a particular theological epistemology that goes beyond and corrects the epistemological and hermeneutical prolegomena of Wright's major project. This is where the constructive theological contribution begins. In the third and fourth chapters the apocalyptic approach is defined and articulated according to a progression from soteriology to Christology to creation. Then, in the fifth chapter, this theological work is directed first to a theology of

---

[7]The reader should bear in mind the difference between apocalyptic as a specific kind of *theology* and apocalyptic as a specific literary *genre*. In order to avoid using scare quotes throughout the book, I have instead left it up to context to determine which meaning of the word is operative. The contested status of "apocalyptic" will be addressed in chapter three and will be the subject of the final chapter, in which the implications of my argument will be traced with specific reference to the way in which Wright interprets the term *apocalyptic* and its usefulness for constructive theological proposals. At this point I simply ask for patience and openness from readers as I employ this term.

history and then finally to a theology of historiography that is presented in critical dialogue with Wright's historical method. The sixth and final chapter brings together the apocalyptic theology and evaluation of Wright's method into critical engagement with the question of apocalyptic literature and Pauline apocalyptic. What does it mean to say that Paul was an apocalyptic thinker? How does Wright articulate this, and how might the methodological and theological arguments presented in the previous chapters respond to Wright's concerns, as well as open doors to new ways of imagining the relationship between history and theology? Finally, this chapter argues for an apocalyptic theology that takes seriously both the covenant with Israel and the new creation in such a way that holds together a commitment to the present reality of history and, at the same time, to the radical rupture and discontinuity that the apocalypse of Jesus Christ is for this history.

1

History and Theology
According to the Historian

N. T. Wright's Historical and Theological Method

IN ONE SECTION OF N. T. WRIGHT'S *Jesus and the Victory of God*, the repetition of the phrase *serious history*[1] signals one of the underlying concerns of Wright's entire project, a project that aims at restoring the relationship between Christian theology and methodologically rigorous historical scholarship. This concern for renewed attention to the work of historians for the sake of theological discourse signals a renewed confidence in the *results* of historical scholarship to both encourage and correct orthodox Christian faith. This occurs through a more nuanced and careful understanding of the relationship between Christian theology and the historical events that gave rise to the Christian movement.

> The Christian is committed to the belief that certain things are true about the past. . . . This belief will drive the Christian to history, as a hypothesis drives the scientist to the laboratory. . . . The appeal to history with which the Enlightenment challenged the dogmatic theology of the eighteenth century and after is one which can and must be taken on board within the mainline Christian theological worldview.[2]

---

[1]See *JVG*, 83-89.
[2]*NTPG*, 136. See also Wright, "Whence and Whither Historical Jesus Studies in the Life of the Early Church?," *JPPG*, 155-56.

Here Wright makes two points that need to be foregrounded before going further. First, his entire project is premised upon the commitment of the Christian faith to the reality of the events to which it refers. This commitment, however, leaves the description—both historical and theological—open to be informed and corrected by a proper historical method.[3] Second, the critical turn to rigorous history during the Enlightenment, while seemingly detrimental to faith, is nevertheless a necessary development if the first point is to be taken to be axiomatic.

In light of these two points, Wright's project develops within his own telling of the history of the relationship between theological and biblical scholarship as it has been shaped by historical forces, whether political, philosophical or theological. His account is at once both a declension narrative and a hopeful, programmatic call for a renewed commitment to serious history. In short, the Enlightenment's historical project rejected the a priori of faith because, in the eyes of the enlightened, it skewed the results of historical investigation away from that which could be known as fact. It did this unaware that it was making just as questionable assumptions under the guise of freedom and objectivity. Yet even as it imported its own problematic set of assumptions, the Enlightenment nevertheless provided an important turn to the significance of scientific historical investigation and the importance of the historical question for the Christian faith. This is a lesson that the church is still struggling to learn. Without history, and the corrective that the discipline provides, "there is no check on Christianity's propensity to remake Jesus, never mind the Christian god, in its own image."[4] The historian stands as an important point of contact between the past events that make up the source of Christianity's confessions and the theologian's efforts to articulate the significance of those events for contexts that present themselves ever anew.

In *NTPG* Wright identifies three movements within the history of Western culture that transformed the way the New Testament is read. These three historical movements are the following: (1) pre-Enlightenment: pre-critical reading; (2) Enlightenment/modernity: historical and theological reading; and (3) postmodernity: postmodern reading.[5] This chapter will

---

[3]See, for example, *JVG*, 121.
[4]*NTPG*, 10.
[5]Ibid., 7.

begin by examining the way in which Wright depicts the dynamic relationship between history and theology as it undergoes significant philosophical, theological and political pressures during each of these three periods, and how this history has come to determine the place of history vis-à-vis theology today.[6] Moving from Wright's narrative to his constructive proposal, I will focus on the history/theology relationship that is corrected by his account of "critical realism" (CR). This means looking for the way he articulates the problems relating history and theology from the perspective of his constructive, critically realist proposal. My articulation of Wright's method will largely be based upon a reading of his account of the various quests for the historical Jesus in *JVG*, and his methodological reflections in the first two parts of *NTPG*.

The thesis of this chapter is that Wright's methodological proposals are specifically designed to reconcile theology and history, and to do so in such a way that their reconciliation is philosophically justified according to a particular epistemological theory (CR). Wright's version of CR is designed to answer the problem of history and theology, but in doing so he leaves the ontological and metaphysical questions unanswered. Yet it is just these questions that need to be addressed in order for Wright's CR to be true to the unique objects of both history and theology. In support of this thesis, the broad task of this chapter will be to describe (1) the threefold historical context in which Wright has set this return to the historian's task, (2) Wright's specific critique of this context in his constructive account of CR and (3) an examination of the questions that his critical realist proposal raises for a continued program of reconciliation between history and theology.

THE HISTORICAL CONTEXT

From the Precritical Period to the Reformation

Wright bases his programmatic retrieval of the discipline of history for the-

---

[6]Wright names three disciplines that the study of the New Testament involves: literature, history and theology. I am focusing my attention on the latter two, leaving the literary questions aside. This is not because they are unrelated, for I take it that these three disciplines are integral to one another, but rather for the sake of clarity and as a way of limiting the following discussion. In any case, Wright sees the core issue at the heart of each discipline to be epistemological. See *NTPG*, 31.

ology and biblical studies in a narrative that begins with the Reformation. When reading Wright's work it is hard to find an ecclesial situation or historical moment when things were exactly right. Yet if he is telling a declension narrative, it is one that has its high point in the simple, pre-Enlightenment assumption that the Bible reports actual occurrences and that the veracity of its stories are what we would consider today to be "historical." The Bible was assumed to be speaking of real events. This is not to say that this assumption is without its own problems, only that the assumption that Christian belief is inextricably bound together with beliefs about historical events is the right assumption to have. Nevertheless, prior to the critical movements of the Enlightenment, the situation of Christians vis-à-vis history was such that it could "today be criticized on (at least) three grounds . . . : it fails to take the text seriously historically, it fails to integrate it into the theology of the New Testament as a whole, and it is insufficiently critical of its own presuppositions and standpoint."[7] Without the safeguards of a proper historical discipline, these criticisms come to characterize Wright's declension narrative. In *JVG*, Wright tells the story of modern historical Jesus studies by beginning with the pre-Enlightenment, precritical context of the sixteenth-century Reformers. What particular shift, in Wright's view, did the Reformation effect that might signal a declension away from a more healthy—if only intuitive—union of theology and history?

Pro me. During the Reformation, as Wright tells it, a significant shift occurred as doctrines became centered around the question of benefits *pro me*,[8] or how the teachings of the Christian church were soteriologically efficacious within the current situation of the individual Christian living in Europe.[9] This meant that the narrative contexts in which the Christian teachings made sense were discarded in favor of more propositional formulations that could be articulated in a variety of confessions with certainty and clarity. In the practical use of the Bible, this looked like a favoring of the more theologically oriented epistles over the more narrative-based Gospels.[10] While this benefitted the need for doctrinal clarity in the face of ecclesial abuse, the negative

---

[7]Ibid.
[8]*JVG*, 15.
[9]Ibid., 16.
[10]Ibid., 14-15.

result was that the stories that made sense of the doctrines and in which they found their proper horizon of meaning were lost precisely as the crucial hermeneutical context for the teaching of the church. Jesus' death and resurrection made sense according to the demands of a newly reinvigorated personal soteriology, yet the stories that made up the bulk of the Gospels, that made sense "historically" of why Jesus was crucified (i.e., social, cultural, political and economic reasons), were seen to be of lesser importance. Thus, the ecclesiological and political break with Rome can be seen to be analogous to the theological movement away from the historical particularity of Jesus and its significance for the pressing questions of the day.[11] According to this narrative, we could say that the doctrinal controversies that made up the Reformation took the historical basis of the Christian faith for granted, focusing instead on the sources of the tradition, the texts themselves, as the basis of the propositional content of Christian theology. The Bible itself came to replace the historical events to which the Bible bore witness.

For Wright this is all quite nicely displayed in Philip Melanchthon's (1497–1560) dictum, *Hoc est Christum cognoscere, beneficia eius cognoscere*: to know Christ is to know his benefits. After quoting the dictum in *JVG*, Wright quotes Melanchthon's following question: "Unless one knows why Christ took upon himself human flesh and was crucified what advantage would accrue from having learned his life's history?"[12] In *NTPG* and *JVG*, the *pro me* of the gospel is identified with the benefits of Christ that Melanchthon prioritizes, and Wright interprets these benefits against the historical question of Jesus. Melanchthon's dictum stands for this rupture between Christology and the historical Jesus. In the context of politically charged theological disputes, in which rupture and discontinuity were both threat and possibility, the Reformation, on the side of discontinuity, set the stage theologically (and politically) for the major philosophical shifts that were to come with the Enlightenment. According to Wright, by prioritizing doctrines over history according to the criterion of *pro me*, the Reformers could, in principle, ignore the historical question and instead settle theological disputes in abstract, conceptual terms. Their concern to break eccle-

---

[11]Ibid., 15. It should be noted that here Wright makes his claim based upon his reading of the modern heirs of the Reformation: Lutherans Martin Kähler and Rudolf Bultmann.
[12]Quoted in *JVG*, 15. Cf. *NTPG*, 22.

sially and politically with the medieval church in favor of continuity with Christ and the apostles by faith came with a similar break with the history of Jesus, the first-century Jew. "Continuity with Christ meant sitting loose to the actuality of Jesus, to his Jewishness, to his own aims and objectives."[13] The Jesus of history could easily be transposed into the abstract, conceptual Christ. By opening this door, the Reformers made it possible for theology, in its movement forward from the Reformation into the crucible of the Enlightenment, to adapt to a variety of new historical claims. This in turn would give theologians an increased freedom to articulate theological claims regardless of changing historical understanding.

History and doctrine. In Wright's account, this "divorce" between history and doctrine became a key moment in the history of theological development. Politically, the question of authority was of such significance during the Reformation that theological innovations surrounding the source of religious authority determined the rise and fall of cities, states and empires. The Reformers set the question up in terms of Scripture, and answered with the doctrine of *sola scriptura*, making the Bible, but especially the proclamation of its doctrines, the source of authority over and against the Roman Catholic magisterium. While this break with the authority of Rome was based upon the Bible itself, the question of authority was never directed to the Bible's historicity, but rested with the teaching of either "pope or preacher."[14] In Wright's understanding, the debates assumed the abstract Christ: "The icon was in place, and nobody asked whether the Christ it portrayed—and in whose name so much good and ill was done—was at all like the Jesus whom it claimed to represent."[15]

The Enlightenment: Idealism and Realism

The Enlightenment and the movement of modernity can be characterized according to a certain paradoxical tension between materialistic empiricism and subjective idealism. The Enlightenment was the era in which the prioritization of reason, following the Renaissance, was realized first in the elevation of objective scientific investigation. The remarkable scientific and

---

[13]*JVG*, 15.
[14]*JVG*, 16.
[15]Ibid.

technological successes that were transforming almost every area of life and inquiry were validations of the transformative power of reason. It was also the era of Immanuel Kant (1724–1804), who radically transformed philosophy into its modern form and made subject-oriented standards of universal reason and criticism dominant. In a paradoxical way, with the Kantian revolution, Gary Dorrien writes, "the seemingly unstoppable march of materialistic empiricism was stopped in its tracks."[16] The Cartesian search for the foundation of knowledge of the external world in the thinking subject turned, by means of Kant's "transcendental move," toward a subjectivism that tended to reject the very possibility of knowledge of external reality. And yet the empirical tradition continued alongside the subjective, leaving us with a modern legacy of profoundly significant technological advancement and conceptually abstract philosophical systems. These two emphases uniquely positioned theology and biblical scholarship in such a way that the tension between them came to determine the next several hundred years of Christian intellectual effort.

On the one hand, there was that which in a broad sense can be termed *realism*, bolstered by empiricism, which was confidently committed to the correspondence between what one observed and what a thing is *in itself*. The successes of the natural sciences in the rapidly expanding knowledge of the physical world were taken as sure evidence confirming the validity of the realist's confident march toward a holistic account of a thoroughly demystified natural world. On the other hand, and in a seemingly contrary move, was the Kantian turn to the subject, the emergence of various manifestations of idealism and the critical theory that developed in the wake of increasing suspicion that any meaning could be found in an object that was not determined by the knowing subject. These two divergent paths, realism and idealism, become crucial to understanding Wright's programmatic retrieval of the study of history for biblical studies and theology.[17] Christian theology

---

[16]Gary Dorrien, *Kantian Reason and Hegelian Spirit: The Idealistic Logic of Modern Theology* (Chichester, West Sussex: Wiley-Blackwell, 2012), 13.

[17]See for example, Wright's use of both terms as he describes the alternative paths taken, with the path from Lessing to Bultmann describing idealism, and Wrede, Räisänen and the "biblical theology" school standing in for realism. See *NTPG*, 21, 25. Colin Gunton, whom Wright cites positively, also makes this distinction by using these two terms. See Gunton, *Enlightenment and Alienation: An Essay Toward a Trinitarian Theology* (Eugene, OR: Wipf and Stock, 2006 [1985]), 46-47; cf. *NTPG*, 32n3.

could take either path. The first path, that of realism, would move down the road of rigorous historical inquiry—and suffer the consequences. The second, that of idealism,[18] would pick up Christian doctrines and take them away from their historical rootedness and along multiple paths that would include subject-oriented idealism, existentialism and speculative, progressive Hegelian systems. Here, the Hegelian approach is exemplified by D. F. Strauss,[19] while Rudolf Bultmann exemplifies the neo-Kantian trajectory within New Testament interpretation and theology.[20] The latter does so according to modified Heideggerian categories.[21]

The Jesus of history and the Jesus of faith. One way Wright narrates the split between realism and idealism is by telling the story of the origins of the quest for the historical Jesus (in *JVG*). Along the first path, that of historical inquiry, the Enlightenment followed the lead of Reimarus (1694–1768) who in his posthumously published *Fragments* (1788) sought, according to Wright, to "destroy Christianity (as he knew it) at its root, by showing that it rested on historical distortion or fantasy."[22] Following Colin Brown, Wright claims that Reimarus was influenced by the antisupernaturalism of English Deism[23] and instigated the "Quest" for the historical Jesus "as an explicitly anti-theological, anti-Christian, anti-dogmatic movement."[24] Given the political climate and the Enlightenment radicals' motivation (Spinoza, Lessing et al.)[25] to break free from the constraints of tradition, the

---

[18]See *NTPG*, 23, for Wright's use of *Idealism* to describe the philosophical context of much Protestant theology, "happier with abstract ideas than with concrete history."

[19]D. F. Strauss, *The Life of Jesus Critically Examined*, 4th ed. trans. George Eliot (London: Swan Sonnenschein & Co., 1902), 783: "In his discourse to the church [the theologian] will indeed adhere to the forms of the popular conception, but on every opportunity he will exhibit their spiritual significance, which to him constitutes their sole truth, and thus prepare—though such a result is only to be thought of as an unending progress—the resolution of those forms into their original ideas in the consciousness of the church also."

[20]Anthony C. Thistelton, *The Two Horizons: New Testament Hermeneutics and Philosophical Description with Special Reference to Heidegger, Bultmann, Gadamer, and Wittgenstein* (Grand Rapids: Eerdmans, 1980), 205-12.

[21]Ibid., 217. Cf. Roger A. Johnson, *The Origins of Demythologizing: Philosophy and Historiography in the Theology of Rudolf Bultmann*, Studies in the History of Religions (Leiden: E. J. Brill, 1974).

[22]*JVG*, 16.

[23]Ibid., and cf. Colin Brown, *Jesus in European Protestant Thought, 1778–1860* (Grand Rapids: Baker Books, 1985).

[24]*JVG*, 17.

[25]Cf. Jonathan I. Israel, *Radical Enlightenment: Philosophy and the Making of Modernity 1650–1750* (Oxford: Oxford University Press, 2001).

discovery of Reimarus by Lessing was an opportunity to further their goals. The point of all of this was not to provide a more accurate historical basis for the Christian faith, but rather to free the individual from the constraints of religion and, in this newfound freedom, to discover what are the eternal and universal truths of reason.

This brings us to Lessing's "broad ugly ditch."[26] On one side of the ditch are the contingent truths of history, the events that we know through sense perception and experience, whether in the present or in the past; and on the other are the necessary truths of reason, those truths that are not contingent because they are not based upon historical events, events that could have been otherwise. Lessing's ditch essentially was a deepening of the divide indicated by Melanchthon's dictum. The payoff with respect to Christian theology was that an abstract Christ could now be associated with the universal truths of reason, while the historical basis of Christian faith, along with the ecclesiastical forms of authority that were related to it, could easily be dismissed as irrelevant. As Lessing wrote, "I do not deny for a moment that Christ performed miracles. But since . . . they are merely reports of miracles . . . I do deny that they can and should bind me to the least faith in the other teachings of Christ. I accept these other teachings for other reasons."[27] The point that historical investigation was after, apart from simply the desire to know the past, was akin to the willingness of the Reformers to break with the traditions of the past, to introduce a rupture in history that would free the individual from dogmatic claims (and old political loyalties) based upon past history. If that history could be put in question, then those binding claims could be undone and humanity would be free to live and govern according to the universal authority of reason. So for the theologians following the path of rigorous historical investigation, the only possibility was to abandon church teaching in the face of a discredited historical foundation, or to abandon history as a foundational component of Christian identity.

In *JVG* Wright describes the work of Reimarus as "simply exploiting the split between history and faith implicit in the emphasis of Melanchthon's dictum. . . . [Reimarus] claimed that the gospels were records of early

---

[26]Gotthold Ephraim Lessing, *Philosophical and Theological Writings*, trans. H. B. Nisbet, Cambridge Texts in the History of Philosophy (Cambridge: Cambridge University Press, 2005), 85-87.
[27]Ibid., 86.

Christian faith, not transcripts of history, and that when we study the actual history we discover a very different picture."[28] This emphasis on the study of history, while aimed at discrediting the historical foundation of the Christian faith, nevertheless opened the door for an important corrective to the Reformation's emphasis on the abstract conceptual Christ. Wright points out the irony of the turn to history following Reimarus. "The fascinating thing, looking back two hundred years later, is that the appeal to history against history, as it were, has failed. History has shown itself to contain more than the idealists believed it could."[29] Historical investigation, it turns out, is not only essential for retaining the historical basis of the Christian faith, but good historical method—serious history—is in fact less damning of a historically grounded Christian faith than Reimarus, Lessing, Strauss and others thought. The realist path, the path that chased down the empirical but contingent truths of history, led ever further into a discovery of a past that affirmed the Christian faith even without the help of the ecclesial authorities who had always predetermined what one would find at its end.

By using the term *idealist* in the passage just cited to refer to the Reformation split between history and faith, Wright points us toward the other path from this division through the Enlightenment. While somewhat anachronistically used to refer to the direct intellectual heritage of the Reformation, Wright's use of *idealism* first gains meaning in reference to the abstract conceptual nature of Christian theology, as opposed to the concrete historical reference that Christian thought has always assumed. The idealist path can in this sense be traced from Melanchthon's dictum to Lessing, through Kant and all the way to Bultmann and Barth. In this trajectory, if attention was paid to the past, it was to the experience of the believing subject that bore theological significance, and not to the historical events themselves. This became a major force in German theology through the modern period. "Bultmann in his way, and Karl Barth in his, ensured that little was done to advance genuine historical work on Jesus in the years between the wars. Attention was focused instead on early Christian faith and experience, in the belief that there, rather than in a dubiously reconstructed Jesus, lay the key to the divine revelation that was presumed to have taken place in early

---

[28]*JVG*, 17.
[29]Ibid., 18.

Christianity."[30] The fact that historical-critical work has continued alongside the idealist movement can be attributed to the enduring significance of Lessing's ditch. These two trends, both a thoroughgoing realism in historical investigation and the speculative retreat into the realm of the subject, idealism, were able to be maintained because of the assumed incompatibility between contingent historical events and the universal truths known to the rational subject. The idealist is not interested in learning about reality as if events in themselves were meaningful, but, as Wright argues, "one looked at the history in order then to look elsewhere, to the other side of Lessing's 'ugly ditch,' to the eternal truths of reason unsullied by the contingent facts of everyday events, even extraordinary ones like those of Jesus."[31]

The intellectual context that Wright is outlining can, at this point, be described along the lines of a significant split between the Jesus of history and the Jesus of faith. The Jesus of history, the real man who lived and taught in Palestine, is understood apart from faith and, perhaps most significantly, apart from the miraculous. As Murray Rae notes, the Enlightenment quest for the historical Jesus that Reimarus and Lessing introduced was committed, as was Spinoza, to the category of immanence.[32] The Jesus of history is limited to explanations that make sense within known possibilities. The Jesus of faith, on the other hand, is an open possibility, a figure who can be molded and articulated according to various speculative schemes and ideals, and whose true reality may indeed be simply but powerfully existential. So, for example, Wright characterizes Albert Schweitzer's final portrait of Jesus like this: "He thus took upon himself the Great Affliction which was to break upon Israel and the world. The bridge between his historical life and Christianity is formed by his personality: he towers over history, and calls people to follow him in changing the world. The very failure of his hopes sets them free from Jewish shackles, to become, in their new guise, the hope of the world."[33] If we go back to the ruptures, ecclesial and theological, of the Reformation, we can see the way in which doctrines, if they are to be maintained despite being ruptured from their narratival contexts, can move in

---

[30]Ibid., 22.
[31]Ibid., 18.
[32]Murray Rae, *Kierkegaard's Vision of the Incarnation: By Faith Transformed* (Oxford: OUP, 1997), 85. Cf. Benedict de Spinoza, *Ethics*, trans. Edwin Curley (London: Penguin Books, 1996), 114.
[33]*JVG*, 19.

either direction. They can be picked up and transported into an idealist framework, or, if historical foundations remain significant, doctrines can be the theological commitments that predetermine our reading of history.

The dilemma for faith. This last point regarding the priority of theological commitments is significant, because it identifies what remained for many the only possibility for the church if it is to maintain its commitment to the necessary relationship between history and theology: a commitment to the affirmation of biblical history even in the face of the severe dismantling of the historical sources of Christian faith. Those who took this path had to do so in faith and against increasing pressure in the opposite direction from academic historians. If the path of idealism is rejected and an affirmation made that the historicity of the Christian faith ultimately matters, then this appears to be the only option. Indeed, for Wright it is the case that "the rootedness of Christianity in history is nonnegotiable."[34] The temptation for orthodox Christians can be simply to avoid the Enlightenment critique of the historical events that gave rise to the Christian faith. In the case of Jesus, this often involves a prior commitment to the divinity of Jesus, ahead of historical investigation, and then whatever historical work follows must reflect this commitment. The result is a portrait of Jesus that is iconic, "useful for devotion, but probably unlike the original subject."[35] If, however, we commit ourselves to rigorous historical investigation, leaving the question of divinity aside, there is the fear (for some) that "we will thereby 'disprove,' or at least seriously undermine, orthodox theology."[36] This is precisely what happened for those who followed the trajectory represented by Reimarus. The picture that emerges in this telling of the relationship between Christian theology and the pressures of the Enlightenment is of the difficult position in which Christian faith finds itself. On the one hand faith relies upon history to make sense of its very existence, and yet historical investigation following the Enlightenment has been highly critical of Christianity's historical claims.

If the church forsakes history for the idealist side of the picture, Christian faith retreats to a subjectivism, insulated and safe from the pressures of historical research. Yet here it becomes unclear that what we have is genuine

---

[34]*NTPG*, 9.
[35]*JVG*, 8.
[36]Ibid.

Christianity, if genuine Christianity depends upon a particular history. The tension between realism and idealism that emerged during the Enlightenment forced Christian theology into the difficult position created by these polar forces working against each other. Wright's theological dialogue partners,[37] those who represent the most serious declension in his narrative, are primarily those who have done theology on the idealist end of the spectrum. These theologians have attempted to protect the Christian faith from the work of the historian and, like the older brother in the parable of the prodigal son, remain distrustful of the historian's return to the household of faith.[38] Wright's project is intended to resolve this tension through a fully committed and rigorous historical investigation, and by bringing to the table equally rigorous theological questions, all the while maintaining the nonnegotiable relationship between history and theology. "The underlying argument . . . is that the split is not warranted: that rigorous history . . . and rigorous theology . . . belong together, and never more so than in discussion of Jesus."[39]

Wright's project, then, can be understood to be a thoroughgoing attempt to halt the decline in the relationship between theology and history with a comprehensive methodological approach that takes seriously both poles of the Enlightenment, realism and idealism, and effects a kind of synthesis of the two that can maintain an orthodox Christian faith in an intellectually rigorous and philosophically credible way.

Postmodernism

Wright's account of the postmodern turn, while only cursory, emphasizes the dialectic of realism and idealism. His account focuses on the world of postmodern literary criticism as a turn toward an emphasis on the act of reading rather than on the reality of the events to which texts refer.[40] His response to this is both appreciative and critical. The postmodern focus on the reader can

---

[37]See the description of a *via negativa* in Jesus studies represented at the outset of *JVG* by quotations from Schweitzer, Bultmann, Barth, Lightfoot and Bornkamm. *JVG*, 3.

[38]The parable of the prodigal son is used by Wright to describe the relationship between the theologian (elder brother) and the historian (prodigal). See *JVG*, 9. Of course, there is no evidence in the parable that the younger son repented of his ways. The emphasis is on the Father's acceptance, not the wayward son's transformation!

[39]Ibid.

[40]*NTPG*, 9.

be seen as an extension of the Enlightenment's turn to the subject, where the question of external reality is only answered in terms of subjectivity and not objectivity. Postmodern reading focuses on the reader's experience of the text. This can point to an important aspect of the hermeneutical enterprise that is neglected if the text is seen as a simple window into another world, but the opposite danger is that the text becomes only a mirror, reflecting only the reader to the reader's self.[41] The text as object, to be dealt with as external to the reader, locates the positive aspect of the postmodern literary turn in light of the concern for a realist account of reading. On the other hand, the subjective element—in other words, the focus on the reader and her experience in reading—points to the idealist strand and the critical aspect of the hermeneutical question. Wright's own project takes significant strides toward addressing these issues in the third chapter of *NTPG*, where he takes up and provides a detailed account of both story and worldview.

Significantly, we see Wright continuing to hold together the idealist and realist strands as essential correctives to each other in a generous movement, welcoming the insights of the postmodern critique while retaining a sense of the necessary grounding of Christian thought in a reality external to the subject. The postmodern text is one possible open door to this ground, while the postmodern account of the reader provides the critical distance needed for appropriate epistemological humility.

FROM CRITIQUE TO CONSTRUCT

Introduction: Idealism, Realism and Critical Realism

The previous section described the way in which N. T. Wright articulates the tension between history and theology by attending to the narratives he tells about the Reformation, the Enlightenment and postmodernity. In both *JVG* and *NTPG* we find a variety of terms that can generally be clustered around two intellectual trajectories from this narrative, two trajectories I have already begun referring to as *realism* and *idealism*. The choice of these terms is not meant to refer to their technical philosophical use, although the terms can include them, but rather to indicate the twin poles

---

[41]See ibid., 54.

of the epistemological tension between the knowing subject for whom the
world is subjectively and rationally determined (idealism), and the reality
of the external world that presents itself, as it is, to the subject (realism).[42]
This choice is suggested by Wright's methodological proposal, his particular account of "critical realism" (CRw),[43] which relies upon a critique
and reformulation of these two poles.[44] Wright himself admits that at
times the concepts he is working with are "deliberately general" and that
he is using a "broad-brush" to set up the "rival theories" that make his
methodological account necessary.[45] This should be kept in mind, both as
a restraint to quick dismissals from more nuanced perspectives of CR, and
as an encouragement that continued work within the framework that
Wright has offered is warranted. It is to Wright's account of this framework,
his CRw, that I now turn.

Critical realism (CRw), in Wright's own words, "offers an account of how
we can take full cognizance of the provisionality and partiality of all our
perceptions while still affirming—and living our lives on the basis of—the
reality of things external to ourselves and our minds. This method involves,
crucially, the telling of stories within the context of communities of
discourse."[46] The threefold form of this description—provisionality, reality,
communities of discourse—will guide the organization of this section, although I will change the order slightly. The tension between provisionality
(idealism) and reality (realism) is overcome in the positive aspect of Wright's
methodology—namely, the attention paid to the stories that constitute the
discourse and worldviews of communities. Each of these elements will be
dealt with in turn, beginning with realism and ending with the synthetic

---

[42]Cf., e.g., Gunton, *Enlightenment and Alienation*, 46-47.

[43]When referring to Wright's version of critical realism, I will use the letter *w*, as in "CRw." This is similar to the practice in the appendix of Donald L. Denton Jr., *Historiography and Herme-neutics in Jesus Studies: An Examination of the Work of John Dominic Crossan and Ben F. Meyer* (London: T&T Clark, 2004), 218-19.

[44]Wright explicitly juxtaposes these two terms against one another in the fourth chapter of *NTPG*, even though he also questions the distinction as "ultimately misleading." Yet here the point is not that the terms can be apt descriptors of intellectual movements, but rather that "swings from one to the other are not much help in terms of an actual historical investigation such as ours." As we will see, CRw is precisely a way out of this false dilemma. Nevertheless, the dilemma ex-ists, and use of this language can help to characterize the intellectual trajectories that have led to the particular conflicts between theologians and historians. See *NTPG*, 96.

[45]Ibid., 32.

[46]Wright, "In Grateful Dialogue: A Response," *JRI*, 245-46.

resolution of the tension in an appropriate methodology. The purpose of this section, then, is to provide an account of CRw according to these terms, as the synthetic overcoming (*Aufhebung?*) of the dialectic between idealism and realism. Theology, since at least the Reformation, errs when it tends toward the idealist end of the dialectic, and history (e.g., Enlightenment historiography)[47] errs when it is overdetermined by its commitment to realism. The overcoming of this dialectic is facilitated by Wright's attention to the contexts of human knowing, contexts that are given coherence according to narratives, stories and, ultimately, worldviews. Knowledge occurs in the dynamic relation between reality and the conceptual makeup of our engagement with that reality.[48]

Realism

Realism can be associated with the intellectual trajectory from the Enlightenment that pushed against the traditional historical content of Christian teaching with a confidence in the ability of a modern historical method to know the truth, with varying degrees of objectivity, about the past. That is the historical context of realism in Wright's narrative. Philosophically understood, realism names a confidence in the independent existence of objects apart from observers.[49] Historians, to the extent that they are realists about their subject matter, are confident that the events that they study have (really) occurred in time and space and that texts and testimony do, in happy cases, refer to those events. This is the case regardless of whether or how one has access to those events. It may be the case that we cannot know the events, but a realist nevertheless believes that events really occurred that, through human intention, become objects of inquiry. Thus realism, broadly conceived, implies the allowance in epistemology for the reality of objects external to the knower, objects that must be considered in their externality.

---

[47]*JVG*, 117.

[48]It should be made clear that a dualism based on these two concepts is not, in Wright's understanding, finally helpful, but rather represents a false separation that needs to be overcome. As we will see, CRw is presented as a "relational epistemology" that is meant to collapse the "hard-and-fast distinction between objective and subjective" (*NTPG*, 44-45) by integrating the two in such a way that a new epistemology emerges.

[49]Alexander Miller, "Realism," in *The Stanford Encyclopedia of Philosophy*, 2012 edition, http://plato .stanford.edu/archives/spr2012/entries/realism/.

Positivism

Realism could be said to simply describe the epistemological assumptions of most people before coming under the Enlightenment critique. How one came to know a thing was not a question of the reality of the thing itself (this was not in question), but rather a problem of appropriate method with respect to a given object. Scientific method and historical method were seen to be epistemological developments that would aid the observer in coming to know an object as it really is, without regard for what the observer brought to the task of observation. *Positivism* names this "optimistic" epistemological position.[50] As Wright understands it, positivism is simply a position that assumes the ability to make claims about reality external to the observer based solely upon sense data. One of the problems that Wright sees on the positivistic side of realism is that it ignores the prejudices that always accompany observation. For positivist historians, this looks like a "value-free and dogma-free historiography as though such a thing were attainable."[51] For positivist theologians, either the biblical text is read "straight" as if they have avoided all presuppositions, or, "because one cannot have 'direct access' to the 'facts' about Jesus, all that we are left with is a morass of first-century fantasy."[52] Another problem that Wright sees with positivism is its rejection of other types of knowledge, presuming them to be less secure compared to the direct and unmediated knowledge of empirical verification. Positivistic knowledge, if it is methodologically controlled through empirical testing, must either reject other claims to knowledge, for example, philosophy, theology and so on, or these claims are generally "downgraded"[53] because they are not subject to empirical verification. Wright notes that positivism has generally been rejected by philosophers after undergoing the critique leveled against it by the sociological study of knowledge and the reconsideration of the philosophy of science by philosophers such as Michael Polanyi and Thomas Kuhn. Even so, positivism hangs on in popular opinion. This understanding of realism is pejoratively referred to as "naïve realism" by Wright

---

[50]On Wright's account of positivism, see *NTPG*, 32-33.
[51]Ibid., 16.
[52]Ibid., 33-34.
[53]Ibid., 33.

and identified as a "common-sense level"[54] of realism that, in positivistic fashion, would seek both an objective point of view and claim unmediated correspondence of perception between subject and object.[55]

Phenomenalism

Phenomenalism names the realist position taken to the other extreme, what Wright calls "the pessimistic side of the Enlightenment programme. . . . The reverse of this belief is that, where positivism cannot utter its shrill certainties, all that is left is subjectivity or relativity. The much-discussed contemporary phenomenon of cultural and theological relativism is itself in this sense simply the dark side of positivism."[56] This "dark side of positivism"—phenomenalism —is similar to the idealist/subjectivist thread from the Enlightenment, except that rather than having its roots in the Kantian turn to the subject, it has its roots in the realist side of critical realism, and specifically in the commitment to empirical observation. Phenomenalism begins with the humble recognition that all phenomena from the external world are mediated through our senses, but instead of taking that as a positive account of how we have knowledge of external reality, phenomenalism takes this as an absolute barrier to knowledge: all we can do is speak in terms of what we perceive rather than what really is. For Wright, an unchecked phenomenalism is a step onto the slippery slope to solipsism, the "belief that I and only I exist."[57] "When I seem to be looking at a text, or at an author's mind within the text, or at events of which the text seems to be speaking, all I am really doing is seeing the author's view of events, or the text's appearance of authorial intent, or maybe only my own thoughts in the presence of the text . . . and is it even a text?"[58]

What is rejected by Wright is the idea that external reality can be immediately known, that is, unmediated, apart from larger mediating contexts of meaning. This gets at the heart of Wright's critique of the Enlightenment's historical method. All historical knowledge is knowledge that is mediated. By assuming that scientific methodologies function positivistically, any his-

---

[54]Ibid.
[55]Ibid., 37.
[56]Ibid.
[57]Ibid., 35.
[58]Ibid.

torical methodology that claims objectivity will simply ignore the imported a priori commitments and broader narrative contexts that predetermine conclusions about historical events. In Wright's words, "The positivist . . . traditions are wrong to imagine that perception is prior to the grasping of larger realities."[59] The twin problems of positivism and phenomenalism represent for Wright dangers of a realist epistemology that is not corrected or checked by a properly critical realism. It is to this critical, and in some respects idealist, end of Wright's account of epistemology that we now turn.

Idealism: Two Branches

In its most basic sense, idealism, and the cluster of terms associated with it from *NTPG*, can be understood to correspond to the subjective turn of the Enlightenment. The term *idealism* shows up more frequently in *JVG* than in *NTPG*, primarily because in the former Wright is dealing with the particular intellectual trends that contributed to the scholarly projects associated with the various quests for the historical Jesus. In *NTPG*, Wright refers to idealism as the philosophical context of much modern Protestant theology, which, when read together with the introduction of *JVG*, links it together with the historical trajectory from the Reformation to Kant and beyond. The extent to which Wright's realist epistemology is critical will need to be articulated in contrast to the idealist trajectory of the Enlightenment in order to see how his constructive proposal attempts to overcome the idealist critique. In Wright's account, the idealist trajectory can be demonstrated according to two major branches that influence the relationship between theology and history: conceptual abstraction and subjectivism.

Conceptual abstraction. Wright's narrative of the idealist trajectory begins, chronologically, with Melanchthon's dictum, the *pro me* of the Reformation, and the abstraction of doctrine from history that it implied. It ends with the radical subjectivism of postmodernity. When Wright speaks of the way in which theology deviates from its proper relationship with history, he does so in reference to this abstraction from the historical and concrete, and he uses, at times, the term *idealism* to draw attention to its conceptual nature. For example, when discussing the many problems to be

---

[59]Ibid., 43.

found within the field of New Testament theology, Wright identifies "Idealism" as the distinct philosophical context in which the field developed. This development favored abstraction rather than "concrete history," with the outcome being that abstract theology became the privileged discipline set free from the historian's attempt to ground theology in the reality of actual events in time and space.[60] This has been a consistent emphasis within Wright's critique of the relationship between theology and history, and it is implicit in more recent critiques of abstract theological categories such as "divinity" and "humanity" when they take precedence over more biblically rooted concepts such as the kingdom of God or Jesus as Messiah.

> In fact, one might suggest sharply that it is the mainstream dogmatic tradition (arguing about the "divinity and humanity" of Jesus) that has actually falsified the canon by screening out the Gospel's central emphasis on the coming of the kingdom and by substituting for this the question of the divinity of Jesus, as though the point of the Gospels' high incarnational Christology were something other than the claim that this is Israel's God in person coming to claim the sovereignty promised to the Messiah.[61]

The abstraction of theological concepts from the historical narratives is a mistake that has significant theological and even political ramifications. By locating theological doctrines in their historical contexts, the Christian faith is necessarily rescued from its "charmed faith-based circle" so that it might "go out and address the world, in order to rescue the world."[62]

Subjectivism. The other branch of idealism is subjectivism. Subjectivism holds that the only knowledge we can have of objects is of their appearances, as they appear to the observer, and not as they are in and of themselves.[63] With Immanuel Kant's epoch-making shift in philosophy, the idea that all reality actually conforms to a priori categories that belong to the mind of the human subject, the independent reality of objects in the world was put into question. In Wright's discussion of epistemology, surprisingly little attention

---

[60]Ibid., 23, cf. 21. Another example comes from *JVG*, 24: "This . . . is true to the reformation emphasis: The purpose of Jesus' life was to *say* things, to teach great truths in a timeless fashion. It was also true to idealist philosophy: what matters ultimately is ideas, not events."

[61]*JPPG*, 134.

[62]Ibid., 154.

[63]William Bristow, "Enlightenment," in *The Stanford Encyclopedia of Philosophy*, Summer 2011, http://plato.stanford.edu/archives/sum2011/entries/enlightenment.

is paid to Immanuel Kant.[64] Where subjectivism is mentioned, it is associated with phenomenalism,[65] the outworking in a negative direction of the trajectory of positivism that I have associated in Wright's work with realism. Nevertheless, the Kantian turn to the subject is an essential part of the idealist trajectory. The *pro me* and corresponding theological abstraction of the Reformation was followed by the turn to the subject and the radical subjectivism that followed. Put in question by this move was the very reality of the external world. What might have simply been Cartesian doubt regarding our knowledge of the world, knowledge in search of an external foundation that Descartes found in God, was now with Kant grounded in an account of the metaphysical priority of the human subject. This move placed the reality of the nonsubjective world, that is, the world of objects, into question. Seen from the perspective of Wright's project, the major problem with this strand of the idealistic turn is that it makes what should be independent, concrete historical events completely dependent on the subjectivity of the one interpreting history. All history involves interpretation, but for the thoroughgoing idealist it is *only* interpretation. Kant's description of his project as a "Copernican shift" is an apt metaphor for the sort of shift that occurs when the critical element overcomes the primacy of the reality of the external world.[66] For in Kant it was the object that must conform to the subject, and not the other way around. The center of the universe has become the subject, and the universe itself is only understood around that center. This is exactly opposite for Wright in the sense that Wright is committed to the existence of external reality and that our knowledge ought to conform to that reality. But how does one account for externality if we cannot escape our subjectivity? How do we remain epistemological realists while at the same time acknowledging our own subjective limitations?

Wright's Critical Realism (CRw)

CRw fits into Wright's project as an epistemological position that attempts to resolve the tension between realism and idealism in such a way that re-

---

[64]He is only mentioned in two footnotes: *NTPG*, 35n12; 107n49.

[65]E.g., ibid., 37.

[66]Immanuel Kant, *Critique of Pure Reason*, trans. and ed. Paul Guyer and Allen W. Wood (Cambridge: Cambridge University Press, 1998), 110.

gains the central role of historical knowledge for theology and, at the same time, to justify theological inquiry as undertaken by the historian. It is specifically intended to overcome the rejection by theologians of the biblical historian's conclusions, while at the same time it functions to expose the a priori commitments of the historians who reject the theological claims of their historical subjects. Above these polemical goals, however, CRw is meant to be an epistemology that conforms to the reality of the world as the good creation of God, and to provide a way of investigating that world free from the dualisms that we have seen through Wright's narration of the intellectual heritage extending from the Reformation and the Enlightenment. The dualisms of idealism and realism, subjective/objective, phenomenalist/positivist, and so on, are present in the split between theology and history.[67] In Wright's words, "The challenge is now before us to articulate new categories which will do justice to the relevant material without this damaging dualism—and without, of course, cheating by collapsing the data into a monism in which one 'side' simply disappears into the other."[68] CRw will be an attempt to meet these twin challenges: to reject the false dualisms that beset Christian discourse and avoid the temptation of favoring one side or the other. CRw must be a new way of accounting for the reality to which the Christian faith must bear witness.

The primary dualism that provides the immediate context in which Wright introduces CRw is that of positivism and phenomenalism. This highlights the primary tension that we have been dealing with—namely, the tension that exists between the reality of the external world and the subjectivity that determines the way in which we experience it. After giving a brief description of CRw (to which we will come in a moment), he comments that "critical awareness . . . challenge[s] a naïve realism or a mainline positivism."[69] This is another way of referring to the phenomenalism/positivism duality. A few paragraphs later he attempts to preempt the conclusion that in CRw it appears that the "phenomenalists, or the subjectivists, have won after all."[70] It is this cluster of terms, and the inherent dualistic tension between what I

---

[67]*NTPG*, 24-25.
[68]Ibid.
[69]Ibid., 36.
[70]Ibid., 37.

am calling idealism and realism, that Wright identifies in order to set up the context in which he presents CRw. In Wright's own words, CRw is a

> way of describing the process of "knowing" that acknowledges *the reality of the thing known, as something other than the knower* (hence "realism"), while also fully acknowledging that the only access we have to this reality lies along the spiraling path of *appropriate dialogue or conversation between the knower and the thing known* (hence "critical").[71]

The point that needs to be made, and the key to understanding how CRw can avoid falling onto one side or another, is that knowledge, for Wright, is only achieved along this "spiraling path" described as "appropriate dialogue" or "conversation." It is this "path" that holds the key to understanding what Wright is doing with CRw.

Knowledge as contact. Against the empiricist or positivist assumption that separates the knower and the known into the categories of *subject* and *object*, CRw prefers to understand this fundamental epistemological relationship in terms of *humans* and *events*. This eliminates the distance between the knower and the known by refusing to abstract each from within the social contexts or "frameworks" that contribute to identity and meaning.[72] Rather than assuming a basic distance between the knower and the known, something that the language of subject and object do, the language of *human* and *event* necessarily involves the inclusion of each within stories that make sense of them as conversation partners. In other words, knowledge is not empirical verification or, in a positivistic sense, an objective comprehension of what a thing is in itself; rather, knowledge is fundamentally relational. CRw is a "relational epistemology."[73]

Wright identifies CRw within a tradition of CR spanning several disciplines, including theology, philosophy, science and history. A brief look at two scholars from whom Wright draws for his understanding of CR will be helpful for understanding what "relational epistemology" means. First, theologian Colin Gunton's book *Enlightenment and Alienation* argues that one of the problems with Enlightenment epistemology is that it operated under the false assumption that there exists a fundamental distance between the observer and the world (alienation). Drawing on the work of Michael Polanyi,

---

[71]Ibid., 35. Italics in original.
[72]For this account, see ibid., 43-44.
[73]Ibid., 45.

Gunton describes the contrast between the Enlightenment assumption of alienation and a critical realist epistemology as the difference between two different metaphors of seeing. On the Enlightenment side, normal seeing is the primary metaphor, and the observer is assumed to be at a distance from the object seen. On the critical realist side, seeing is likened to a blind person with a white cane, feeling the world through the cane. Knowing, according to this metaphor, is a process of learning through contact. Polanyi's arguments, the source of this change of metaphor, "all circle around his central claim that knowledge of any kind, whether it be of mathematics, natural science, philosophy or literary criticism is personal and not, for example, to be understood on the analogy of the machine or of omniscience."[74]

Another of Wright's influences, Ben F. Meyer, whose own work of biblical interpretation draws heavily upon the transcendental method of Bernard Lonergan, points to Lonergan's *Insight* for a similar rejection of the metaphor of seeing: "Insight demystified the conflicting epistemologies of the modern era (naïve realism, empiricism, idealism), tracing them to a common root, namely, the fallacy that knowing is like seeing, that knowing the real is, or would be, akin to seeing it."[75] Lonergan's own words are helpful in elucidating further the epistemological position of Wright:

> For knowing is an organically integrated activity. . . . To conceive knowing one must understand the dynamic pattern of experiencing, inquiring, reflecting, and such understanding is not to be reached by taking a look. To affirm knowing it is useless to peer inside, for the dynamic pattern is to be found not in this or that act, but in the unfolding of mathematics, empirical science, common sense, and philosophy; in that unfolding must be grasped the pattern of knowing and, if one feels inclined to doubt that that pattern really exists, then one can try the experiment of attempting to escape experience, to renounce intelligence in inquiry, to desert reasonableness in critical reflection.[76]

For both Lonergan and Polanyi, knowing is a type of experience or encounter with the world. Knowing is coming into contact with that which is

---

[74]Gunton, *Enlightenment and Alienation*, 38.

[75]Ben F. Meyer, *Critical Realism & the New Testament* (Eugene, OR: Pickwick Publications, 2009 [1989]), 150.

[76]Bernard Lonergan, *Insight: A Study of Human Understanding* (London: Longmans, 1968 [1957]), 415-16. Cf. Lonergan, *Method in Theology*, 2nd ed. (London: Darton, Longman & Todd, 1973), 239.

to be known. In this way it is a realist epistemology. In CRw, this contact with the real is uniquely accounted for in Wright's account of story and worldview.

In Wright's words, worldviews are "the basic stuff of human existence, the lens through which the world is seen, the blueprint for how one should live in it, and above all the sense of identity and place which enables human beings to be what they are."[77] The concept of worldview is not a constructive proposal of Wright's, but is rather based in what he sees as a particular honesty regarding how humans engage and interact epistemologically with the world. By countering both the idealist and realist strands of thought, what remains is an account of human interaction with reality that can only be understood in terms of a holistic vision of humanity in integrated contact with the world. The concept of a worldview provides a way of talking about this integrated nature of human contact with reality. Worldviews do this by providing stories that give coherence to our experience of reality. They answer basic questions that arise out of these stories and out of human experience, and the answers to these questions are always bound within stories. Worldviews also include cultural symbols that express the stories and questions that make up worldviews, and they are sustained and formed in the context of praxis, of particular ways of being in the world.[78] This account of worldview is basic for CRw and provides the context that makes sense of the human as knowing subject, an integral part of the whole of reality.

One function of the role of worldview and story in CRw is to be a critical check on any aspirations to a positivist epistemology. This can be seen in the way that story and worldview function with respect to the process of hypothesis and verification.

Hypothesis and verification are the normal scientific means by which one comes to know things about reality external to oneself. Wright understands the methods of hypothesis and verification according to the "usual accounts of 'scientific method.'"[79] For Wright, it is important to make the claim that in the natural sciences, the data that we gain from our senses always has a prior framework of understanding, a hypothesis and theoretical context that makes sense of experience, and that focuses the scientist or historian in which di-

---

[77]NTPG, 124.
[78]Ibid., 123-24.
[79]Ibid., 37.

rection to look and with what tools to use in their inquiry into an event, person or other object of knowledge. Sense data is then interpreted according to an existing framework or theory that can make sense of it. In order to successfully inquire regarding an experience or an object, "one needs a larger framework on which to draw, a larger set of stories about things that are likely to happen in the world."[80] In Wright's method, worldviews provide the frameworks within which knowledge can occur. There is no knowledge apart from worldviews, and it is in the interaction between worldviews, through the processes of hypothesis and verification uniquely enabled by worldviews (just as a theory or hypothesis enables data based on observation to gain meaning in a scientific research program), that knowledge can take place. In this way, knowledge is never abstracted from stories, and it is in the context of stories that contact with external reality takes place.

But in what sense can we speak of this as "contact" with reality? There are at least four explicit ways in which Wright accounts for "contact" in his articulation of the relationality of CRw. First, Wright articulates the theological and biblical claim that humans are made in the image of the Creator and so are given responsibility within the created order. This means that human presence in the world is necessarily interactional and can be described in moral terms as "stewardship." Wright even suggests that his CRw might be understood as an epistemology of love.[81] This is clearly a claim internal to Wright's own Christian worldview and subject to the same critique as any other worldview. That Wright uses this argument suggests his willingness to admit his own bias, an admission that is consistent with his understanding of the impossibility of a point of view outside of any worldview. Second, the dialogical nature of the epistemological process implies contact,[82] a contact exemplified by the fact that the knower may be changed in the process of knowing. Third, the content of stories, the basic components of our knowledge about the world, are necessarily and "irreducibly" about the "interrelation of humans and the rest of reality."[83] Knowledge cannot escape this interrelationality. Fourth, and finally, stories

---

[80]Ibid.

[81]*JPPG*, 146-47; *NTPG*, 64.

[82]For an example outside of Wright but to which Wright refers, see Thistelton, *Two Horizons*, 440: "fusion of horizons."

[83]*NTPG*, 45.

are told. It is the human act of telling stories that communicates information about reality; storytelling is that unique practice in which knowledge is passed from one community to another across time and space.

Stories and worldviews, then, provide the appropriate critical check to a realist epistemology in CRw. They do this ostensibly without risking the realism that is essential to Wright's Christian commitments, preventing both abstraction and the subjectivism that would isolate the knower from the contexts that provide meaning. There can be no abstraction of knowledge apart from frameworks of meaning that permit knowledge to be classified as knowledge. "The fact that *somebody*, standing *somewhere*, with a particular *point of view*, is knowing something does not mean that the knowledge is less valuable: merely that it is precisely *knowledge*."[84] Knowledge could thus be defined as the appropriate fit of a fact or object within the worldview of a knower. This means that we can only know what an object or a fact is (any "small" piece of knowledge) if we can place it within a story, or, in another term Wright uses, an "event."[85] There are no isolated facts or objects: "Stories . . . are more fundamental than 'facts'; the parts must be seen in light of the whole."[86] Knowledge therefore must be understood as the successful location of objects or facts within a true story or worldview.

But what makes a story true? Here Wright seems to leave us with a coherentist account of truth. At several points the proof of his account of CRw, or epistemology, is simply given over to the coherent outcome of his project: "And, as always, the proof of the pudding remains in the eating. . . . Simplicity of outline, elegance in handling the details within it, the inclusion of all the parts of a story, and the ability of the story to make sense beyond its immediate subject-matter: these are what count."[87] All external reality, if it is to be the subject matter of knowledge, is necessarily story bound. In other words, reality is only perceived as an object for knowledge of the knowing subject within stories. These stories situate the object of knowledge within a spatial and temporal framework of meaning. Therefore reality can only be known in a meaningful way if we get our stories right. This means that the

---

[84]Ibid., 89. Italics in original.
[85]Ibid., 43-44.
[86]Ibid., 83.
[87]Ibid., 42; cf. 45.

epistemological process, as a process that moves toward true stories about the world, will have to pay critical attention to the stories and worldviews that make sense of both the knower and the person or event to be known. This can only be done through contact with the storied existence of reality. But this contact is always contact between stories and worldviews.

In sum, CRw attempts an account of epistemology that overcomes the historic dualisms that have separated the knower from the known through a critically realist epistemology of contact. Knowledge that has traditionally been defined according to the subject/object distinction is redefined in CRw according to the categories of human and event, worldview and story. Knowledge is what we know to be true according to our worldview, according to the *meaningful* contact that we have with reality. The next two sections will look at the way in which this epistemological method is appropriated in the disciplines of history and theology.

Historical knowledge in CRw. Wright defines history as "the meaningful narrative of events and intentions."[88] If we keep in mind that in CRw there is a fundamental commitment to external reality, then "events and intentions" names the "things" that historians are after. History is not simply an exercise in reading texts, although it certainly is that, but it is looking through texts (and artifacts) at events and the human intentions present with those events that actually happened.[89] Yet this realism is simultaneously complemented by the critical qualifier that would resist the positivist temptation to posit a factual essence, or bare event, free from interpretation.[90] The goal of the historian, through appropriate methodological tools (e.g., hypothesis and verification, worldview investigation, narrative criticism, historical-critical methodology), is to gain "the 'inside' of the event."[91] That is, the historian aims at the inner logic, in narrative and worldview terms, of the meaning of an event according to the perspectives of those involved. In a later essay Wright quotes R. G. Collingwood with respect to this point: "The historian's task, as seen by Collingwood, is to 're-think' or inwardly re-enact the deliberations of past agents, thereby rendering their behavior

---

[88]Ibid., 82. Italics removed.
[89]Ibid., 90-91.
[90]Ibid., 91.
[91]Ibid., 92.

intelligible."[92] In this way historical knowledge is unique in comparison with other scientific disciplines since it is not trying to discern laws or causal links that are repeatable, but rather investigating particular one-time events and their unique causal contexts.[93] Historical method properly moves from the event itself to the meaning of the event through the "inside" of the event.

Wright indicates three aspects to this methodological movement, or "three levels of understanding,"[94] as the historian moves between the historical event itself and the meaning of that event.[95] The first is that a proper historical method makes human intentionality a necessary object of investigation. Human intentionality involves the aims, intentions and motivations that make sense both of particular actors and also entire communities and societies.[96] The next movement after the investigation of human intentionality is the attempted integration of events, their interiors, intentions, motivations and so on according to a coherent story or narrative. The historian tells a story and attempts to give a harmonious account of the whole of historical data.[97] The best way to understand this narrative aspect of historical method may be to understand the story as a particular community tells it. So looking at the inside of an event, such as the messianic event of Jesus of Nazareth, would involve seeing it as the community telling the story, the early Christians, would see it. That means that to understand an event or person would require understanding it from within the resultant tradition rather than having to establish a position outside of it.[98] Third, from telling a story the historian moves on to the meaning of the story, the meaning of past events. Meaning, in CRw, is always found within worldviews. But since CRw operates according to an externalist premise, any worldview cannot simply become an idealist or phenomenalist subjectivism, a private worldview that would obscure the reality of events. Events and

---

[92]Wright, "In Grateful Dialogue," JRI, 250.
[93]This point will become important when Wright wards off the accusation of methodological naturalism.
[94]NTPG, 109.
[95]These are not necessarily sequential, but rather ought to be understood according to the "spiral of epistemology" that characterizes human inquiry according to CRw. Ibid.
[96]Ibid., 109-12. Cf. Ben F. Meyer, "The Primacy of the Intended Sense of Texts," in Critical Realism & the New Testament, 17-55.
[97]NTPG, 114.
[98]Ibid., 115.

intentions are essentially public.[99] They are available to investigation, critique and change. CRw makes sure this happens by preventing worldviews from being seen as private (because of the insistence on external reality) and by insisting that the knowledge of an event is always an interpretation of its reality and therefore always open to dialogue with alternative interpretations or theories.[100] As I have shown above, this dialogical nature of CRw is essential to making sense of it as an epistemology of contact, rather than an epistemology of alienated "seeing."

N. T. Wright's historical method, understood within the context of his critically realist epistemology, can be summarized as follows:[101] it is an epistemology that acknowledges both the reality of the object of investigation, external to the knower, and the fact that any external reality is only known through a process in which the worldview of the knowing subject mediates knowledge of that reality.[102] Following this way of knowing, Wright's historical method proceeds according to the method of hypothesis and verification that guides normal scientific inquiry in other fields.[103] Because knowledge itself is made possible by worldviews, all reality comes to us saturated with meaning, a meaningfulness determined by the worldview through which we perceive that which is external to us. Thus, the historian's own worldview will always direct questions of meaning to the events of history that are under investigation. The questions the historian asks are appropriate questions of meaning, inquiring into aims, intentions and motivations of historical subjects. These questions and their answers guide the historian to hypothesize, to formulate meaningful stories about events and then to verify those meaningful stories, testing them against the historical data. The method is not necessarily sequential, but rather spirals[104] through

---

[99]Wright offers "public" and "private" as an alternative to "objective" and "subjective" earlier in *NTPG*, 44.

[100]Ibid., 117.

[101]See Wright's brief summary in *RSG*, 29.

[102]"The knower cannot know without being involved." *NTPG*, 103.

[103]Here Wright would be concerned to clarify that history is not after repeatable phenomena, nor is it too concerned with maintaining the criteria of analogy as Troeltsch asserted. See *RSG*, 16-17.

[104]Cf. Ben F. Meyer: "The movement of understanding is a recurrent spiral from the pre-understanding of things through the understanding of words to a firmer, sharper, more differentiated and penetrating understanding of things." *The Aims of Jesus*, Princeton Theological Monograph Series 48 (Eugene, OR: Pickwick Publications, 2001), 96.

the process of hypothesis and verification in a self-critical way as stories are refined and unnecessary complexities resolved.[105] In this way the historian learns to see the world through the eyes of the subjects under investigation.[106] The stories that emerge are always subject to the challenge of critique and falsification, but only by enduring critique do they come to be "fair and true statements about the past."[107]

With this summary of Wright's historical method, what remains is to show in what way CRw as an epistemological position determines Wright's theological method and the unique claims involved in the investigation of God.

Theological knowledge and worldviews in CRw. At the beginning of his chapter on theological method in NTPG, Wright states that his aim in the chapter is to provide an account of theology that is a "composite" of theological, literary and historical investigation and to see in what way such an account might function as "normative or authoritative."[108] Wright does precisely this by locating theology as a questioning discipline within his concept of worldview, together with literary and historical readings. He defines theology accordingly as the "god dimension of a worldview."[109] This raises questions as to the nature of theological knowledge with respect to its unique object, God, and God's place within Wright's critically realist epistemology.[110] What can we say about the knowledge that theology gives? In what way does Wright claim that God can be known in and through his critically realist epistemology? Answering this question will involve a brief look at how Wright positions theology within a worldview, and then a close look at the type of knowledge that CRw can gain with respect to the question of God.

Wright approaches theology as a unique aspect of the sociology of knowledge, understandable as part of the "worldview pattern"[111] that conditions all forms of knowledge.[112] While acknowledging that theology can be

[105]See the discussion on simplicity in NTPG, 106-9.
[106]Ibid., 118.
[107]RSG, 29.
[108]NTPG, 121.
[109]Ibid., 130.
[110]Wright addresses this question in NTPG, 126-37.
[111]Ibid., 126.
[112]See the quotation from Norman Petersen (ibid., 127) with regard to explicitly identifying worldviews, in the context of a discussion of theological knowledge, within the sociology of knowledge.

narrowly defined as "the study of gods, or a god,"[113] Wright opens up his
account of theology to pay particular attention to the way that theology
functions according to the four points of the grid that make up his account
of worldviews: symbol, story, questions and praxis. Theology deals with, or
"turns the spotlight on," the interaction between these four aspects as it raises
questions and answers them with respect to transcendence or to the divine.

As we have seen, for Wright, a worldview is the basic, foundational and
usually invisible grid through which people see and interpret the world in
which they live. People look through them, not at them.[114] But, even though
we do not usually see them, they can still be taken up and examined;[115] they
are always in process, being refined, altered or rejected—implicitly and, at
times, explicitly. Theology as a particular type of discourse belongs within
the larger comprehensive category of worldview, and should be understood
as a crucial component of the manifold discourses that make up the way in
which humans articulate and understand their relationship to reality. This
final claim can be clarified by seeing how theology in Wright's view is related
to its subject matter: transcendence or the divine.

Throughout the chapter on theological method in *NTPG*, Wright works
with a particular graphic depiction to illustrate the possible epistemological relations between humans and god(s). The basic illustration looks
like figure 1.

Figure 1

The sequence of Wright's account follows a sequence that moves from left
to right, from humans to knowledge of god(s). Humans tell stories that
speak of transcendence. If we are going to assume the basic nature of worldviews for human knowing, then the stories humans tell need to be shown to
function according to the internal logic of the worldviews in which they
operate, and not dismissed because they do not fit within the particular
worldview that determines an outsider's way of seeing. This allows us to keep

---

[113]Ibid., 126.
[114]Ibid., 125.
[115]Ibid., 117.

the question of transcendence open against the modern temptation to fore-
close on its possibility; transcendence and the theological questions it poses
are important regardless of the further question of actual or true reference.
So the actual phenomenon of human language of the transcendent allows
us to ask questions that interrogate this transcendence.[116]

Wright's commitment to asking questions of intention is also significant
here, since what the historian is after in understanding an ancient worldview
is the intended meaning, the thing expressed by the texts in question. To
illustrate, an example provided by Ben F. Meyer is instructive: "Bultmann
understood what the writer [John] meant by 'the Word was made flesh';
namely, 'a pre-existent heavenly being became man.' Over and above such a
meaning, however, there remains the question, 'But did a pre-existent
heavenly being actually become man?'"[117] The Johannine claim is intended
to mean what Bultmann claimed it meant. That is a claim open to the historian, and even more of interest to the theologian. But how does one move
from the interpretation of the Johannine claim to the more direct (some
would say, first-order) claim that John was right, that "a pre-existent heavenly
being became man"? In Wright's account of theology, the difference between
the two claims is overcome according to an account of metaphor and story.

The stories humans tell that reference the transcendent signal the presence
of "something we may as well call 'revelation.'"[118] This points us to the possibility of actual revelation, that is, the presence of language (or something
else)[119] that uniquely affirms transcendence.[120] But instead of being positivistic direct speech about god(s), Wright argues that god language is fundamentally metaphorical. Metaphors are "mini-stories" and as such preserve
the reality of the other as being greater than that which positivistically referring language can disclose.[121] But it is also metaphorical language that pre-

---

[116]This is a significant move for biblical studies, allowing the historian of the Bible to include
theological questions as part of a properly disciplined methodology.

[117]Meyer, *Aims of Jesus*, 105.

[118]*NTPG*, 129.

[119]Wright acknowledges that revelation might be understood by some to include part or all of the
following: the Bible, Christian stories, the beauty of creation, human beings or something deep
inside human beings. Judging between them would involve detailed arguments according to
the different worldviews involved. Ibid.

[120]Ibid.

[121]Ibid., 130.

vents the movement along the line from revelation to god(s) to be a direct line of reference. This places theological language "on the same footing as language about anything else."[122] As mini-stories, metaphors, and in our case language about god(s), belong within larger stories and therefore within worldviews. CRw, since it is committed to external reality, and in theology to the possibility of a divine referent, must ask questions with regard to the possibility that revelation speaks of a real god, but it must do this as a question within the critical context of worldviews. If revelation moves from its language in reference to god(s) to actual knowledge of God by way of metaphorical language and story, the question can be raised of criteria.

What are the criteria for successful reference? Or, given that all theology is worldview bound, what sort of criteria might exist to evaluate God-talk as truthful speech about its referent? In answer to this question Wright appeals to the criteria present in CRw that have already been established in the other three fields of discourse that his work engages: epistemology, literature and history.[123] First, and crucially, CRw admits that theological questions and their answers have to do with an external reality. This is not to beg the question of whether or not God exists, just to clarify that the subject matter in the question of theological speech is a reality (or unreality) external to the knower. But, in order to clarify further the way in which CRw understands the criteria for reference, the question can be split into two even more specific questions. First, what are the internal criteria for a claim to successfully refer? This question interrogates the claim according to the internal logic of the worldview within which the claim is made. Second, what are the public criteria according to which the claim can be judged? This second question interrogates the worldview itself along with its particular claims according to criteria from without (though not necessarily in contradiction with it) and always within another or overlapping worldview (there is no extra-worldview point of view). In CRw, as we have seen, the criteria for determining the truth of an event or a person (the subject matter of inquiry) is always provisional (within and without); it never rests upon an objectively known foundation. So the first question of internal criteria is answered by a demonstration of internal coherence, and the second is answered through comparison with

---

[122]Ibid.
[123]Ibid., 128.

alternative accounts of the reality in question. For example, in the case of the incarnation mentioned above, the claim would be judged according to its own coherence within the worldview of the community making the claim (first century, Johannine). The second question, that of external criteria, is answered by way of critically evaluating the claim based upon other possible explanations for the Johannine worldview and the historical data in question. In other words, for the question of criteria, we are directed to ask: What larger stories, internal and external, make sense of this particular theological belief?

Theology may indeed successfully refer—its claims may truly correspond to the being/nature of a real god(s). This is a possibility, but as we have seen, it is one that can never refer in a direct, positivistic way. Rather, theology refers through metaphor and story, forms of speech and knowledge that make sense and cohere only within comprehensive, yet provisional, accounts of reality. For Christian theology, a "Christian critical realism," stories, metaphors and myths are the ways in which "words in relation to the creator and redeemer God can be truly spoken."[124] Christian theology is an attempt to make sense of these stories and metaphors and the way they refer from within a coherent worldview. All theology, Christian or otherwise, does this by answering the four basic questions of any worldview: "Who are we?"; "Where are we?"; "What is wrong?" and "What is the solution?"[125] In this way, in other words, as an essential component of a worldview, theological language is, as we have seen, "on the same footing as language about anything else."[126] It is equally provisional, equally subject to critique and equally integral to a worldview. Theology drives toward knowledge of god(s) according to the questions that determine its worldview.

The claim that theological language is "on the same footing as language about anything else" points to the fact that theological language is public; it is open to investigation and critique from within and without. Worldviews do not protect their adherents from critique. This is precisely because of the realist dimension of CRw: the claim that language refers to external reality means that that reality is open to investigation, to the normal scientific pro-

---

[124]Ibid., 135. Wright suggests the argument that in the Jewish and Christian worldview(s) human speech is in principle adequate to the task of speaking about God because humans are made in the image of the God of whom they speak. Ibid., 130.

[125]Ibid., 132-33; cf. 123.

[126]Ibid., 130.

cesses that include hypothesis and verification, and to the critique to which all worldviews are subject.[127]

If theological language is integral to the task of answering the key questions that determine all worldviews (not excluding atheistic worldviews),[128] then crucial to understanding any human perspective in an even remotely comprehensive way will include questions of a theological nature. And since talk about god(s) refers, we can inquire about its referent. But if we follow Wright's graphic depiction of the movement of humans to knowledge of god(s), the point needs to be made that it is the (possible) objects of revelation—namely, texts and their stories, human experience, natural beauty, and so on—that are the subject matter of theological investigation, not god(s) directly.[129]

Christian theology, to which Wright turns after providing a more general account of theology, operates in this same way. "Christian theology only does what all other worldviews and their ancillary belief-systems do: it claims to be talking about reality as a whole."[130] Wright then goes on to fill out this picture of a Christian worldview according to the answers it provides to the four basic worldview questions. Furthermore, like all worldviews, the Christian one is a "public statement" and can therefore be brought forth, examined and debated.[131] It is not "just a private game, in which the players agree on the rules while outsiders look on in perplexity, it must appeal to some sense of fittingness or appropriateness. There must be, as in a scientific theory, a sense of clean simplicity, of things fitting together and making sense."[132] To be absolutely clear, Christian theology, according to Wright, is determined as a discipline according to the epistemological commitments of CRw, commitments that are *not* derived theologically. Rather, they are based upon an account of the general way in which humans know things. This does not mean that theological commitments cannot interrogate the very assumptions of CRw, for even CRw itself must be an epistemology subject to its own method of hypothesis and verification, and its own criteria of coherence. "All epistemologies have to be, themselves, argued

---

[127]See ibid.
[128]Ibid., 131.
[129]Ibid., 129.
[130]Ibid., 131, cf. 471.
[131]Ibid., 135.
[132]Ibid., 136.

as hypotheses: they are tested not by their coherence with a fixed point agreed in advance, but . . . by their simplicity and their ability to make sense out of a wide scope of experiences and events."[133]

In Wright's account, then, theology is a discipline that interacts with the givenness of human discourse about gods or a god and not, in a positivist sense, directly with gods or a god. In other words, in Wright's account theology appears to be a second-order discourse since it deals with talk about God ("god-talk-talk") and does not, as a first-order discourse, speak directly about God ("God-talk").[134] Or, if Christian speech about God does directly refer, it is only through story and metaphor, thereby qualifying and mediating theological speech by the critical context of worldviews. And yet it would be misleading to describe Wright's position in terms of "first-order" discourse and "second-order" discourse. CRw, if interpreted consistently as an attempt to reject epistemological dualisms, would reject as well the distinction between first-order discourse and second-order discourse. Claims about God and claims about what someone has said about God are treated in exactly the same way and are subject to the same criteria of verification. Language only successfully refers after it has gone through the critical process described by CRw, and then what counts as successful reference or knowledge is understood in terms of this process and not as if in a final stage of direct positivistic reference.[135] Normative statements about God (God-talk) would be subject to the same sort of criteria as knowledge about anything else. Of course, within worldviews theological language does make direct claims about God. God-talk happens. The point is that no theology can ever claim first-order status since it is always caught up within the complexities of worldviews. The desire to be able to speak in a way that would have the epistemological benefit of being able to be described as first-order is a desire to do something that assumes a positivist epistemological commitment, something that CRw does not allow. The best we can do is speak of the way in which worldviews demand theological talk because of the questions that they raise with respect to matters of ultimate concern.

---

[133]Ibid., 45-46. Italics added.

[134]For the use of "God-talk" and "god-talk-talk," see Alan J. Torrance, "Can the Truth Be Learned? Redressing the 'Theologistic Fallacy' in Modern Biblical Scholarship," in *Scripture's Doctrine and Theology's Bible: How the New Testament Shapes Christian Dogmatics*, ed. Markus Bockmuehl and Alan J. Torrance (Grand Rapids: Baker Academic, 2008), 144.

[135]*NTPG*, 128.

That Wright's account of theology is an account that is primarily concerned with human discourse regarding human discourse (even if it is discourse that refers to the divine) can be seen in the way he introduces the problem of Christology within the "Third Quest" for the historical Jesus in *JVG*. Wright begins with the question, "Is it possible to proceed, by way of historical study, to a portrait of Jesus which is sufficient of itself to evoke, or at least legitimate, that worship which Christianity has traditionally offered to him?"[136] The language here of *evoke* and *legitimate* is vague with respect to our question of criteria, but shortly after asking the above question Wright speaks of "three recent attempts to write about Jesus . . . in which history may be thought to lead to a positive christological conclusion."[137] It would be fair to conclude from these two statements that what Wright is asking about is the warrant for making strong theological claims about Jesus, claims such as Jesus is God incarnate and, therefore, worthy of worship. And, indeed, he clarifies this as "the attempt to move from Jesus to christology."[138] The "positive christological conclusion" that Wright leaves on the table is, or would be, warranted by proper historical method, which would include the questioning role of theology, but within the epistemological limits of worldviews. The approach that Wright takes in *JVG* attempts to do just this, to move from Jesus, historically understood, to a reconsideration of the high Christology of the church. This is a move from history to theology according to the epistemological criteria of CRw that we have been describing. Part of the motivation of Wright's program is to avoid the critique that would claim that his historical study itself is motivated by high christological concerns, an a priori commitment that favors the outcome. Against this critique, and as we have already seen, Wright says, "But, if we play the game properly—if, that is, we leave the meanings of 'divine' and 'human' as unknowns until we have looked at the material—then there can be no advance prediction of what the result may look like."[139] The result, in the last paragraph of *JVG*, looks like this:

> Forget the "titles" of Jesus, at least for the moment; forget the pseudo-orthodox attempts to make Jesus of Nazareth conscious of being the second

---

[136]*JVG*, 120.
[137]Ibid.
[138]Ibid., 121.
[139]Ibid.

person of the Trinity; forget the arid reductionism that is the mirror-image of that unthinking would-be orthodoxy. Focus, instead, on a young Jewish prophet telling a story about YHWH returning to Zion as judge and redeemer, and then embodying it by riding into the city in tears, symbolizing the Temple's destruction and celebrating the final exodus. I propose, as a matter of history, that Jesus of Nazareth was conscious of a vocation; a vocation given him by the one he knew as "father," to enact in himself what, in Israel's scriptures, God had promised to accomplish all by himself. He would be the pillar of cloud and fire for the people of the new exodus. He would embody in himself the returning and redeeming action of the covenant God.[140]

True to Wright's epistemology, the claims in this conclusion are relegated to considerations of Jesus' own aims and beliefs as a "matter of history." There are no first-order claims being made with respect to God. Wright avoids the trap of concluding with the claim, "Therefore, Jesus can be affirmed as the Son of God." In the three attempts to write about Jesus that Wright mentions, attempts that move from Jesus to Christology, the progression away from the temptation to make first-order claims can be seen. Edward Schillebeeckx, Wright reports, "at the end of his massive work, declares that he chooses to say, 'Jesus is the Son of God.'"[141] Anthony Harvey, moving further from this sort of claim, focuses his attention on the *possibility* that historical inquiry "will enable us to understand better what it might mean to claim that 'God was with' a person of history . . . and become an object, not only of our endless and fascinated study, but of our love and worship."[142] Schillebeeckx made a statement of faith while Harvey hoped to be able to make the claim based on historical inquiry. Ben Witherington, as the third example, turns his attention to the way in which Jesus saw himself: "Having argued in detail that Jesus believed himself to be Messiah, [Witherington] opts for a cautious but open-ended possibility: that Jesus saw himself 'not merely as a greater king than David but in a higher and more transcendent category.'"[143] This illustrates the significant move from direct claims

---

[140]Ibid., 653.

[141]*JVG*, 121. Cf. Edward Schillebeeckx, *Jesus: An Experiment in Christology* (New York: Seabury Press, 1979 [1974]).

[142]*JVG*, 121. Cf. Anthony Harvey, *Jesus and the Constraints of History: The Bampton Lectures, 1980* (London: Duckworth, 1982), 10.

[143]*JVG*, 121. Cf. Ben Witherington III, *The Christology of Jesus* (Minneapolis: Fortress Press, 1990), 276.

made about who Jesus was to what Jesus, as a historical figure, believed about himself. This latter quest limits the claims of historical method, but requires theology to help make these claims, since theology is needed to accurately interrogate the beliefs and aims of historical figures. Yet it is a move from history to theology that does not allow theology to be engaged in first-order speech about God.[144] The question with regard to the church's high Christology comes to the fore when we ask whether or not Jesus was correct in his beliefs, and whether or not the church is warranted in its belief that Jesus not only had these aims and beliefs (and Wright makes a per- suasive case that he did), but that he was, indeed, *Emmanuel,* God with us.

Is theology, according to Wright, unique with respect to its object? If the- ology is considered within the field of the sociology of knowledge, then it appears that it must remain a sociological project, that is, a project that is rooted in the social dimensions of inquiry, and not in some unique way at- tached to a transcendent object.[145] The object of theology would thus be human discourse and praxis with respect to the divine (or gods and/or god). If God is to be known within human discourse about God, then our episte- mological limits are no different than human knowledge about anything else. They are subject to the same sort of criteria. This seems to be exactly what Wright is arguing.[146] Within a worldview we might be able to extend our inter- rogation to ask questions and articulate answers about God directly, but it is not clear that this sort of task would provide us any different epistemological considerations than were we to interrogate past historical events that were not divine. The question that this begs is precisely the question of the nature, the metaphysical and ontological nature, of the object of theology—namely, God. How is God to be known if, according to the Christian worldview, God is

---

[144]It is important to be reminded here that Wright's epistemology would consider such direct claims to be erroneously positivistic if they were not caught up in the limitations of worldviews. If they are part of worldviews, then their epistemological status is not different than claims about anything else.

[145]See, e.g., *NTPG,* 472.

[146]It is important not to exclude from this the consideration that Wright pays to the role of faith. Faith, for Wright, is not to be divorced from history. Considered together with history it can be episte- mologically fruitful. Wright characterizes this sort of knowledge as personal knowledge, yet as it plays out in his methodology, faith knowledge seems to be a component of the larger epistemology of worldviews. See his discussion of faith in Marcus Borg and N. T. Wright, *The Meaning of Jesus: Two Visions* (New York: Harper Collins, 1999), 25-27.

"active within the world but not contained within it"?[147] It is precisely this line of questioning that will be taken up in the following chapter.

Wright's Challenge to Theology

Before moving on to that discussion, however, it is important to conclude this chapter with a brief summary of the critical challenges that Wright poses for the theologian. As we have seen, Wright's attempted retrieval of the historian's role for theology is grounded in his account of the Reformation's abstraction of theology and doctrine from the historical narratives that made sense of them. Broadly conceived, this can be called the problem of abstraction. Against the tendency to abstract theological concepts from the history in which they are based, the story that makes up the historian's concern

> is precisely the story of the real world, the world of space, time and matter, of actual events. My first real problem of not doing history properly is that we shrink the story of God and God's kingdom in Jesus, and the story of Jesus bringing Israel's story to it's climax—which two stories are not two but one—to the thin, abstract categories of "divinity" and "humanity." It is much safer, less risky, to do that; much more in line with "the tradition" but much less like the real Gospels, or the real gospel.[148]

In Wright's understanding, Christian doctrines are like "suitcases" that function as compact, portable stories and symbols that must be unpacked from time to time to make sure we have them in the right narrative context. The problem comes when they are abstracted from particular narratives and then replaced into other narratives to which they are not germane.[149]

Theological abstraction away from the narratives of the Bible makes the misplacement of theological concepts a very real danger.[150] Against this, the

---

[147]NTPG, 135.

[148]JPPG, 137. See also his characterization of the definition of Chalcedon (without rejecting it) as reimagining divinity and humanity "within a partly de-Judaized world of thought." Ibid., 135.

[149]This argument is made in Wright's essay "Reading Paul, Thinking Scripture," in Scripture's Doctrine, Theology's Bible, ed. Alan J. Torrance and Markus Bockmuehl (Grand Rapids: Baker Academic, 2008), 59-71.

[150]This is evident in Wright's polemical engagement with John Piper over Pauline soteriology. Wright counters Piper's commitment to a narrow understanding of Reformed theology with an articulation of what ought to be a shared commitment to the practice of good exegesis: "The more we know about first-century Judaism, about the Greco-Roman world of the day, about archaeology, the Dead Sea Scrolls and so on, the more, in principle, we can be on firm ground in anchoring

task of the historian is to see the story from the perspective, the worldview, of those who told the story in the first place; the historian seeks the intentions, beliefs and aims of the characters in the story in order to understand what they saw and how they believed. Without this attention to the aims and intentions of the biblical writers, the aims and intentions of the interpreters of Scripture will tend to take over. This means that the personal and communal theological commitments of the writers of the Bible belong together with the narratives that they tell and that the reality to which they refer is seen from the perspective of their respective and overlapping worldviews. The theologian who disregards the importance of the constructive contribution from the historian who holds together questions of reality, narrative and theology will inevitably interpret the story in terms of a foreign worldview, importing, for example, modern metaphysical or epistemological distinctions into a story where they do not belong.[151]

On one hand, this is simply the problem of exegesis versus eisegesis. The theological development of doctrine has a long and storied history that makes the theological contribution to the interpretation of Scripture a contribution that often stands on its own. Theological abstractions such as the "humanity" and "divinity" of "Christ" are read into the biblical narratives and determine, with hermeneutical force, the supposed exegetical conclusions of interpretation. This presses the important question of how theological concepts relate to the biblical stories and to the historical data that contribute to, and are derived from, those stories. For Wright, these theological concepts are never free from their own contexts within worldviews, and these worldviews need to be critically examined and brought into dialogue with the worldviews of Scripture, within which the subject matter of theology and the subject matter of the historian coincide. In this view, the theological concepts that have made up the church's teachings need to be always committed to the ideal of *ecclesia catholica semper reformanda*.[152] The

---

exegesis that might otherwise remain speculative, and at the mercy of massively anachronistic eisegesis, into the solid historical context where—if we believe in inspired Scripture in the first place—that inspiration occurred." Wright, *Justification: God's Plan and Paul's Vision* (Downers Grove, IL: IVP Academic, 2009), 47.

[151]See Wright's discussion of faith and history in chap. 2 of Markus Borg and N. T. Wright, *The Meaning of Jesus*, and his brief articulation of an epistemology of love, contra the subject-object dichotomy, in *JPPG*, 146-47.

[152]*JRI*, 248.

reformation of theology is to be guided in this case by the corrective work of the biblical historian. And above all, the concepts of the theologian are to be understood as subservient to the story from which they are derived.[153] We might say that for Wright, the story is the thing, not the doctrine, and that the task of exegesis is getting the story right, not the derivation of abstract principles found within the story.

The theologian, on the other hand, is a crucial aid to the scholar studying the biblical worldview simply because the biblical worldview contains theological questions. As we have seen, the theologian works within the context of worldviews and examines the questions of ultimate meaning that make worldviews what they are. The task of articulating the theological questions and answers of the worldview of the biblical authors is especially aided by theologians who are able to articulate the interrelationships between the various theological convictions that find expression in the text. In this way the theologian deals with the reality of the text and the reality of the writers of the text; the theologian deals with the subject matter of Scripture. This work of theological interpretation also benefits the critical side of CRw by directing attention to the theological questions and assumptions, "the presuppositions, aims and intentions"[154] of the contemporary interpreters of Scripture, as well as the intellectual movements that have influenced interpretation.

Yet, beyond the emphasis on proper exegesis, the critique of abstraction is a more significant critique since it is connected with an account of epistemology that encloses theology within the purview of the epistemological limits defined by worldviews. If all knowledge is critically circumscribed within an epistemology of worldviews, and theological knowledge is no different from other sorts of knowledge in this respect, then theology is limited with respect to its subject matter by the same limits as any knowledge. The air that theological concepts breathe is, as with other disciplines, air that is conditioned by the hermeneutical limits of human knowing. There is no

---

[153]This can be seen in the following statement that Wright makes with regard to Pauline theology: "Underneath all this is the argument . . . that Paul's whole view of Christ and the law can be understood in terms of the *story* of God and the people of God—a story which cannot be reduced to a single formula or proposition, but which when viewed whole can be seen to have the proper integration and coherence that a story ought to have." N. T. Wright, *The Climax of the Covenant: Christ and the Law in Pauline Theology* (Minneapolis: Fortress Press, 1993), 258. Cf. *NTPG*, 138n26.

[154]*NTPG*, 138.

rarefied theological air, privileged because of its subject matter, but rather, theology kicks around in the dust, especially the dust of first-century Palestine (or at least it ought to).[155]

Wright's critique of theology may be summed up as an extended argument for proper, historically grounded exegesis, following the normal scientific procedures of hypothesis and verification, and the limitation of theology to the discursive confines of worldviews with the same epistemological criteria as other forms of knowledge.

CONCLUSION

With these criticisms, Wright challenges Christian theologians to pay close attention to the worldviews that determine their own way of seeing, and to pay equally close attention to the worldviews of those who were both the writers of the Christian story, the New Testament, and the subject matter of that writing, most notably Jesus of Nazareth. It is by paying attention to the way in which all human knowing is caught up in ways of seeing, that is, worldviews, that theologians can avoid the twin dangers inherent in an idealist abstraction that would lead away from the concrete reality of God's involvement with history. By grounding both his historical method and theological method in CRw with its concomitant conception of worldview, Wright offers a holistic vision of human knowledge in integrated, relational contact with the world. Included in this relational contact is that which theologians refer to as revelation, and what Christians refer to as the writings of Scripture; the contact comes at the level of worldview. As our own worldviews come into contact with the worldviews of Scripture, we discover that the Scriptures "are written, in their different ways, to articulate and invite their hearers to share a new worldview which carries at its heart a new view

---

[155]Cf. Richard Hays's essay in *JPPG*, where he reports on Wright's criticism of a collection of essays produced out of "The Identity of Jesus Project" sponsored by the Center of Theological Inquiry in Princeton, NJ: Beverly Roberts Gaventa and Richard B. Hays, eds., *Seeking the Identity of Jesus: A Pilgrimage* (Grand Rapids: Eerdmans, 2008). Hays writes that "Tom greeted the book with sharp criticism, chiefly because he saw its approach to seeking Jesus as insufficiently historical. Our 'pilgrimage,' he said, was overdetermined by dogmatic concerns and theological traditions, and inattentive to the realities of first-century history. Real pilgrims, Tom observed, would get their feet dirty on the dusty roads of ancient Palestine. But this book of essays was instead 'a pilgrimage by helicopter,' and its authors and editors were 'pilgrims with suspiciously clean feet.'" *JPPG*, 43.

of 'god,' and even a proposal for a way of saying 'God.'"[156]

This suggests a way forward. If the question animating Wright's entire project is the discovery of and proposal for a way of saying "God," then this raises the following question: What bearing does the reality of God have on the critical realist project? If God is the object of knowledge, the subject matter of our ultimate concern, how does God's reality impinge upon and even determine the way in which he is known?

---

[156]*NTPG*, 472.

2

Theology According to
the Theologians

CRITICAL REALISM AND THE OBJECT
OF KNOWLEDGE IN THEOLOGY

THE PREVIOUS CHAPTER INTRODUCED the specific contri-
bution of N. T. Wright to the methodological and epistemological questions
regarding the relationship between theology and historiography. Wright's
work, as I have presented it, is a case study in the contemporary allocation
of theological questions oriented within a historiographical framework, and
purposed toward a constructive contribution to a historically grounded theology. In other words, Wright is useful to look at because of his attempt to
bring together a commitment to historical knowledge and a concern for
theological questions. Further, Wright's questions are the church's questions,
and his method is governed by his *theological* commitment to history. Yet
his historical method overtakes his theological commitment by submitting
both history and theology to the epistemological frame of CRw. Fundamental to *both* history and theology is his account of human knowing. Theology is ordered according to human questions regarding ultimate meaning,
and revelation is present in the world as an object of knowledge in the same
way as other objects of knowledge are present in the world. One way of
clarifying this would be to say that Wright's formal account of epistemology
relies upon the material content of human questions regarding ultimate
meaning; it starts with the questioning subject. In this way, his epistemology

has a transcendental structure, one that gains knowledge according to the rational answers to human questioning, even if that questioning is regarding revelation.[1] As we will see, the theological approach I will describe in this chapter begins with the material content of revelation and orders an epistemology around that content, especially the divine object of knowledge.[2] What this looks like is the task of this chapter.

This chapter and the next aim to reverse the direction of Wright's epistemology in order to see *theology* from the perspective of the theologian. Following these chapters we will then look at *history* from this newly articulated theological perspective. What does theology, with its methodological assumptions and commitments, have to say about the historian's work? By letting Wright have the first word in the present chapter, the following discussion intends to be shaped by his critically realist concerns, and so begins by asking the following very specific question: What is the epistemological significance of the object of knowledge *if* the object of knowledge is God?

A brief look again to Wright will be followed by a clarification of the subject-object distinction in modern theology and philosophy, and then our attention will be turned toward two theologians, T. F. Torrance and Søren Kierkegaard,

---

[1]That Wright's epistemology has a transcendental structure is further suggested by his close reliance on the work of Ben F. Meyer and Meyer's account of critical realism. In *The Aims of Jesus*, Meyer, discussing the relationship between theology and history, endorses in his approach the "transcendental method" of Bernard Lonergan (Ben F. Meyer, *The Aims of Jesus*, Princeton Theological Monograph Series, vol. 48 [Eugene, OR: Pickwick Publications, 2002], 280n30). Meyer articulates this according to a "morality of knowledge" at work in a "pre-critical" way: "It is the confident supposition that human intelligence intends the real and attains it. . . . By this route [i.e. questioning] it brings to light the realized conditions of the possibility of attaining the real by intelligence, thereby disclosing the further possibility that men should be 'hearers of the word'" (ibid., 108-9). The purpose of Meyer's comments in this section of *Aims* is to move from the skeptical hermeneutics of Cartesian criticism to the positive and engaged hermeneutics of a precritical approach in full faithfulness with the creedal tradition of the church. This positive assessment of history (and a quick dismissal and mischaracterization of Barth; 107) is theoretically bound to a deeper epistemological commitment to the transcendental Thomism of Lonergan. *In nuce*, as Robert Sokolowski writes, "Lonergan infers from the complete intelligibility of being to the affirmation that God exists" (Robert Sokolowski, *The God of Faith and Reason: Foundations of Christian Theology* [Washington, DC: The Catholic University of America Press, 1995], 109). The account of theological epistemology that I will provide in this chapter overcomes Meyer's dichotomy between critical and precritical, rejecting any hint of a transcendental methodology, by moving deeper into the space opened up by Karl Barth's theology, here represented by T. F. Torrance.

[2]Wright is suspicious of words like *divine* to the extent that they force into the abstract an ideal concept of the very historical and particular God revealed in the Hebrew and Christian Scriptures. Here and elsewhere where I use such language I am mindful of the problem, but have been unable to find a less awkward alternative.

both of whom deal in depth with the concepts of objectivity and subjectivity, respectively. Torrance, perhaps more than any other theologian, has emphasized the objectivity of God in the theological enterprise; and Kierkegaard, through his pseudonymous works as Johannes Climacus, powerfully turns objectivity into a radical subjectivity. The goal of this chapter, then, is to begin to articulate the relationship between the object of knowledge and the human subject's relationship to that object if that object is the God revealed in the Bible.

CRw and the Object of Knowledge

As we saw in his methodological proposal, Wright gives theological knowledge the same epistemological status as knowledge about anything else. But are all objects of knowledge the same? In Wright's articulation of a Christian worldview he describes God as "active within the world but not contained within it."[3] If this is the case, what does this unique ontological category "active but not contained" with respect to the world mean, and in what way does an external reality of this sort effect the way in which it can be known? In order to answer this question we will pursue a further examination of the way in which CRw is positioned as an epistemology with respect to ontological and metaphysical questions. To do this, I will first show how CRw compares with some other forms of CR and suggest that what needs expansion in Wright's account are particularly the metaphysical and ontological questions that bear upon the status of the "real" in CRw. This claim will be deepened with a close examination of the nature of the object in theology and its bearing on the subject-object relationship.

Realism is the determinative epistemological commitment for Wright. The problem of historical method is how we can know this past reality and know it in a meaningful way. Wright's solution, as we have seen, depends upon redefining knowledge itself within the complex structure of a conceptualized account of worldviews. But to speak of the knowledge of reality begs the question of the ontological status of the reality in question. For Wright, CRw is exclusively concerned with epistemological questions and leaves open the question of the nature of reality, even though it is committed to a realist ontology. By doing so, Wright leaves open a significant point at which a corrective to his method can be introduced. In his book *Critical Scientific Realism*,

---

[3]*NTPG*, 135.

Ilkka Niiniluoto identifies "six different problems of realism," which include the problems of ontology, semantics, epistemology, axiology, methodology and ethics.[4] He includes table 1 to clarify each sort of problem:[5]

Table 1

Ontological: Which entities are real? Is there a mind-independent world?	(OR)
Semantical: Is truth an objective language-world relation?	(SR)
Epistemological: Is knowledge about the world possible?	(ER)
Axiological: Is truth one of the aims of inquiry?	(AR)
Methodological: What are the best methods for pursuing knowledge?	(MR)
Ethical: Do moral values exist in reality?	(VR)

Wright's methodological contribution, CRw, if we were to classify it according to Niiniluoto's categories, lines up nicely with the middle four questions but leaves aside the first (OR) and the last (VR). The premise that Wright assumes at the outset—namely, that external reality exists—is clearly a claim regarding OR, but the philosophical arguments that would fill in that claim are left for others. He does mention the problem of an "undiscussed metaphysic" if attention is not paid to "presuppositional matters";[6] however, the ontological status of reality external to the knower is left largely untouched. His program works if we grant his limited foundational claim that there is an external reality and that it exists independently of the knower. In this way he does pay attention to this aspect of his presupposition, but the ontological content of this metaphysical assumption is left for others. All three areas of concern that he is addressing—history, theology and literature—include ontological and metaphysical assumptions that require articulation if the epistemology of each is going to be adequately defended. Wright understands this: "If this means we end up needing a new metaphysic, so be it. It would be pleasant if, for once, the historians and the theologians could set the agenda for the philosophers, instead of *vice versa*."[7]

---

[4]Ilkka Niiniluoto, *Critical Scientific Realism* (Oxford: Oxford University Press, 1999), 2.
[5]Ibid.
[6]*NTPG*, 31.
[7]*JVG*, 8. With this offhand comment it seems there is reason to suggest that Wright and Barth would be sympathetic to each other regarding the primacy of theology over philosophy. It also serves to highlight the question to which this book is directed—namely, the relationship between history and theology. In what way can *both* contribute to a new metaphysics?

For now it should be clear that Wright is attempting to address an epistemo-logical question while allowing the vague term "external reality" to hold the place of a yet-to-be-articulated ontology and metaphysics.

It could be argued that ontological questions are beside the point if CRw is concerned primarily with the sociology of knowledge. That is, if an un-derstanding of how people know things is understandable apart from the things themselves, if questions of correspondence are never asked, then on-tology can be pushed aside in favor of pragmatic concerns regarding the usefulness of beliefs for the present.[8] In some ways Wright's method has similarities to this aspect of pragmatism. He is concerned with questions of method that are not foundational, but rather reflect the way in which humans know things, a way of knowing that is discovered a posteriori, as a belief is shown to fit into a worldview. But his commitment to reality as externally real and knowable as such (properly nuanced), as that with which worldviews interact, makes his critical realism distinct from pragmatism.[9]

But neither is Wright's realism committed to a presuppositional account of reality that requires certain philosophical or theological commitments a priori in order for humans to know things. His account of critical realism is an ob-servational account of what counts as human knowledge, while arguing that such an account is normative on the grounds that this is simply how it works. Description precedes prescription. One could move from there to a pragmatic refusal to argue for a normative account of human inquiry or epistemological method, but to do so would require disregard for the question of the reality of the external world. Wright, as we have seen, is fundamentally committed to the external reality of the subject matter of inquiry, and it is this question of reality that animates his historical and theological quests. Since, in Wright's view, we cannot escape worldviews, our account of reality must necessarily acknowledge this as a determining factor in what makes knowledge count as knowledge.

Therefore, if Wright's method is not purely pragmatic, but rather is com-mitted to realism in both theology and history, then the question of the

---

[8] On a pragmatic historiography, see the programmatic essay by Colin Koopman, "Historicism in Pragmatism: Lessons in Historiography and Philosophy," *Metaphilosophy* 41, no. 5 (October 2010): 696-703.

[9] For a pragmatist discussion on the difference between Christian worldview philosophy and pragmatism, see J. Wesley Robbins, "Christian World View Philosophy and Pragmatism," *Journal of the American Academy of Religion* 56, no. 3 (Autumn 1988): 529-43.

ontological status of the reality in question will be important precisely because of the way the "real" functions in critical realism. As we have seen, in
his most concise statement of critical realism, Wright points to an interaction, a "conversation between the knower and the thing known."[10] It is this
conversation that provides the "critical" aspect of CRw in a way that Wright
describes as "passive": "realism *subject* to critique."[11] The object of knowledge,
by virtue of its reality and the possibility of a certain qualified contact by the
subject with that reality, is itself a limiting factor in the epistemological
process. Another way of saying this is that the object of knowledge is assumed as real (passive) but comes under critique as critique becomes necessary; knowledge of its reality (*that* it exists) is not the end result of a
process of rational criticism. But the important question with respect to God
as the object of knowledge, as the real, is whether or not God relates to the
knower in a way that upsets the "conversation" of CRw. Can God, as an
object of knowledge, be known in the same way as any other object, or does
his unique ontological identity—unique with respect to every other object
available for knowledge—demand a new, or modified, account of human
knowing *for just this object*?

The Subject-Object Relationship

A realist perspective, at the most basic level, requires that the normal epistemological distinction is maintained between the knowing subject and the
object of knowledge. Reality external to the knower is distinct from the
knower. Retaining the language of *subject* and *object* maintains this distinction
between the knower and the known and preserves the commitment to the
reality of the world external to the knower as something truly other, as object.
In various ways this distinction has been assumed thus far by referring to the
knower and the *known*, or the *knowing subject* and the *subject matter* or *object
of knowledge*, as we have examined the epistemological and methodological
position of Wright. Wright's own definition of CRw depends upon these two
poles, subject and object, as it "acknowledges the reality of the thing known,

---

[10]*NTPG*, 35.
[11]Ibid., 35n12.

as something *other* than the knower."[12] Since the critical philosophy of Kant, the language of subject and object has accrued a long history of nuanced articulations, not the least of which is the assumption of an epistemological dualism, predating Kant, that assumes an *epistemological* gulf between the knower and the thing known. This gulf can be described as "the Cartesian assumption that the nature or reality of everything outside a person is fixed and can neither be known directly by the person nor influenced by the person's interpretation of it."[13] The difference here between the knower and the known becomes a problem, the gulf becomes another "ugly ditch" and the problem of epistemology is set up as the problem of overcoming that ditch.

The normal epistemological pressure, before Kant, was directed *from* the external world *to* the knowing subject. Objects in the world were known as they impinged upon the senses, were interpreted by the knower and were given identifying signs through language. With Kant the direction was reversed, and the epistemological pressure was placed within the knowing subject[14] (the linguistic turn would come later). Kant was, in part, responding to the perceived skepticism of David Hume regarding the possibility of reason to secure universals that could be the basis for metaphysics, "concepts that would extend our cognition."[15] Because of the gulf between subject and object, the experiences of the external world could not be shown to have any bearing whatsoever—no causal connections—on metaphysics. Kant wanted, instead, to establish metaphysics based purely upon thinking, to show how the subject could be the basis for a limited metaphysics that established what it could regarding objects "before they are given to us." At the risk of oversimplification, Kant was trying to make sense of the way we experience the world, not by looking at the nature of the world, but first by looking at the nature of the subject and what the subject brought to the world, according to which the world might make (limited) metaphysical sense. In this way,

---

[12]*NTPG*, 35. Italics added.

[13]This helpful description comes from Roland Daniel Zimany, *Vehicle for God: The Metaphorical Theology of Eberhard Jüngel* (Macon, GA: Mercer University Press, 1994), 50.

[14]And, as James Brown points out, the very terminology of *subject* and *object* and the way those terms are used in English today are dependent upon the use Kant made of them in his first critique (and Coleridge's introduction of them to England). See *Subject and Object in Modern Theology* (London: SCM Press, 1955), 19-21.

[15]Immanuel Kant, *Critique of Pure Reason*, trans. and ed. Paul Guyer and Alan W. Wood (Cambridge: Cambridge University Press, 1998), 110.

"any given phenomenon . . . becomes a clear and definite object only in and through the act of thought itself."[16]

Turning from this to the epistemology of T. F. Torrance, one might have the initial impression that he simply reverses the Kantian move by reverting to the assumption that "all our cognition must conform to the object." If the subject-object distinction remains, as it does in the work of Torrance, it remains without the epistemological gulf assumed by Kant. Discussing the work of John Macmurray, Torrance writes,

> If . . . we start off with pure thought, we at once abstract from action, and so isolate our knowledge from that which sustains it, isolating the self from existence as a purely logical subject concerned only with idea, that is, with the non-existent. It is precisely this radical dualism falsely posited between thinking and existence, knowledge and action, that lies behind so many of our modern problems, and therefore it must be rejected in order that "a new logical form of personal activity" may be developed in which the theory of knowledge occupies a subordinate place within actual knowledge, and in which verification involves commitment in action.[17]

The removal of this epistemological gulf occurs as the relationship between subject and object is defined by subjective action as Macmurray suggests, and by *contact* between subject and object. The subject in this account is not abstract "cognition" or the "mind" but rather the *existing* subject who is not abstracted from the material world. As James Brown argues, Kant's subject, even if it is closer to this material conception because of the attention he pays to the "skeleton" of the mind with his articulation of the manifold of a priori categories to which objects conform in the process of knowing, is nevertheless still a "means to an end" of "necessary knowledge," something that is of greater interest than the subject itself.[18] This, Brown argues, is due in large part to Kant's interest in a more narrow kind of knowledge; knowledge that is true "knowledge" is modeled according to the empiricism of the natural sciences, and Kant's account of the self is ordered to this end. However, there are other objects of knowledge in other areas of

---

[16]Roger A. Johnson, *The Origins of Demythologizing: Philosophy and Historiography in the Theology of Rudolf Bultmann*, Studies in the History of Religions (Leiden: E. J. Brill, 1974), 43.

[17]T. F. Torrance, *Theological Science* (London: Oxford University Press, 1969), 4.

[18]Brown, *Subject and Object in Modern Theology*, 25-26.

inquiry that do not lend themselves so readily to the sharp division between subject and object. Art, morality and religion are three of these areas, each of which has an objectivity unique to its area of discourse.[19] This points out the fact that the subject-object distinction on its own is not sufficient to make metaphysical claims; rather, each area of knowledge brings with it its own unique metaphysical assumptions.

> In Kant's own system, from which the terms "subjective" and "objective" take their modern origin, the scales seem heavily weighted in favour of scientific naturalism. . . . But this is semblance only. Kant is sure of the moral law within his breast as equally self-authenticating in its majestic and even numinous splendour with the starry heavens above. If he seems to rest assurance of God, freedom and immortality on the inferior testimony of faith rather than knowledge, we may see in this the effects of a ready-made metaphysics which he brought to his task, which presupposed that knowledge is of phenomena only. What is this but to say that he held without argument to the existence of noumenal reality? . . . The entire scheme of things is not explicable in terms of natural science, nor is final truth bound by [natural science's] conception of objectivity.[20]

The subject-object distinction solves no ontological problems. These problems are assumed into the subject-object relation based upon other arguments, arguments that are determined according to the nature of the variety of particular objects of knowledge.

The point here is to clarify an account of the subject in the subject-object relation that is not an abstraction into the realm of the ideal, but rather remains, for lack of a better word, "embodied." If there is an epistemological gulf, it is one that has been created by the attempt to establish an idealistic basis for it, abstracted from the realm of objects. If knowledge is to be freed from epistemological dualism, it must be freed from the idealism that would posit the subject as proximally separate or isolated from the object of knowledge. Instead, the self must be understood not as a concept derived from the abstraction of thought, but rather from the unity of experience as the unity of the self. In this way the theory of knowledge is replaced by an account of "actual knowledge" in which the self is understood in relation to

---

[19]Ibid., 29.
[20]Ibid., 31.

the world and not in abstraction from it.[21] At this point the similarity with
Wright's account should be apparent.

But the object of theological knowledge is God and not simply "external
reality." What sort of "object" might God be said to be, and what does the
subject-object distinction look like if we place God as one of the pair? If the
epistemological gulf is overcome through an epistemology of contact, then
we cannot abstract "god" from the God, say, of Israel.

We must simply reinforce the point made earlier, that we already begin
in a knowing relationship to the God under question. The God we are
seeking to know is the God of the Bible, the God of Israel, and the God who
has revealed himself as Jesus the Messiah and has done this and continues
to do so in the church for the world.[22] We, as subjects, are proximal to this
God. For Christian theology it is *this* relationship we are investigating and
no other. Therefore the question of the knowledge of *this* God is not going
to be abstracted either from the history of his relationship to his people or
the world, and it is not going to be abstracted from the dogmatic content of
Christian teaching or proclamation.[23] If we are going to avoid a radical
epistemological dualism between subject and object, then the resolution to
our question regarding the relationship between theological knowledge and
historical knowledge will need to follow Torrance when he writes that "how
God can be known must be determined from first to last by the way in which
He actually is known."[24] It is this *actuality* of the knowledge relationship
between the human subject and God, who is the object of knowledge, that
determines the nature of the subject-object relationship in Christian theology. I take this to be fully consistent so far with Wright's epistemology.

The Object of Knowledge in Theology

The knowledge of "god" in N. T. Wright. In *NTPG* the knowledge of God is
treated no differently than the knowledge of reality external to the knower

---

[21]John Macmurray, *The Self as Agent* (London: Faber and Faber, 1962), 82.

[22]This is similar in many respects to Wright's acknowledgment of the Christian worldview that he
assumes in *NTPG*, 131-34.

[23]Cf. T. F. Torrance: "What is offered in this discussion presupposes the full content of theological
knowledge, and is the attempt to set forth the way of proper theological knowledge in accordance
with that content" (*Theological Science*, 10-11).

[24]Ibid., 9.

in general. Wright's epistemology subsumes God ("god"), de facto, within the "class" of objects for our purview, that is, all those objects external to the knowing subject. In the chapter in which he introduces CRw, Wright claims that this epistemology is useful for a wide variety of fields of inquiry including everything from literature to theology.[25] That Wright is committed to this epistemology with respect to the question of God is suggested by the purposeful yet idiosyncratic use of the lower case when writing *god*. Conversely, using the capital letter "would be begging the question" and "follow[ing] a usage which seemed to imply that the answer was known in advance."[26] CRw is an epistemological method that approaches the knowledge of God in the same way as knowledge of history. In fact, this seems to be a significant characteristic of Wright's entire project. In an autobiographical passage, written in a book he coauthored with Marcus Borg, Wright describes his personal liberation through an interweaving of faith and history free from a "split-level" world of faith divorced from history.[27] In rebellion against the "tyrannical thought-forms in whose split-level world I had grown up," he describes how his study of first-century Judaism "led me, at length, out into fresh epistemological air, and the new, risky choices of a single world with multiple interlocking dimensions."[28] Presumably, this "single world" is the single context in which knowledge of God and of history are of one kind, our knowledge of which can be described according to the process of CRw. This metaphysical framework leaves significant questions, and demands further clarity. The question remains: Is the epistemological process of CRw adequate to the metaphysical and ontological demands of a proper epistemology in both areas of knowledge—history and theology?[29] Can theology be treated within this "single world" with "interlocking di-

---

[25]*NTPG*, 32.

[26]Ibid., xv. I will not follow Wright's convention in this book.

[27]N. T. Wright and Marcus Borg, *The Meaning of Jesus: Two Visions* (New York, Harper Collins: 1999), 16.

[28]Ibid.

[29]Wright's comments on the resurrection being the "starting-point for a Christian epistemology" are an interesting case that suggests that the weight of the demands that the resurrection makes upon historical methodology have been taken into consideration. Nevertheless, he uses the resurrection as a validation of his epistemological method rather than something that might call it into question. This point will be taken up later in the discussion. See Wright, "Resurrection: From Theology to Music and Back Again," in *Sounding the Depths: Theology Through the Arts*, ed. J. Begbie (London: SCM Press, 2002), 206-11.

mensions"? And what is a proper epistemology if God is the object, or subject matter, under investigation?

The argument to be pursued here is that the relationship between epistemology and history in Wright's method, theologically understood, ought to begin with a theological epistemology determined by the object of knowledge. Historical knowledge, to the extent that it is focused on the knowledge of God (or "god"), must grapple with the nature of this unique object. Therefore a prior examination of theological epistemology will set the proper context in which to open up a subsequent examination of the epistemological and theological issues inherent in the historical knowledge of God and his acts. This will, in turn, set up an opportunity to articulate a constructive proposal for a theology of history in dialogue with the one that Wright has offered. This chapter begins the epistemological task by reading together T. F. Torrance and Søren Kierkegaard.

T. F. Torrance's theological science: knowledge in relation. Theology is concerned with the knowledge of God, so the question of the adequacy of CRw to the object of theological discourse is the question of the adequacy of an account of epistemology to the subject matter of theology. In T. F. Torrance's *Theological Science*, the knowledge of God is approached in a way that is in fundamental agreement with the formal shape of Wright's epistemology; Torrance begins with what we already know, that is, he begins within the knowledge relation itself. Similarly, Wright begins with the understanding that when we articulate an epistemology we find that we are already in a relation to the thing known,[30] what I have described as an understanding of knowledge as "contact." Torrance, drawing on philosophers as diverse as Husserl, Macmurray and Kierkegaard, begins his account of the knowledge of God with the claim that "in any branch of knowledge we begin within the knowledge relation where we actually are, and seek to move forward by clarifying and testing what we already know and by seeking to deepen and enlarge its content."[31] For both Wright and Torrance then, the actual relationship between the knower and the known is prior to the epistemological task. As Torrance goes on to say, in the epistemological task we "seek to move forward by clarifying and testing what we already know and by seeking to deepen and enlarge its content. To do this we are forced at

---

[30]*NTPG*, 45.
[31]Torrance, *Theological Science*, 2.

some time to raise questions as to the ground and reality of this knowledge."[32] This is the principle that Torrance then goes on to elaborate in more detail, moving beyond the mere formal structure of knowledge in general to the material content of a specifically theological knowledge.

For theology, this means that theological knowledge begins with an already existing relation between the knower and the one known. Theology investigates this relation a posteriori, and therefore is determined externally by the unique dynamic *in actuality* of the relationship between God and the subject who knows God. Torrance defines theology that begins this way as "scientific theology," in which "we begin with the actual knowledge of God, and seek to test and clarify this knowledge by inquiring carefully into the relation between our knowing of God and God Himself in His being and nature."[33] What this suggests is that the way forward, if we are to stay centered on the concerns of Wright's methodological proposals in epistemology, theology and history, must interrogate the nature of the *existing* relationship between the knower and the God who is known.

Expounding in more depth the nature of the knowledge of God and its implications, and drawing heavily on Karl Barth's theological epistemology in *CD* II/1, Torrance sets his epistemological task so as

> to focus our attention on the area where God is actually known, and to seek to understand that knowledge in its concrete happening, out of its own proper ground, and in its own proper reference to objective reality. . . . It would be uncontrolled and unscientific procedure to run ahead of the object and prescribe just how it shall or can be known before we actually know it, or to withdraw ourselves from actually knowing and then in detachment from the object lay down the conditions upon which valid knowledge is possible.[34]

This means that an account of theological epistemology will be derived from the material content of theology, from the actuality of God's self-revelation, rather than according to the ontological implications of a formal epistemology. Torrance develops this line of thinking according to three aspects of the knowledge of God, understood from within the actual divine-human knowing relationship.

[32]Ibid.
[33]Ibid., 9.
[34]Ibid., 25-26.

Actuality of knowledge. First, as we have described above, Torrance begins with the *actuality* of the knowledge of God. This means that the knowledge of God takes place within time, space and history, in Jesus Christ.[35] "We do not therefore begin with ourselves or our questions, nor indeed can we choose where to begin; we can only begin with the facts prescribed for us by the actuality of the object positively known."[36] This means that the knowledge of God begins with what is given from beyond knowledge, from its external (to us) source in God. Even though we experience the knowledge of God within the complexities of human experience and the givenness of human consciousness, the knowledge of God and the subject matter of theology cannot be reduced to the givenness of human experience or consciousness, but must remain "that stubborn element in them which cannot be reduced to anything else and which we cannot reproduce at will, the ultimately hard objective reality without which we would have no such knowledge and which we must distinguish from our knowing of it."[37] While this has the formal characteristics of scientific objectivity, the material content must be the reality of God who reveals himself. In this way, theological epistemology must confess that its object is a God who is *"not a mute fact."*[38] Rather, the object of theology is the living God who is personal, speaking to us in person (*Deus loquens in persona*)[39] through and in and as his Word. But because of this, we have to learn to hear the speaking as something distinct from our "interpretative processes in which we engage in receiving and understanding it."[40] Theological knowledge begins already knowing this particular, acting and self-communicating God. Theological epistemology is therefore an a posteriori reflection on the nature of this relationship in its concreteness and historical reality; and it is *"empirical, thinking out of real experience of God determined by God."*[41]

Objectivity of knowledge. The second aspect of theological knowledge that Torrance draws our attention to is that theological knowledge is properly termed

---

[35]Ibid., 26.
[36]Ibid.
[37]Ibid., 27.
[38]Ibid., 28. Italics in original.
[39]Ibid.
[40]Ibid., 30. We could describe this in Wright's terms as the reality that comes to us distinct from our worldviews.
[41]Ibid., 33.

objective as it is "devoted to and bound up with . . . its own proper object."[42] This he described further as the essential rationality of theology that loosens its hold on all other presuppositions not determined by its object.[43] Objectivity is understood by Torrance not in terms of detachment from the object of knowledge, as it might be according to the common use of the term, but rather as *attachment* to the object and detachment from all other a priori commitments. "To be actively attached to the object and therefore free from preconceptions, to be detached from the bondage of preconceptions and therefore free to submit to the object, is the aim of scientific objectivity. And it is also the concern of theology."[44] While the possibility of this sort of objectivity may be doubted, Torrance at this point is emphasizing the realism that determines theology—that even though the knowing subject is bound up within his or her way of seeing the world, nevertheless the reality of the object, God, by virtue of his reality external to the knower, is always concretely active over and against the preconceptions brought to the subject-object relation. The point, then, is that theology is not concerned with a detachment from its object in the interest of a false objectivity, but rather commits to an attachment to its object so that its rationality might conform itself to the reality of the object and might learn to *think along with* the object as the object, by virtue of its externality, requires.

Torrance goes on to list seven factors that need to be considered regarding the objectivity of God, some of which repeat things already said, but two of which bear recounting here because of their importance for what will follow. The first is that God is to be known objectively according to his action toward us in grace in our own historical existence. We do not discover God according to our own efforts of investigation as we might discover objects in the natural world. He objectifies himself for us, but he does this "within the movement of time where we have our being and our knowing, so that we cannot know Him by seeking to step outside of this historical existence, or by seeking to abstract knowledge from that movement or relationship in time and turn it into timeless ideas or propositions that have their truth timelessly."[45] Theological knowledge is not idealism. Second, God's action

---

[42]Ibid., 34.
[43]Ibid.
[44]Ibid., 36.
[45]Ibid., 40.

in history is purposive, so its truth is "teleological truth."[46] That means that "we cannot truly know God without being reconciled and renewed in Jesus Christ. Thus the objectivity of our theological knowledge is immutably soteriological in nature."[47] It is this final point that gets at the heart of the material content of theological epistemology according to Torrance, and suggests the next aspect of theological knowledge to be considered from within the knowledge relationship.

Possibility of knowledge. The third aspect that Torrance articulates concerns the *possibility* of theological knowledge. By beginning in the actual knowledge relation, the possibility of knowing of God is only given according to its actuality and not from some standpoint outside of that relation. The importance of the question of the possibility of knowing God lies in the nature of theological knowledge as objective; in other words, the knowledge of God is dependent upon the nature of God himself, who makes possible his own knowledge. This is important to acknowledge because the possibility of our knowing God lies outside of us, is given to us in grace and is given in such a way that it can be said to save us (hence, "soteriological").

The importance of this aspect has an impact on how we understand method. There is no method for knowing God that does not derive from God himself. There are no outside criteria according to which we can judge our knowledge of God and its possibility apart from its actuality, and its actuality is wholly determined by the "fact that God has given himself to be known by us in Jesus Christ."[48] This focuses Torrance's account of the possibility of knowledge of God into the following two questions: "(a) How does God give Himself to be known?" and "(b) How does [one] truly receive and know what is given?"[49] Taken in the light of Christology, the material center of theological epistemology, this movement is entirely fulfilled according to "three 'moments' in the realisation of our knowledge of God in Jesus Christ."[50] In sum, it is Jesus Christ who in himself fulfills the "how" of both sides of the question. God gives himself as Jesus Christ to us, and Jesus Christ, as fully human, truly and faithfully receives what is given.

---

[46]Ibid., 41.
[47]Ibid.
[48]Ibid., 45.
[49]Ibid.
[50]Ibid., 46.

He is, in Himself, not only God objectifying Himself for man but man adapted and conformed to that objectification, not only the complete revelation of God to man but the appropriate correspondence on the part of man to that revelation, not only the Word of God to man but man obediently hearing and answering that Word. In short Jesus Christ is Himself both the Word of God as spoken by God to man and that same Word as heard and received by man, Himself both the Truth of God given to man and that very Truth understood and actualized in man. He is that divine and human Truth in His one Person.[51]

The possibility of theological knowledge for human beings is realized in the person of Jesus Christ. Thus the possibility of knowledge of God for humanity is understood in terms of *participation* in the knowing relationship between the Father and the Son. The incarnation itself reveals to us that we stand outside of "that relation with God in which true knowledge of Him is actualized."[52] We are outside of the "closed polarity" that, remaining within the language of the subject-object relation, is determined on one side by God who reveals himself (as object) and on the other side by the human knower, the subject.[53] Yet this relationship is only truly realized (in this sense, "closed") in the knowing relationship between the Father and Son (the "polarity").[54] The human situation into which the Son comes is determined by human sinfulness that, in terms of the subject-object relation, characterizes the natural relationships of objectivity humans have with the world. That means that as subjects we objectify that with which we come into contact in natural knowing relationships, seeking to "subjugat[e] the external world to the processes of our thought in order to give us power and control over them so that we may use them to reassure and establish ourselves in the world."[55] It is into this context, into the context of the sphere of our own self-alienation from him, that the Son comes in a movement of God's own self-objectification. The

---

[51]Ibid., 50. Cf. Torrance, *Karl Barth: An Introduction to His Early Theology, 1910–1931* (London: SCM Press, 1962), 142.

[52]Torrance, *Theological Science*, 50.

[53]Ibid.

[54]We should acknowledge the absence of the Holy Spirit in this economy, an absence that Torrance himself notes, and he directs us toward another "moment" in the knowing relation that is not yet an additional "moment." That is, it is not additional "in the sense that anything has to be added to the objective reality and possibility of our knowledge of God in Jesus Christ." The Holy Spirit "comes to us as Presence from within us and so to open us up subjectively toward Himself." Ibid., 52.

[55]Ibid., 48.

polarity of human sinfulness is a subjectivity that is closed in on itself. "In
Jesus Christ God has broken into the closed circle of our inability and inad-
equacy, and estrangement and self-will, and within our alien condition has
achieved and established real knowledge of Himself."[56]

It is important to note here that Torrance draws our attention to the bro-
kenness of the natural subject-object relationship with respect to God, so that
when God does come to us it is into a broken and sinful context; his coming is
described as a "breaking-in" to the human sphere of knowing. More than just
a faulty epistemology made so by the natural limitations of human finitude, the
problem with humans knowing God is one of sinfulness. It is important to
clarify which of these two dynamics, finitude and sin, is at work.

The epistemological barrier between humans and God that is present
simply because of human creatureliness means that God "condescends," and
communicates himself to us in our finite, creaturely language and human
ways of knowing. Human sinfulness, on the other hand, means that this
condescension must be salvific. The fact that human knowledge of God is
known in the reconciled relationship between God and humanity means
that the natural barrier that exists by virtue of our creatureliness remains a
barrier revealed only from the a posteriori perspective of actual reconciliation. The solution cannot then be a resolution of the merely human barriers
to knowledge, as if solving the formal problem of epistemology will help. In
other words, a sociology of knowledge that articulates clearly the way
humans know things in general is of no help with respect to the knowledge
of God, since the very question of knowledge of God implies at the same
time the answer.[57] Rather, the problem is material; knowledge of God confronts a very real and concrete barrier in human sinful alienation and rebellion that can only be resolved from outside.

Since we have distinguished between human creatureliness and human
sinfulness and given priority to the problem of sinfulness, the metaphorical
use of *outside* (and also *above* and *below* metaphors) signals a soteriological
barrier rather than a metaphysical/cosmic dualism. Because our human
limitation vis-à-vis God is understood in the context of our accomplished
reconciliation with God, that means that we are permitted, methodologi-

[56]Ibid., 51.
[57]Ibid., 44.

cally, to understand the ontological distinction between the creature and the Creator in the context of the richness of Christian doctrine. Knowing *this* God means that we understand him according to the full content of his revelation of himself. The pressure of interpretation moves from justification to metaphysics, and not in the other direction.

For now the primary epistemological problem is represented by the Christian doctrine of the fall. The problem is that "our ideas and conceptions and analogies and words are twisted in untruth and are resistant to the Truth, so that we are prevented by the whole cast of our natural mind from apprehending God without exchanging His glory for that of a creature or turning His Truth into a lie."[58] We can see here that human knowing does not just run into the limits set for it by creation, but that human knowing apart from the soteriological dimension is actively rebellious and idolatrous. This human alienation from the knowledge of God means that when he comes he must bring to us a way of reconciliation, the possibility and actuality of a renewed mind. As God breaks in to the sphere of human knowing, he does not come in any other way than as an object for us to know; that is, he does not disturb the natural way of knowing given to humans as part of God's creation, the rationality that makes human knowing possible. What God must do in response to human sin is to demand repentance (μετάνοια).[59] "But," Torrance asks, "how can we repent like that? How can we expel the untruth that distorts our reason and falsifies the habits of our knowing unless we receive the Truth into our minds, and yet how can we receive the Truth into our minds unless the whole shape of our mind has been altered so that it can recognize it, and unless we are made appropriate to receive it?"[60] This question contains strong echoes of Johannes Climacus's argument in Kierkegaard's *Philosophical Fragments*, to which we now turn.

THE CONDITION: SØREN KIERKEGAARD

If Torrance provides us with a scientific account of divine objectivity articulated in dogmatic terms according to a soteriological model of God as object, Søren Kierkegaard provides an account of divine objectivity from the per-

---

[58]Ibid., 49.
[59]Ibid.
[60]Ibid.

spective of subjectivity, with focused attention on subjectivity as it characterizes the knowledge of God. This is no less an account of God's objectivity,
as we will see, but it is an account from the prior perspective determined by
the human subject. For this account of Kierkegaard, we will limit our investigation to the *Philosophical Fragments* and its companion volume, the *Concluding Unscientific Postscript*, each written under the pseudonym Johannes
Climacus. The *Fragments* offers Kierkegaard's most succinct framing of the
epistemological question,[61] and the *Postscript* his account of subjectivity. Climacus himself is a more or less agnostic character who performs a thought
experiment guided by the opening question in the *Fragments* that sets the
program for the entire work: "Can the truth be learned?" The answer to the
question posed by the thought experiment addresses the epistemological
issue, but it does so most significantly by exploring and clarifying the relationship between the metaphysical question and the question of sin: To what
extent is the epistemological problem determined by the ontological distinction between Creator and creature and the moral distance between humanity and the truth? It does this by "discovering" the condition that must
be given to the knowing subject, a condition that reveals and overcomes
both the metaphysical and the moral distance between the knower and the
truth. This section will explore Climacus's question and his answer as a way
of deepening Torrance's account of the implications of God's objectivity for
theological knowledge. The argument that will be advanced, using these two
texts from Kierkegaard, is that the God of Christian revelation, as an object
of knowledge, determines the knowing subject both in terms of the rationality necessary to know God and also in terms of the subject's metaphysical
relationship to God. What is determined is that the knowing subject is rela-
tionally dependent upon God's ongoing revelation of himself as subject. This
latter determination is what Kierkegaard identifies as the "condition."

Familiar Ground

At the outset it ought to be noted that, with Kierkegaard, we are again on
familiar ground regarding two basic epistemological perspectives. First, if Climacus can be said to have a commitment a priori for his epistemological ques-

---

[61]This is, of course, in dialogue with the idealism of his time, represented to a large degree by Hegel.

tioning, then it would be a commitment to the priority of the existence of the knowing relationship in a way similar to what we have seen first in Wright and then in Torrance. Climacus writes, "I never reason in conclusion to existence, but I reason in conclusion from existence. For example, I do not demonstrate that a stone exists but that something that exists is a stone. The court of law does not demonstrate that a criminal exists but that the accused, who does indeed exist, is a criminal."[62] Second, the similarity of Kierkegaard's concerns to those of Wright can be seen in the rejection of the idealist priority in favor of realism in the existential commitment to the actuality of the object of faith.

> The object of faith is the actuality of another person; its relation is an infinite interestedness. The object of faith is not a doctrine, for then the relation is intellectual, and the point is not to bungle it but to reach the maximum of the intellectual relation. The object of faith is not a teacher who has a doctrine, for when a teacher has a doctrine, then the doctrine is *eo ipso* more important than the teacher, and the relation is intellectual. . . . But the object of faith is the actuality of the teacher, that the teacher actually exists.[63]

How the object of faith is an object for historical knowledge will be addressed in a later chapter, but for now it should be clear that for both Wright and Kierkegaard the ground of realism in epistemology is, at a basic level, common ground.[64] The point at issue here, as it was with Torrance, is to further interrogate the knower's relation to the object of knowledge if the object of knowledge is the God of Christian confession.

Subjectivity and Objectivity

It might seem misplaced to include Kierkegaard in a discussion of divine objectivity for the very reason that he is often associated with aggressive

---

[62]Søren Kierkegaard, *Philosophical Fragments/Johannes Climacus*, ed. and trans. Howard V. Hong and Edna H. Hong, Kierkegaard's Writings, vol. 7 (Princeton, NJ: Princeton University Press, 1985), 40.

[63]Søren Kierkegaard, *Concluding Unscientific Postscript to* Philosophical Fragments, ed. and trans. Howard V. Hong and Edna Hong, Kierkegaard's Writings, vol. 12.1 (Princeton, NJ: Princeton University Press, 1992), 326.

[64]There is some disagreement on the realism of the metaphysics of the *Postscript*. In support of a realism in Kierkegaard similar to Wright's, see M. G. Piety, "The Reality of the World in Kierkegaard's *Postscript*," in *International Kierkegaard Commentary: Concluding Unscientific Postscript to Philosophical Fragments*, ed. Robert L. Perkins (Macon, GA: Mercer University Press, 1997), 169-86.

polemics *against* objectivity while advocating (through Climacus) that "truth is subjectivity."[65] In this vein Kierkegaard is often understood as advocating subjectivity with respect to truth that amounts to an epistemological relativism,[66] a commitment to subjective determination of objective truth that is, therefore, a contradiction to the very objectivity and realism emphasized by Wright and Torrance, an emphasis in which the external reality of the object is distinguished from the subject. Yet, if we read Climacus in the light of Kierkegaard's polemic against Hegelian systematizing and idealism, we can see that Kierkegaard was resisting the absorption of the subject into the absolute by inserting a radical break between the subject and the truth. If Wright and Torrance emphasize realism at the objective end of a subject-object continuum, Climacus emphasizes it at the subjective end. In order to see this in Climacus's pseudonymous authorship, we will start with a brief look at the object of knowledge, "truth," and how it is defined and understood by Climacus, before moving on to a more involved discussion of the relationship between subjectivity and objectivity in these works.

The truth in question is not truth in general, which would include the world of immanent and mundane facts;[67] the truth that Kierkegaard's pseudonymous project is dealing with is "essential truth, or the truth that is related essentially to existence."[68] The knowledge of the truth that is of concern here is the sort of knowledge that makes one human, "an ethical and religious [truth], the fulfillment of the pupil's being as human."[69] For Climacus, the knowledge of God is the example and the focus of the question regarding the truth, and because of this it goes beyond what might be termed *objective knowledge* or knowledge *about* something. In Climacus's terms, objective knowledge falls under the category of answering the question, "What?"[70] and as such, "goes along leisurely on the long road of approxi-

---

[65]Chapter 2 of the *Postscript* is titled "Subjective Truth, Inwardness; Truth is Subjectivity," 189.

[66]For examples, see C. Stephen Evans, *Kierkegaard's 'Fragments' and 'Postscript': The Religious Philosophy of Johannes Climacus* (Atlantic Highlands, NJ: Humanities Press International, 1983), 115-16.

[67]Cf. Robert C. Roberts, *Faith, Reason, and History: Rethinking Kierkegaard's Philosophical Fragments* (Macon, GA: Mercer University Press, 1986), 18, and Jacob Howland, *Kierkegaard and Socrates: A Study in Philosophy and Faith* (Cambridge: Cambridge University Press, 2006), 41.

[68]Kierkegaard, *Concluding Unscientific Postscript*, 199.

[69]Roberts, *Faith, Reason, and History*, 18.

[70]Kierkegaard, *Concluding Unscientific Postscript*, 202.

mation." But "to subjective knowledge every delay is a deadly peril and the decision so infinitely important that it is immediately urgent."[71] In the *Postscript*, the knowledge in question is this "subjective" knowledge, knowledge that is concerned with the question "How?" in the sense that the very existence of the knower is at stake in the answer to the question. The difference between the two is expressed in the following quotation:

> When the question about the truth is asked objectively, truth is reflected upon objectively as an object to which the knower relates himself. What is reflected upon is not the relation but that what he relates himself to is the truth, the true. . . . When the question about truth is asked subjectively, the individual's relation is reflected upon subjectively. If only the how of this relation is in truth, the individual is in truth, even if he in this way were to relate himself to untruth.[72]

When the knowledge of God is the example, as it is immediately following this passage, the subjectivity of knowledge is described in terms of relationality: "The individual relates himself to a something *in such a way* that his relation is in truth a God-relation."[73] The *way* in which one is involved with the truth makes all the difference.

> Now, if the problem is to calculate where there is more truth . . . whether on the side of the person who only objectively seeks the true God and the approximating truth of the God-idea or on the side of the person who is infinitely concerned that he in truth relate himself to God with infinite passion of need—then there can be no doubt about the answer for anyone who is not totally botched by scholarship and science.[74]

The truth is the sort of truth that engages one's entire being. Regarding the present question of objectivity in the knowledge of God, Climacus's subjectivity is just the sort of *way* one must know an object if that object is God. Therefore, subjective knowledge of this sort is the right and proper concern of a theological epistemology if theology is to be faithful to its object. In other words, what Climacus is telling us is that the truth is not knowable without it making an existential difference for the knower, or learner. Truth, then, is not an objective concern for detached knowing, but

---

[71]Ibid., 200.
[72]Ibid., 199. Italics removed.
[73]Ibid. Italics in original.
[74]Ibid., 201.

rather something that must become a condition of the learner in order for the learner to be fulfilled as a human subject.

Truth, in this case, is the truth about existence, not mundane facts about the world; it is the truth about God. This allows for "scientific" objectivity as a way of reasoning determined by the object (Torrance), but Kierkegaard's reflections on this sort of objectivity force his own epistemology into a radical subjectivity. What was written a few paragraphs above, that for Climacus knowledge of the truth "goes beyond" objective knowledge, needs to be restated. Rather, knowledge begins in subjectivity and only after the subject is made subject with respect to the object of truth can we ask the question of objectivity. For Climacus, it is objective knowledge of God that goes beyond the subjective knowledge of the truth. For existence is *in concreto*, and the truth about existence engages the subject and is engaged by the subject in his or her concrete existence, which is in subjectivity. Objectivity is the abstraction of concreteness into the realm of the ideal. In other words, existence is interested in existence, not essence.[75] It is how the truth can be known to existence, in actuality, that is the interest of the subject and not abstract essences, the latter being the interest of objectivity.

Objectivity, as Climacus conceives it, is a movement away from subjectivity, which means that it is a movement away from existence. This can happen either in the movement toward the abstract ideal (in which existence is replaced by essence), or in the movement toward objective knowledge to the diminution of the subjective (the opposite of inwardness). Brown writes, "All the errors of Hegel, according to Kierkegaard, arise in the end—or rather, in the beginning—from ignoring the fact that thought implies a thinker, a concrete, individual, existing thinker, having his being in time, i.e. in 'becoming.' . . . Hegel has *not* incorporated existence into his system, contends Kierkegaard, but only the *idea* of existence."[76] Against this idealism, Kierkegaard asserts the *existence* of the subject. Again, Brown clarifies,

> The Subject in Kierkegaard is neither an abstract logical presupposition of knowledge and experience, nor a *noumenal* mystery inevitably conceived

---

[75]Cf. Lore Hühn and Philipp Schwab, "Kierkegaard and German Idealism," in *The Oxford Handbook of Kierkegaard* (Oxford: Oxford University Press, 2013), 78; and Kierkegaard, *Concluding Unscientific Postscript*, 316.

[76]Brown, *Subject and Object in Modern Theology*, 41.

after the analogy of material substance. It is neither a mathematical point without surface or qualities, nor yet a block of being sculptured in metaphysical marble or psychological mind-stuff. It is a living, active, self-making, self-choosing, self-renewing energy, genuinely set in time, process and becoming, with its life in ethics, religion *and* knowledge vitally affected thereby.[77]

The objectivity of the truth is such that it cannot be objectified but can only present itself as subject to subjectivity.[78] This means that the person who would come to know the truth can only do so in his or her concrete existence with actual concrete concern—passion and infinite interest. This is not to deny objectivity or objective existence—far from it—but only to assert that the *how* of the question of knowledge (how one knows the truth) is of ultimate and prior importance. Compared to how objectivity has been described in Torrance, Climacus's focus on subjectivity can be described in objective terms: *how one knows the truth is determined by the nature of the truth that is known.* When the truth is God, Climacus is right to offer such an account of subjectivity. What Climacus adds by way of emphasis is that the nature of the truth is never known except in subjectivity.

The Thought Experiment

By turning our attention to Climacus's thought experiment, we will be able to see in what way theological subjectivity is realized for the individual, or in other words, how God brings about the unique subjectivity that is the necessary condition for knowledge of himself. The question that Climacus asks, "Can the truth be learned?" is a more basic form of Torrance's question with which we ended the previous section: Torrance asks, "How can we expel the untruth that distorts our reason and falsifies the habits of our knowing unless we receive the Truth into our minds, and yet how can we receive the Truth into our minds unless the whole shape of our mind has been altered so that it can recognize it, and unless we are made appropriate to receive it?"[79] Specifically, with respect to repentance, the question might be rephrased as, How are we to repent if we cannot know that toward which we are to turn? Or,

---

[77]Ibid., 45.
[78]Kierkegaard, *Concluding Unscientific Postscript*, 200.
[79]Torrance, *Theological Science*, 49.

How can we repent and turn if the very sin that blinds us, blinds us toward that which is the standard for repentance? As Climacus poses the problem on the opening page of the *Philosophical Fragments*' "Thought-Project," "A person cannot possibly seek what he knows, and just as impossibly, he cannot seek what he does not know, for what he knows he cannot seek, since he knows it, and what he does not know he cannot seek, because, after all, he does not even know what he is supposed to seek."[80] Torrance's question, read together with Kierkegaard's Climacus, is simply following the pattern of thought present in Plato's presentation of the problem of knowledge in the *Meno*, a problem Socrates goes on to resolve by appealing to the preexistence of souls and the claim that all knowledge is, therefore, recollection.[81] Climacus's response is to work out a thought experiment to resolve the problem in a way that is not Socratic, by supposing that knowledge is not recollection, but rather must come from outside the learner: a teacher must bring the truth. Climacus identifies the event that brings the truth as that which he calls the *moment*. With Socrates, the moment is simply the temporal point of departure for recollection brought forth by questioning. But since it is recollection, the moment is "nothing, because in the same moment I discover that I have known the truth from eternity without knowing it, in the same instant that moment is hidden in the eternal," and for Climacus this means that the moment of recollection disappears into an "*ubique et nusquam* [everywhere and nowhere]."[82] The thought experiment is intended to explore the implications if the moment is of decisive significance, if in the moment "the eternal, previously non-existent, came into existence [*blev til*] in that moment."[83] If the teacher must bring the truth in the moment, the truth must be something that is not available to the learner otherwise.

Because the truth is given in the moment, and in order to avoid the Socratic situation in which the truth is recognized as something always already known, it comes to the learner as a true novelty. There is something about the truth that is contradictory to the reasoning of the learner, so that the truth is not a rational possibility for the learner apart from the teacher's act

---

[80]Kierkegaard, *Philosophical Fragments*, 9.
[81]Plato, *Meno* 80e.
[82]Kierkegaard, *Philosophical Fragments*, 13.
[83]Ibid.

of revealing the truth. In this way, the truth comes to the learner as a paradox. But the paradoxical nature of the truth means that the learner, if she is to truly learn, must be given the condition to receive the truth, even to recognise the truth *as* paradox.[84] Once given the condition, however, the truth is no longer paradoxical since it brings with it, in the condition, its own rationality.[85] The object of knowledge is operative in this thought experiment in a determinative way as it was in Torrance's *Theological Science*, determining the rationality appropriate to the apprehension of the object.

But this presents a problem for Climacus's method. As Jacob Howland observes, "Climacus claims that we have learned through divine revelation that we need divine revelation in order to learn the truth, yet he must be aware that his alleged demonstration has fatal flaws."[86] Citing Anthony Rudd, Howland suggests that Climacus's thought experiment is itself evidence that the "absurd" of Christianity is entirely possible as a human invention. On one hand this seems to be an obvious problem, since Climacus appears to be outside of the condition himself and yet "discovers" the absurd through a thought experiment. Yet the issue is more complicated than that. C. Stephen Evans points to the fact that Kierkegaard himself was writing in the context of Christendom, in which the Christian story of the incarnation was common fare for every child who grew up in Sunday school ("what any child knows"[87]).[88] Climacus is thus pointing out that what has become common and ordinary is, in fact, a very real offense. This suggests that the source for Climacus's imaginings is not his own, but is somehow dependent upon the god having made himself known. If this

---

[84]Ibid., 51.

[85]Here I am following Murray Rae's argument that for Kierkegaard, "the Incarnation is not itself intrinsically absurd or paradoxical but only appears that way from within the pervasively dualist framework of human reason." Reason, in this sense, is understood not "as a framework or paradigm, much less an absolute or neutral one, but must rather be understood as a tool, very likely among others, which makes possible the heuristic functioning of a particular paradigm. . . . Reason is constrained by the paradigm in which it operates and cannot be the means by which that same paradigm is undermined and replaced." Murray Rae, *Kierkegaard's Vision of the Incarnation: By Faith Transformed* (Oxford: Oxford University Press, 1997), 113, 124. Cf. also Sylvia Walsh, "Echoes of Absurdity: The Offended Consciousness and the Absolute Paradox in Kierkegaard's *Philosophical Fragments,*" in *International Kierkegaard Commentary:* Philosophical Fragments *and* Johannes Climacus, ed. Robert L. Perkins (Macon, GA: Mercer University Press, 1994), 33-46.

[86]Howland, *Kierkegaard and Socrates*, 52.

[87]Kierkegaard, *Philosophical Fragments*, 35.

[88]C. Stephen Evans, *Passionate Reason: Making Sense of Kierkegaard's* Philosophical Fragments (Bloomington, IN: Indiana University Press, 1992), 56-57.

is the case, the presence of the poem is, in fact, pointing to a hidden premise, a rhetorical enthymeme according to which the reader is meant to supply the intended response: "This story that is so familiar is the great paradox and the proof of the god's presence with us!" Climacus betrays the source of his thought experiment and responds in wonder to this poetic venture in which the god is the agent who writes the poem, poeticizing himself in the likeness of a man: an event that Climacus can only plagiarize.[89] If this is the case, then Climacus is fully consistent since he is not the source of the poem—and yet he has the poem, which must mean that the god has revealed himself in this way. Climacus's poem, it turns out, is not Socratically gained, but rather has come from the god himself, even if it has become domesticated.[90]

This points to an important distinction that must be made (again) with respect to theological claims. If we take Climacus at his word that all he is doing is performing a thought experiment, then with him we can, indeed, make discoveries of the rationality necessary to understand Christian proclamation vis-à-vis the Socratic. That is, we can understand how the object of knowledge, the god, will determine the rationality necessary for making theological claims. Accordingly, we may be able to discover the necessity for divine revelation.[91] Nevertheless, Climacus cannot make first-order theological claims (God-talk), only second order, "experimental" claims (God-talk-talk). Were Climacus to venture into the area of first-order claims about God, he would immediately find that his claims were suspect, since they would be thrust back upon Socratic, immanent reasoning. Anyone can recognize that we are in untruth—the one thing we *can* know in Socratic fashion[92]—and this presses us on, passionately, to discover the truth, but unless the condition is given to us, from the truth itself, we only move further into untruth. To know one is in the untruth, then, is not necessarily to know anything about the truth. This is why the project of the *Philosophical Fragments* can only be a thought

---

[89]Kierkegaard, *Philosophical Fragments*, 36.

[90]Cf. Torrance's comment regarding the natural tendency of humans to objectify and thus control the objects of their knowing.

[91]It is debatable, I think, that Climacus claims precisely what Howland says he claims—namely, that divine revelation is necessary for us to know that divine revelation is necessary. The entire thought project is an exercise in understanding what the alternative to the Socratic is, finding absolute epistemological significance in the moment. Revelation through the teacher is the assumption, not the result of revelation.

[92]Kierkegaard, *Philosophical Fragments*, 14.

experiment. A thought experiment can only approach the truth as object, and therefore can never arrive at the truth, for objective knowledge is always only an approximation; it never finally arrives. If we were to build a dogmatic theology upon a thought experiment, or objectivity, the result could only be untruth. This is significant when thinking about the deliverances of historical knowledge for theology. Without the condition, with respect to theological claims, the positive deliverances, however seemingly congruent with the revelation of Christianity, must nevertheless be considered suspect from this epistemological perspective and without the requisite subjective condition from God, and therefore in error.

Yet Climacus is not so simple as to ignore this implication. As we saw above, the "poem" that animates his thought experiment turns out to be a sort of revelational "deposit" in the cultural Christendom of Denmark, explainable only on revelational terms. If this is so, then Climacus occupies the position of theological plagiarist—a title he is willing to claim—and so is, himself, beginning within the knowing relationship of the object of knowledge. How does the condition required for knowledge of God relate to the presence in history of the "poem"? The question that must finally be addressed is whether or not this "poem" of the incarnation, the paradox of the god becoming a man, is something that can become part of our immanent knowing so that it can be understood as historical fact, as any historical fact can be known. If the incarnation can become an immanent deposit, knowable as the incarnation of the god, then the knowledge of such a historical object is given to objective knowledge as opposed to subjective knowledge. It can be held at a distance, and remain closed to the appropriate rationality determined by the object itself. If the incarnation is historical reality, and objectively so, then it can only be truly known subjectively in accord with its true object. Since this knowledge is given to subjectivity, it continues to depend on the presence and action of the teacher, the god himself, who continues to make himself known—as subject. "Even when the learner has most fully put on the condition and then, by doing so, has become immersed in the truth, he still can never forget that teacher or allow him to disappear Socratically."[93]

The condition is absolutely necessary for knowing the truth and for

---

[93]Ibid., 18.

being a human subject who is in the truth. What then is this condition? We have already seen that this condition is related, epistemologically, to subjectivity. For Climacus, the condition is that state of the understanding in which the learner is given the truth regarding the absolute. "We shall call it *faith*. This passion, then, must be that above-mentioned condition that the paradox provides."[94]

What has been said thus far regarding the paradox has focused on its epistemological implications, but now it is necessary to briefly go further and say something about the paradox itself, since the paradox is not simply a concept or an idea, but an actuality, an objective historical reality—or it must be so if Climacus's thought experiment is to succeed. The paradox must be the god, the only one who is able to provide the condition. The obvious model for this paradox is the Christian doctrine of the incarnation: the God who becomes a man. He does this in order to give the condition, to restore the relationship of knowledge between himself and humanity. Because of the infinite, qualitative distance between the Creator and the creation, and because—here following Socrates—the only way for there to be true understanding for the human is through equality,[95] the god must enter into the lowliness of human creaturehood in order to bestow the condition, which is a restored relation to himself, on the creature. The infinitely other has become known in this paradox of equality.

> But that which makes understanding so difficult is precisely this: that he [the learner] becomes nothing and is yet not annihilated; that he owes him [the teacher, the god] everything and yet is not annihilated; that he owes him everything and yet becomes boldly confident; that he understands the truth, but the truth makes him free; that he grasps the guilt of untruth, and then again bold confidence triumphs in the truth.

Climacus goes on to assert that this paradox must be overcome by the act of the god, "whose love is *procreative*."[96] We might say that the god, in order to return the human to the place of knowledge, must do, or bring about, something new and creative. "Whereas the Greek pathos focuses on recollection, the pathos of our project focuses on the moment, and no wonder,

---

[94]Ibid., 59.
[95]Ibid., 25.
[96]Ibid., 35.

for is it not an exceedingly pathos-filled matter to come into existence from the state of 'not to be'?"[97]

The condition, then, is not in the nature of the learner, that is, a condition that is possessed as a fundamental ontological aspect of being human, but rather must be given by the teacher.[98] It is a gift. "For if the learner were himself the condition for understanding the truth, then he merely needs to recollect, because the condition for understanding the truth is like being able to ask about it—the condition and the question contain the condition and the answer. (If this is not the case, then the moment is to be understood only Socratically.)"[99] And yet the condition is distinctly connected to an anthropological account of the learner. "Now, inasmuch as the learner exists [*er til*], he is indeed created, and, accordingly, God must have given him the condition for understanding the truth (for otherwise he previously would have been merely animal, and that teacher who gave him the condition along with the truth would make him a human being for the first time)."[100] The condition belongs to the creation of humanity as a gift given and, in some way is maintained as a predicate of what it means to be human. Yet the condition is lost or forsaken. In metaphysical terms what stands between the learner and the condition is the ontological distinction between creature and Creator. The condition is the knowledge of the creator, the "understanding of the eternal"[101] that can only be had as a gift, and yet is an essential component of what it is to be human. In other words, the anthropological concern here is to maintain that persons without the condition are not any less human, having once been given the condition, but the condition is still proper to anthropology. We might say that the condition is anthropological in a protological and teleological way since it is both the original state and the proper telos of humanity. It belongs, then, to humanity as that relationship with God that is God's loving intent for humanity.[102] The problem

---

[97]Ibid., 21.

[98]Here we can see a precursor to Barth's rejection of Brunner's *Offenbarungsmächtigkeit* or "capacity for revelation." See Emil Brunner and Karl Barth, *Natural Theology: Comprising "Nature and Grace" by Professor Dr. Emil Brunner and the Reply "No!" by Dr. Karl Barth*, trans. Peter Fraenkel (Eugene, OR: Wipf and Stock, 2002), 91-94.

[99]Kierkegaard, *Philosophical Fragments*, 21.

[100]Ibid., 15.

[101]Ibid., 64.

[102]God's motivation by love is a theme of the *Philosophical Fragments* that must be recognized but, because of space, set aside.

is, of course, that humanity is not in receipt of the condition—a situation that, as with Torrance, can be attributed to two important but distinct issues. This distinction can be seen in the difference between the metaphysical distance between the Creator and the creature and the moral distance between the two, the sin that keeps the learner in the untruth.

Metaphysical and Moral Distance

Kierkegaard is well-known for his assertion that "there is in fact an infinite, a qualitative difference betw. God and the hum. being."[103] This statement, made infamous by Karl Barth's *Der Römerbrief*,[104] is explained in the opening to the journal entry of November 20, 1847, from which the first quotation came: "The whole basic confusion of modern times (which reaches into logic, metaphysics, dogmatics, and the age's whole way of life) rlly consists in this: that the qualitative yawning chasm has been removed from the difference between God and hum."[105] This distinction makes sense of the need for the condition to be given to the human since an infinite qualitative difference between God and humanity can only be overcome by God granting himself to be known. Presumably, based on the logic of the *Philosophical Fragments*, this distinction is necessary as a metaphysical assumption that makes the moment to be of decisive significance. There must be an other, a radical transcendent difference, that contains within itself, apart from the human, the possibility of overcoming the qualitative difference. Only such a metaphysic could allow there to be something other than the Socratic way of knowing. Only such a metaphysic could make sense of the moment. This means two things. First, it means that the human qua human is not in possession of the condition. Humanity must be qualitatively and therefore ontologically distinct from the Creator. The inequality inherent in this distinction makes the knowledge of God as object impossible unless God himself becomes subject[106] in an act of equality or unity.[107] Second, it means

---

[103]Søren Kierkegaard, *Kierkegaard's Journals and Notebooks*, ed. Niels Jørgen Cappelørn et al., Journals NB–NB5, vol. 4 (Princeton, NJ: Princeton University Press, 2011), 252.

[104]Karl Barth, *Der Römerbrief*, 2nd ed. (Zürich: TVZ: 2005), xx.

[105]Kierkegaard, *Journals*, 250. Abbreviations in original.

[106]Cf. Kierkegaard, *Concluding Unscientific Postscript*, 199-200.

[107]Kierkegaard, *Philosophical Fragments*, 25: "Out of love, therefore, the god must be eternally resolved in this way, but just as his love is the basis, so also must love be the goal, for it would

that the condition is something that has been lost. This point takes us to the moral aspect of the problem.

Climacus makes it clear that the loss of the condition is due to its willful rejection, so that its loss is neither accidental nor due to an act of the god, but remains an actual and perpetual state. By this is meant that the learner exists in an actual state of existence without the necessary condition to know the truth and that beyond this the learner is, in fact, actively "polemical against the truth."[108] Climacus calls this sin.[109] On the first of these aspects Climacus, in a textual note, cites several parables to help elucidate the situation of the person without the condition, culminating in this citation of Aristotle: "The depraved person and the virtuous person presumably do not have power over their moral condition, but in the beginning they did have the power to become one or the other, just as the person who throws a stone has power over it before he throws it but not when he has thrown it."[110] The problem that humanity finds itself in is that of actively pursuing untruth by virtue of having lost the condition and being unable to restore it for the very reason that the condition itself is a gift completely dependent upon the god to grant. Only the god can overcome the Creator/creature distinction.

When the god overcomes both of these barriers, what we might settle into calling the metaphysical and the moral barriers, the god is understood as more than simply a teacher; the god must be seen as a savior, deliverer, reconciler and judge.[111] All of these are qualities attributable to the person of the teacher in response to the situation of the learner, who is estranged from the truth. If the truth (e.g., the knowledge of God in a knowing relationship with him) is that which the god brings to the human learner, and that knowledge must come with the condition, then the condition is occasioned by the god himself, which is to say that the god communicates *himself* to the learner. In this way the moment is that point at which the eternal enters time and space,

---

indeed be a contradiction for the god to have a basis of movement and a goal that did not correspond to this. The love, then, must be for the learner, and the goal must be to win him, for only in love is the different made equal, and only in equality or in unity is there understanding."

[108]Ibid., 15.

[109]Ibid.

[110]Ibid., 17n. From Aristotle, *Nicomachean Ethics*, III, 5, 114a. The editors comment that Kierkegaard's translation of Aristotle is "a free but substantially correct rendering of Aristotle" (Kierkegaard, *Philosophical Fragments*, 280n33).

[111]Kierkegaard, *Philosophical Fragments*, 15-17.

the moment at which the transcendent enters into the world of created immanence.[112] "Let us call it," says Climacus, *the fullness of time.*[113] And so Kierkegaard brings the Christian doctrine of the incarnation into focus in Climacus's thought experiment. "The presence of the god in human form—indeed, in the lowly form of a servant—is precisely the teaching, and the god himself must provide the condition."[114] That means, in Climacus's terms, that the moment has a historical point of departure, focused as it is on an actual historical occurrence, the incarnation of God in the person of Jesus Christ.

The theological import of the thought experiment of Climacus for our question of the objectivity of God can be summarized along the following lines. God as an object of knowledge is only available as such to the learner, the subject, who is the recipient of the condition that restores the knowing relationship between God and humans. This restoration is possible only as an act of God and brings about a distinct and particular novel relation that has no immanent precedent. This condition is called faith and comes to the learner as a gift. This gift is not germane to humanity—there is no ontological point of contact—but is an original gracious *relation* between God and humanity that has been lost. God as an object of knowledge is not known *objectively*, as detached objective reason would have it, but *subjectively* as passionate knowledge of a real person who makes himself known, not finally as *object*, but rather as *subject*.

It is important to remember that the thought experiment, as I have tried to show above, is dependent (parasitic?) upon the narrative of the New Testament. It turns out that the thought experiment grows out of that narrative, and like Torrance, Kierkegaard's effort is not to abstract *from* the narrative, but rather to go deeper *into* the subjective involvement of the believer in the inner workings of the narrative and its particularly located logic.[115] The answer to the question that the thought experiment poses addresses the epistemological

---

[112]Hong and Hong note that "the Danish *blev til* . . . refers to temporal and spatial modes of becoming and being. The eternal as timeless being does not come into being but comes into time and space as a specific embodiment of the eternal. The moment, therefore is an atom of eternity and has a significance qualitatively different from that of transient instants of time." Ibid., 280n25.

[113]Ibid., 18. Italics in original.

[114]Ibid., 55-56.

[115]This deeper penetration into the narrative, rather than an abstraction away from it, is described in depth by Torrance in *The Christian Doctrine of God: One Being Three Persons* (London: T&T Clark, 1996), 73-111.

issue, but it also explores and clarifies the relationship between the metaphysical question and the question of sin: To what extent is the epistemological problem determined by the ontological distinction between Creator and creature and the moral distance caused by human sin? It does this by "discovering" the "condition" that must be given to the knowing subject, a condition that reveals and overcomes both the metaphysical and the moral distance between the knower and the truth. It is a condition that is, in the final analysis, relational and not essential, of real existence and not abstract essence.

The objectivity of the truth, once run through the critique of Kierkegaard, demands an appreciation of the personal involvement of the subject in the apprehension of the truth. Knowledge of the truth—knowledge of God— must fundamentally change the subject so that both the metaphysical and moral distance between the subject and the object are overcome. But such knowledge is gained neither through ascent nor descent (as recollection), but only as a gift from the object as subject, from the personal God himself. What Kierkegaard adds to the argument (begun with Torrance's claim regarding God's objectivity) is the observation that God's objectivity, if taken seriously, must be rooted in his subjectivity. This is an acknowledgment that God can never be an object to our knowledge without first being a subject given to us in our subjectivity. His objectivity is only an objectivity looking back from the perspective of faith. It cannot be seen from the other vantage point. It is an analogical move, but one that runs from the reality of God to the rationality of human knowing and not the other way around. But as the Subject given to subjectivity, God is revealed in time and space, in the concrete reality of human existence, as a king, incognito, loving a humble maiden. It cannot be otherwise. This is the God who is known as he gives himself to be known to the individual in faith.

JOHN 3:1-21

What Kierkegaard has labeled the condition, the Bible calls "newness of life" (Rom 6:4), being "born anew" (Jn 3:3, 7),[116] being "raised with Christ" (Col

---

[116]Γεννηθῇ ἄνωθεν, alternatively, "born from above." N. T. Wright prefers this translation. See Wright, *The Kingdom New Testament: A Contemporary Translation* (New York: HarperOne, 2011), 176.

3:1; Eph 2:6), being "in Christ"[117] and a "new creation."[118] Perhaps the most explicit biblical text to draw from is that of John 3:1-21, Jesus' visit with Nicodemus. This Pharisee and ruler of Israel affirms Jesus in the cover of night: "Rabbi, we know that you are a teacher who has come from God; for no one can do these signs that you do apart from the presence of God." Jesus answers him, "Very truly, I tell you, no one can see the kingdom of God without being born from above" (Jn 3:2-3). The NRSV has changed the translation of γεννηθῇ ἄνωθεν from "born anew" (RSV) to "born from above." Wright appears to favor the same translation, rendering the verse, "Let me tell you the solemn truth. . . . Unless someone has been born from above, they won't be able to see God's kingdom."[119] It is clear that the words can be translated in both ways,[120] but it should also be clear from the context that Nicodemus's response makes sense only if Jesus has said the more surprising thing, that one must be born anew, even "born again" (NIV).[121] Whether we are to find the source of the misunderstanding in what Jesus said or in how Nicodemus understood it, Nicodemus's "misunderstanding" in the direction of physical birth nevertheless does not miss the rhetorical force of what Jesus is saying, but rather heightens the sense of rupture that Jesus, with his response in John 3:5, takes in a new direction.[122] This new direction is *literally* carried in the construct γεννηθῇ ἄνωθεν yet needs further elucidation if Nicodemus is to understand what Jesus is saying. This interaction illustrates the point that Jesus is making: you see one thing, but you need me to tell you (ἀμὴν ἀμὴν) what really is the case. But the claim, "You must be born anew/from above" (Jn 3:7) is a requirement in order for there to be knowledge of the kingdom of God. So Marianne Meye Thompson writes,

---

[117]Citations are too numerous to list, but see, e.g., 2 Cor 5:17.

[118]Again, see 2 Cor 5:17 among others.

[119]See Wright, *Kingdom New Testament*, 176.

[120]Cf. the entry "ἄνωθεν" in Frederick William Danker, ed., *A Greek-English Lexicon of the New Testament and Other Early Christian Literature*, 3rd ed. (Chicago: University of Chicago Press, 2000), 92.

[121]"At the level of the text, Jesus could not have said 'unless one be born from above' because this could not have led Nicodemus to think he meant reentry into the maternal womb. Johannine misunderstanding is based on misplaced literalness in interpreting what is said, not on a failure to understand the actual words." Sandra M. Schneiders, "Born Anew," *Theology Today* 44, no. 2 (1987): 191-92.

[122]C. K. Barrett, *The Gospel According to St John: An Introduction with Commentary and Notes on the Greek Text* (London: SPCK, 1962), 208. In Barrett's words, the "misunderstandings . . . provide a step on which the discourse mounts to a further stage."

"But in order to recognize this One as God's Messiah—to see, enter, and understand the kingdom that is genuinely God's kingdom (3:3, 5; 18:36)—the work of the Spirit of God is required."[123] The recognition of the kingdom is not just seeing, as in John 3:3, but also a reality into which one must enter. This discourse suggests that these belong together: one sees the reality of the kingdom only when one is in that reality, and that reality is only known through a new kind of birth. In terms used previously, one knows the kingdom from within the knowing relation. Those who are in this reality are like the wind, born of the Spirit, and their source and destiny are unseen except by those who are, in Climacus's term, given the "condition." In Edwyn Hoskyns's words,

> Knowledge, true theological knowledge and apprehension, capacity to see the dominion of God, is not secured by acquiring more and more information. Nicodemus already possessed quite sufficient information, both acquired and hereditary. The knowledge of God demands a re-orientation, a new creative beginning, so ultimate and fundamental that the initial fact of birth provides the only proper analogy; the only proper analogy, in the sense that all other analogies depend on it.[124]

It is worth pointing out that several tropes are at play in the interaction of John 3 between Jesus and Nicodemus. Nicodemus comes to Jesus in the dark at night (Jn 3:2), bringing to mind the important Johannine distinction between those who are in the light and those who walk in darkness (Jn 1:5, 8, 9; 3:19-21; 12:35). John 3:19 ends the conversation with a judgment on those who love the darkness more than the light, and John 3:20 continues this with an appraisal of those who do what is true: they come to the light, and it is seen that their deeds have been wrought by God. Another trope John draws on in this pericope is that of the two ages, the present age and the eschatological age to come. This can be seen in the promise of "eternal life" to those that believe. Eternal life (ζωὴ αἰώνιον) is best understood as "the age to come" and is in contrast with the "present evil age" that Paul mentions in Galatians

---

[123]Marianne Meye Thompson, "Word of God, Messiah of Israel, Savior of the World: Learning the Identity of Jesus from the Gospel of John," in *Seeking the Identity of Jesus: A Pilgrimage*, ed. Beverly Roberts Gaventa and Richard B. Hays (Grand Rapids: Eerdmans, 2008), 171.
[124]Edwyn C. Hoskyns, *The Fourth Gospel* (London: Faber and Faber, 1947), 203.

1:4.[125] The third trope is, of course, that of birth. Whether we hear Jesus say "new birth" or "birth from above," either way what is encountered is that knowledge of God's kingdom requires the beginning of a new qualitative state in the human so that what enables one both to see and to live within the kingdom is an act of God knowable only from the new state. With birth, this sense of discontinuity is the strongest precisely because birth is an absolute beginning. It makes no sense to compare an "unborn" state with that of the "born" since there is no "state" for the unborn to be in. They simply are not.[126] One can only know the reality of birth a posteriori. Paul's words to the Corinthians express this clearly in the terms of new creation: "So if anyone is in Christ, there is a new creation: everything old has passed away; see, everything has become new!" (2 Cor 5:17).

In John's Gospel we have already seen this in the one, above all, we might expect to have recognized Jesus on his own: John the Baptist.[127] However, we are told twice in the first chapter that John did not know him (Jn 1:31, 33) until he saw the Spirit descending from heaven like a dove; and he claimed, "I myself did not know him, but the one who sent me to baptize with water said to me, 'He on whom you see the Spirit descend and remain is the one who baptizes with the Holy Spirit.' And I myself have seen and testified that this is the Son of God" (Jn 1:33-34). In John 3 we are told that one cannot see the kingdom of God without being born anew/from above, a birth occasioned by the Spirit (see Jn 3:6), and this reflects what we see here in John 1. We are not given insight into the occasion of transformation in John; the new birth is not seen in a specific moment, nor is it to be read into the text that there at the Jordan John was "born again" or "born of the Spirit" before he could recognize Jesus as the Lamb of God; but what we do have is the epistemo-

---

[125]N. T. Wright, *How God Became King: The Forgotten Story of the Gospels* (New York: HarperOne, 2012), 44-45. In this case Wright is making the point that our common reading of "eternal life" tends to imply a future heavenly existence away from the reality of this world. Instead he argues that what is being assumed here is the eschatological/apocalyptic understanding of the two ages that characterize the one reality of this present cosmos. Cf. also *NTPG*, 252-56, in which Wright cites Gerhard von Rad's discussion in *Old Testament Theology: The Theology of Israel's Prophetic Traditions*, trans. D. M. G. Stalker, vol. 2 (San Francisco: Harper & Row, 1965), 301-15.

[126]Of course, this is not to say anything about the biological state of the fetus! That is a wholly different conversation.

[127]Kierkegaard draws attention to this as well when arguing that the "child-conception of Christ" is essentially a pagan conception compared with the paradox, the form of a servant, that characterizes God with us incognito. See Kierkegaard, *Concluding Unscientific Postscript*, 599-600.

logical priority of God's act of revelation in the recognition of the Messiah, even at the individual level. And this recognition is clearly the act of God as divine subject, making John subject in the true knowledge relationship in which Jesus as Lamb of God becomes an object of knowledge. John 3 brings this epistemological event to the light, referring to it as a new birth.[128]

Each of the images in John 3 require a basic and fundamental transition from a present state (darkness, present age, unbirth/nonexistence) to a new and previously unknowable state (light, age to come, birth/existence). Each transition suggests different degrees of continuity between the previous state and the state within the kingdom of God. To anticipate the conclusion of this chapter, the motifs of light, darkness and new birth are the controlling motifs that determine the historical/eschatological motif of the present age/age to come. Our epistemological arguments are determinative for how history is understood. The rationale for this argument follows from the core of the John 3 text and the hermeneutical centrality of the baptismal motif there (cf. Jn 3:5) representing new birth or birth from above, and then in the theology of Paul as it comes to be centered around the death and resurrection of Jesus.[129] Baptism with water and the Spirit is the event of new birth, birth from above, that in the church's later practice of baptism comes to be associated with the death and resurrection of Jesus. The biblical motif of death and resurrection, founded upon the actuality of the death and resurrection of Jesus, will be articulated as the grammar that controls our understanding of the condition since it is the predominant grammar of the Christian rite of ecclesial initiation as well as the grammar for the birth from above that allows the believer to see. At the center, then, of Christian theological epistemology is the cross and resurrection.

CONCLUSION

This chapter began by asking in what way N. T. Wright's account of epistemology took into consideration the object of knowledge if that object is God. More specifically, it was asked if ontological and metaphysical consider-

---

[128]See 1 Pet 1:3b: "By his great mercy he has given us a new birth into a living hope through the resurrection of Jesus Christ from the dead."

[129]For a helpful discussion of the baptismal context of Jn 3:5, see Everett Ferguson, *Baptism in the Early Church: History, Theology, and Liturgy in the First Five Centuries* (Grand Rapids: Eerdmans, 2009), 142-45.

ations were determinative for his epistemology or if all possible objects were known in the same way. If Wright's method assumes the latter (even if in his theological commitments he does not subscribe to a certain univocity of being with respect to God and the world), then there is a need to examine what it would mean for his methodological commitment to external reality if that commitment were to conform to the rationality required by the theological object. If God is an ontologically unique object of knowledge, then it would make sense to inquire into the way theological knowledge is unique with respect to its object. As it stands, the only metaphysical category that determines Wright's epistemology is that of "external reality." Clearly, more metaphysical nuance needs to be brought to Wright's epistemological picture, something Wright himself seems to encourage. It is toward this end that T. F. Torrance's *Theological Science* was brought into the conversation.

CRw is in fundamental agreement with Torrance's epistemological commitment: let the object of knowledge (its reality) determine the method of knowing from *within* the reality of the subject-object relationship. This means that material content is already given to this relationship *before* epistemological questions arise: one *knows* first, and only then inquires into the nature of that knowledge, as it were, a posteriori. The implications of Torrance's arguments are significant with respect to Wright's method since what we find with respect to God as an object is a theological method that is subject to the uniqueness of the nature of God as object in a way that upsets the unified ground on which Wright's method rests. That is, Wright's method assumes a unified ground of being that treats the knowledge of God as the same kind of knowledge as knowledge about anything else. The nuance that Torrance's account brings is to differentiate between the means of knowing and the content of that knowing. Content determines means: the *way* that we know is determined by the object of knowledge, not the knowing subject. This way of knowing is limited to the basic observations that (a) knowledge takes place within the knowing relationship, a posteriori, and (b) the rationality required must conform to the object itself. The task of this chapter has been to articulate a theological analysis of the epistemological subject-object relationship, pressing the question of the uniqueness of the divine object and what that means for human knowing. At this point we can summarize the conclusions of this chapter as follows.

First, we have seen that for Wright, Torrance and Climacus, the actuality of the knowing relationship is the starting point for knowledge, especially the knowledge of God. In Wright, this is demonstrated by his acknowledgment of the way in which knowledge is always contact between the knower and the world, contact that precedes epistemological analysis. In Torrance, the reality of revelation is the place from which epistemological work is done in theology, just as the reality of light is the starting point for physical analysis of light. In Climacus, it is Plato who introduces us to the philosophical problem of starting the search for the truth if one does not even know what one is looking for.

The theological implications of this starting point are manifold. For Christian theology this means that soteriology is the context in which we know God, making all the considerations of God's prior act of salvation present to the epistemological question. The subject-object relationship is determined first by the moral difference between God and humanity—humans in their sin encounter a God who saves them from this sin. In this encounter humans learn who God is, that he is other than the world, but that he becomes present to the world as subject within his own creation and that this is definitively known in the incarnation of the Son, the Messiah of Israel.

Second, if Torrance gives preference to the objectivity of God in his epistemology, then Kierkegaard, through Climacus, pushes this objectivity to its necessary conclusion in the priority of the subjectivity of human knowledge of God. Climacus forces us to see that the objectivity that characterizes our knowledge of God is, in fact, grounded on a prior subjectivity. This subjectivity is not a human creation, but is rather a *new* creation of God as God gives the gift of faith, a restored but new relation between the knower and the known. The movement of subjectivity and objectivity in the knowledge of God can be summarized like this: God as subject makes the individual subject in a relationship between subjects. This relationship of subject to subject is realized in the paradoxical equality of the incarnation. Yet in being made subject, God gives himself to us as an object to be known, as an object distinct from us—as external reality. It is this final step that ushers in Torrance's account of the objectivity of theological knowledge. But with Climacus what we have is a transgression of the boundary between subject and object; the gulf is overcome in the gift of the actual relation of God to the individual. This is the condition, the subjectivity required for knowing the truth. Again, this roots theological epistemology in the saving, gracious work of God in Jesus Christ.

Third, stepping back to Torrance, of crucial importance is the theological account of the knowing relationship that happens between the Father and the Son according to the empowering work of the Spirit. In this picture the Son is the human knower, the human subject who truly knows the Father in a way that must be the only proper way of knowing God. It is into this relationship that we are called to participate, making participation in the epistemological dynamic between the Father and Son the theological grounding for all subsequent Christian theology and removing the possibility that Christian knowledge can ever be a possession. This also means that Christian knowing is based in an *actualism* of God's self-revelation and self-knowing, since in the trinitarian activity of revealing and being known God is continually active, free and sovereign over the human subject who knows God through the work of the Spirit in participation. This account of participation can be seen as the dogmatic counterpart to Climacus's poetic venture and, if this is the case, makes Torrance's account of objectivity compatible with Climacus's account of subjectivity.

3

Apocalyptic, Continuity and Discontinuity

SOTERIOLOGICAL IMPLICATIONS FOR A THEOLOGY OF HISTORY

THE PREVIOUS CHAPTER ARGUED THAT a truly *theological* epistemology must take the objectivity of God seriously as that unique external reality that constitutes its own methodological point of departure. This means that theology begins with the already-received knowledge of God. We have, as it were, bumped into God, and this is where we begin. God's is the reality that stops us in our tracks, that halts our forward progress and demands an accounting of *this* peculiar barrier in our way. If God's objectivity is determinative for theology, and if we are to keep from thinking "god" in the abstract or ideal, then God must be said to be an object of our knowledge only as the result of his activity as subject, active in his revealing, reconciling and saving work, making human beings subjects in the divine-human knowing relation. God has placed himself before us, bumping into us, confronting us in God's own dynamic freedom and saving us. Human knowledge of God is thus, *from an anthropological perspective*, grounded in our own subjectivity; but that subjectivity is not ours as a possession, as if it were given to humanity qua humanity, but is ours as a gift, ever dependent upon the continuing activity of God who gives us knowledge of himself by making us subject to the knowledge of God as object. This act of making us subject is the gift

of the condition. Up until now this condition has been presented in theological and philosophical terms, derived from the material content of
dogmatic theology, its relation to modern epistemological questions and
limited scriptural reflection. While I have argued that this approach is
not, as Wright might suggest, an abstraction from the biblical narratives,[1]
it still needs to be seen what role both the Scriptures and the material
content of Christian theology play with respect to the condition necessary for true theological knowledge.

The present chapter attempts to go further in this direction through the
consideration of, and an argument for, an "apocalyptic" theology. By
making this move, we can integrate (a) the epistemological arguments that
have already been advanced with (b) a theological approach to history, and
in this way continue a constructive critique and, perhaps, an appreciation
of Wright from within a developing contemporary constructive theological
movement (apocalyptic theology).

At this point we can pause to survey the landscape in front of us and
plot the route to our final destination. The first order of business as we
make our way is to present an argument for a theological hermeneutic that
is intrinsically apocalyptic. This will require a brief statement on the implications for a theology of Scripture if God is a reality already known in
the gift of subjectivity. It will also require a clarification of the way in
which we will be using the term *apocalyptic*. Having thereby cleared some
ground before us in the first section, the following two sections will begin
the constructive, path-making, dogmatic work that needs to follow the
epistemological and hermeneutical arguments. This constructive work is
the articulation of an irruptive apocalyptic logic that, in this chapter, traces
a dogmatic movement from soteriology to Christology. We begin this

---

[1]"Theological activity . . . is not concerned merely with biblical exegesis or with a biblical theology that builds up what this or that author in the New Testament taught about the Faith; it is
concerned with the Truth at a deeper level, in the necessary and coherent thinking of the Apostles as they mediated the divine revelation in Jesus Christ to the world of historical understanding and communication." T. F. Torrance, *Theology in Reconstruction* (London: SCM Press, 1965),
40. This "deeper level" is explained in Torrance's account of the stratification of knowledge as
the "theological level" where the "concern . . . is not primarily with the organic body of theological knowledge, but with penetrating through to apprehend more fully the economic and
ontological and trinitarian structure of God's revealing and saving acts in Jesus Christ as they
are presented to us in the Gospel." T. F. Torrance, *The Christian Doctrine of God: One Being Three
Persons* (London: T&T Clark, 1996), 91.

movement in the second section, building on Kierkegaard, by arguing that the actuality of God's self-revelation is necessarily soteriological. This soteriological starting point introduces the question of continuity and discontinuity with respect both to the subject and to history. In the following chapter (chap. 4) it will be shown how this soteriological starting point determines a particular account of Christology, an account for which we will return to the work of Torrance. The next step in that chapter will be to follow the "irruptive, apocalyptic logic" with respect to the doctrine of creation. This all leads up to the next chapter (chap. 5) with its theology of history. This soteriology-Christology-creation-history sequence will then be brought back into dialogue with Wright, setting the stage for remarks on historical method. Our methodological proposal will, in a final chapter (chap. 6), be brought to bear on the question introduced in this chapter, that of apocalyptic. What vantage points might we reach at the end of this journey that would give us theological clarity on the relationship between history, theology and apocalyptic?

In its simplest form, the argument of this and the following chapter is that an apocalyptic theology is a truly theological commitment to the reality of God for theology. And this reality affects every discipline related to theology. For hermeneutics, this means that revelation contextualizes us. For epistemology, this means locating theological knowledge in the historical event of Jesus the Messiah, an event that is soteriologically defined and so known only in the actuality of reconciliation. For history and anthropology, this means that Jesus' ongoing historical subjectivity and his *enhypostatic* union with humanity in his singular human identity is central and determinative. For the individual who would know God, for the human who would be subject, the reality of God is only given as one participates in Christ's knowledge, his humanity and his history, in and through the Spirit; and this can all be seen and known in terms of the Christian act of baptism[2] with its controlling motif of death and resurrection.

---

[2]I use the term *act* rather than *sacrament* or *practice* as a way to avoid importing needlessly at this point the question of the sacramentality of the act of baptism (although I am not against the idea!), and, likewise, as a way to avoid the problematic use of the term *practice* when an account of church practices becomes a means for inadvertently squeezing the agency of God out of the life of the church.

A RUPTURE IN UNDERSTANDING:
A PROPERLY THEOLOGICAL HERMENEUTIC IS APOCALYPTIC

Scripture and the God Who Is Already Known

If the preceding arguments regarding epistemology are correct, then we should be able to read the Bible accordingly, not seeing it as a text co-opted to support philosophical arguments, but rather as a text that presents us with an account of the objectivity of God to which we must conform our way of thinking in order to understand. But even this is not primary. The Bible is not primarily a book *about* an object, but is itself a witness to God as object *within* the economy of the self-giving of God. God is the unique active subject who gives new life and subjectivity to those who would find God as object in the Scripture. In other words, God as "an" object for human knowledge is given in Scripture only according to the grace that makes us subjects to that knowledge.[3] This means that reading Scripture is a human act determined, not by general hermeneutical theory or rules of reading, but rather by the reality of the God who speaks in and through the Scriptures. John Webster may help to clarify this point:

> It is important at the beginning to register that . . . in discussing the nature of reading: we do not move away from operative language about God, shifting into territory more effectively mapped by a psychology of interpretation, a theory of virtue or, perhaps, a general account of rational acts. Language about the merciful self-presence of the triune God has as much work to do when we are talking about readers as it does when we are talking about revelation and its textual servants.[4]

Because of the unique object of Christian faith and knowing, Christian hermeneutics is a discipline that must be considered within the economy of salvation, and not as an exercise originating outside according to a general theory of language or reading. This does not mean that such theories are irrelevant, but that they, like knowing in general, are determined and con-

---

[3]On the graciousness of God's "being-as-object," cf. Eberhard Jüngel, *God's Being Is in Becoming: The Trinitarian Being of God in the Theology of Karl Barth; A Paraphrase,* trans. John Webster (Grand Rapids: Eerdmans, 2001), 61.

[4]John Webster, *Holy Scripture: A Dogmatic Sketch,* Current Issues in Theology (Cambridge: Cambridge University Press, 2003), 69-70.

ditioned by the object of knowledge or, in the case of Scripture, the object of witness. Webster continues,

> The act of reading scripture—because it is the act of reading Scripture, the herald of the viva vox Dei—is not an instance of something else, but an act which, though it is analogous to other acts, is in its deepest reaches sui generis. For as with all Christian acts, its substance is in the last analysis determined not out of its similarities to the acts of other agents who do not share the Christian confession, but by the formative economy of salvation in which it has its origin and end. In that formative economy, the act of reading partakes of the basic structure of Christian existence, namely its active passivity or passive activity. Like other acts of Christian existence it is a human activity whose substance lies in its reference to and self-renunciation before the presence and action of God.[5]

This preference for a hermeneutic of "active passivity" before the primacy of the active voice of God is just the thing Scripture itself assumes.

> For as the rain and the snow come down from heaven, and do not return there until they have watered the earth, making it bring forth and sprout, giving seed to the sower and bread to the eater, so shall my word be that goes out from my mouth; it shall not return to me empty, but it shall accomplish that which I purpose, and succeed in the thing for which I sent it. (Is 55:10-11)

This text from Isaiah is echoed in the letter to the Hebrews: "Indeed, the word of God is living and active, sharper than any two-edged sword, piercing until it divides soul from spirit, joints from marrow; it is able to judge the thoughts and intentions of the heart" (Heb 4:12).[6] The act of God is significantly diminished when hermeneutics become determinative for hearing, when the voice of God becomes subject to cultural linguistic frameworks, horizons of meaning or worldviews. The problem cannot be resolved, however, according to a naive realist hermeneutic, or a doctrine of the perspicuity of Scripture apart from the priority of the divine act. Where then are we to stand? How do we read Scripture and hear the voice of God if we are apparently given no method for which to do so? How do we know God,

---

[5]Ibid., 72.
[6]These Scriptures are cited in support of a similar argument in ibid., 16.

if God himself cannot be known apart from his act of revelation? If we turn to Scripture, we find that Scripture itself participates in the economy of God's self-revealing act and therefore cannot be an escape from the hermeneutic and epistemic grounding that can only be had in the dynamic of revelation. As difficult as this is, the confrontation of this problematic is demanded by the *reality* of the God who is *already* known. This means that God's reality *is* known (we are not confronted here with the problem of a transcendental method), and this has simply been claimed; this claim has, in turn, been articulated according to an epistemology of contact. The only way of describing this in hermeneutical language is to work backward from God's self-revelation to an understanding of what reading Scripture entails in the light of the primacy of the act of revelation. In this way theological hermeneutics works from a particular center; it looks backward—and forward—from the center that is the fullness of God's self-revelation.

Wright might at this point direct us back to his methodological work in *NTPG*. With that work in mind we can imagine that his response to the above passages from Isaiah and Hebrews would be to point out that the dynamic of God's living and active Word is accomplished in and through the normal methods of reading, a "methodology" that pays attention to the hermeneutical dynamics of worldviews and cultural frameworks. We do not account for the activity of God in reading except through the mundane methods of reading assumed in the way humans know things (epistemology). What follows is the attempt to describe the way an apocalyptic theology affects this reading strategy.

Defining Apocalyptic and Its Implication for Hermeneutics

As we approach the question of hermeneutics, it is necessary to address confusion over the word *apocalyptic*, since this disputed term can be a stumbling block even before the conversation can begin.[7] Is the apocalypse of

---

[7]"This term has proved so slippery and many-sided in scholarly discourse that one is often tempted to declare a moratorium on it all together." N. T. Wright, *Paul: In Fresh Perspective* (Minneapolis: Fortress Press, 2009), 41. Or, more recently: "I . . . find myself in company with several other scholars who have suggested that the word 'apocalyptic' has become so slippery, capable of so many twists and turns of meaning, that it would be safest to confine it simply to a literary genre: that of 'revelations,' which is, after all, what the word basically means." Wright, *Paul and His Recent Interpreters* (Minneapolis: Fortress Press, 2015), 2:9.

Jesus Christ (e.g., Gal 1:12 or Rev 1:1: ἀποκαλύψεως Ἰησοῦ Χριστοῦ) to be understood according to the apocalyptic worldview of the first century, a worldview conditioned by a long tradition of Jewish (although not exclusively Jewish) literature, along the lines of which were written the various and many-faceted apocalyptic texts that have given rise to the modern understanding of the genre that goes by the name *apocalyptic*?[8] Is there an actual apocalyptic genre that would be recognizable as such by certain groups in the first century, or can apocalyptic be appropriated to refer to one event that is the apocalypse? Can apocalyptic be construed apart from the genre, with respect to an actual happening in history that is, to whatever degree, revelatory? If the latter route is taken, as it is in a qualified way by the apocalyptic theologians (more on this qualification below) then the biblical scholars who have been carefully working on discerning and defining both the literary genre and the worldview that makes such literature possible, or who have been working on understanding the cultural and literary imaginations of Second Temple Judaism, find themselves either utterly confused or standing, once again, on shifting lexical sands.

Although somewhat of a lightning rod in conversations with Wright on apocalyptic,[9] Douglas A. Campbell's work in this area can help to draw out an understanding of the term's use with respect to the issues of epistemology and history that concern us in the present work. Campbell is candid with respect to the limits of the word *apocalyptic* and its particular usefulness given the variety of meanings it has in a wide range of differing apocalyptic discourses.[10] Nevertheless, for Campbell apocalyptic helpfully locates us within a particular interpretive trajectory:

> The signifier "apocalyptic" is a useful label at an introductory level of discussion when broad loyalties and orientations are being sketched in relation to different basic approaches to Paul; it denotes fairly that an approach to Paul is being pursued that ultimately aligns with the concerns and readings of—in this context in particular—Lou Martyn, and that therefore is in sympathy

---

[8]See, e.g., John J. Collins, *The Apocalyptic Imagination: An Introduction to Jewish Apocalyptic Literature*, 2nd ed. (Grand Rapids: Eerdmans, 1998), and Christopher Rowland, *The Open Heaven: A Study of Apocalyptic in Judaism and Early Christianity* (SPCK: London, 1982).
[9]See Wright's critique of Campbell in *Interpreters*, 2:64.
[10]Douglas A. Campbell, *The Deliverance of God: An Apocalyptic Rereading of Justification in Paul* (Grand Rapids: Eerdmans, 2009), 190-91, 978n41.

with the alternative texts and soteriological paradigm that he endorses, and sensitive to the tensions that he detects between that paradigm and justification concerns.[11]

Yet if apocalyptic identifies this broad theological reading given by Martyn, it has been taken up in recent contemporary theology, taking Martyn as a cue, and thereby given a more particular theological content and programmatic trajectory, Campbell's work notwithstanding.[12] If Martyn's work energizes an "interpretive trajectory," then the apocalyptic hermeneutic that he offers can be given more content than simply its use in denoting a particular school of thought. At its most basic level, Martyn's Pauline apocalyptic is articulated in Campbell's words:

> When Martyn speaks of Paul's apocalyptic gospel, he generally means to signal certain interrelated concerns: the gospel is visited upon Paul and his churches essentially unconditionally, by grace and by revelation. All Paul's reasoning is conditioned in the light of this initial disclosure and hence proceeds "backward" . . . ; the apostle's epistemology is emphatically retrospective.[13]

Campbell is at this point identifying the *epistemological* dynamic of Martyn's apocalyptic interpretation of the Pauline gospel. This is important to note because so far this is a unique emphasis within the apocalyptic conversation. Campbell is singling out this one aspect of Pauline apocalyptic, apart from the cosmic and historical aspects more at home in considerations of the literary genre. That he does this might lead us to suggest that we drop the term *apocalyptic* and refer instead to *revelational* or some other word to describe this aspect of Paul's theology.[14] Whether or not this is advisable will be left for further analysis, a task to which we will turn in the final chapter.

---

[11]Ibid., 191.

[12]Here I am thinking of work by theologians Nathan R. Kerr, Christopher Morse, Philip G. Ziegler, Craig Keen and Doug Harink, among others. Harink is especially of interest because of the sparring between him and Wright over apocalyptic and the problem of supersessionism. I will weigh in on this debate in the final chapter.

[13]Campbell, *Deliverance of God*, 189-90. "Backward" is attributed by Campbell to E. P. Sanders. The point Campbell makes here is important, but it should be noted that for Martyn apocalyptic is not limited to a retrospective epistemology. It has a more developed historical context as a particular interpretation of apocalyptic texts based in part on the work of his student, de Boer.

[14]In the spirited conversation between Wright and Campbell at a special SBL session on Pauline apocalyptic (2014), this move from *apocalyptic* to *revelational* was suggested by Wright with Campbell's somewhat exasperated approval.

For now apocalyptic remains on the table partly because it is the language of Martyn and those who are working in his wake, and because, as will become apparent, I think the word is particularly helpful for identifying a particular theological orientation—both on epistemological/theological grounds and also on literary/historical grounds.

In terms of hermeneutics, the epistemological issue found in this aspect of Martyn's apocalyptic theology can be framed according to the question of where the gospel finds its contextual home. Does it rely on a prior understanding of a story, a narrative or worldview, of which it makes sense; or does its novelty sweep every story and context off the table and start all over again? Is such a thing even possible? From a hermeneutical perspective, the latter option seems like nonsense. After all, it is axiomatic for hermeneutics that nothing is ever known apart from context. When an appeal to apocalyptic is made from within a hermeneutic framework, it must, necessarily, be understood in full contextual terms, as a more-or-less stable semantic world into which an event comes or out of which an understanding is generated. Its stability fluctuates, but only within the hermeneutical possibilities open to a consideration of interacting worldviews.[15] As such, when theologians or biblical scholars use the term *apocalyptic*, it is taken to identify a worldview or prior contextual world that provides the cultural and linguistic grounding for interpretation and understanding of whatever is described as apocalyptic. The difference to which the apocalyptic theologians point is that, for them, apocalyptic names a unique event, the revelation of God in Jesus the Messiah, which brings with it its own self-determining context. This does not make sense hermeneutically *unless* the context is at once the condition, the gift of subjectivity to the knower, upon which the revelation is dependent. So, for example, when Nathan Kerr writes that "God's interruption of history . . . precludes any perspective on reality, any worldview, historical system"[16] and so on, the verb *precludes* is a theological distinction,

---

[15]The influence of Ben F. Meyer on Wright's method would perhaps suggest that at this point the limitation of a hermeneutical framework can be overcome through a method of questioning. Questions and their answers, in a Lonerganian transcendental method, break out of the limitations of human knowing, allowing us to ascend toward new levels of knowledge. The apocalyptic method I am advocating is precisely the opposite; it is an irruption into the world of our hermeneutical limitations, not a transcendence out of them. See chap. 2, n. 1.

[16]Nathan Kerr, *Christ, History and Apocalyptic: The Politics of Christian Mission* (Eugene, OR: Cascade Books, 2009), 13.

not sociological or hermeneutical. Apocalyptic theology denies, on theological grounds, the priority of the contextual axiom of hermeneutics.

For example, the way in which this "apocalyptic anti-hermeneutic" works can be seen, if somewhat cryptically, in a footnote in Martyn's commentary on Galatians, where, describing a Jewish Christian rectification tradition, he reverses the assumed noetic structure of Pauline thinking that moves from plight to solution[17] to a solution-plight structure. Here Martyn brings Karl Barth into the conversation:

> One recalls that K. Barth was an exegete as well as a systematic theologian; for over a considerable period of time he correctly emphasized that Paul saw Adam in the light of Christ, sin in the light of grace, and so on. Note, for example, the comments " . . . it is only by grace that the lack of grace can be recognized as such" (Church Dogmatics, 2.2, 92); " . . . the doctrine of election . . . defines grace as the starting-point for all reflection and utterance . . ." (93).[18]

This footnote is referenced by Wright in an article surveying "Paul in Current Anglophone Scholarship," calling it evidence of Martyn's "Barthian *a priori*." Wright characterizes Martyn's starting point as a radical rejection of history: "Everything must now be known, and can only be known, through the fresh revelation in Christ."[19] This comment brings to the fore the problem and the confusion. Barth's theology is not a hermeneutical theology. It is a theology of revelation. But, if read within a hermeneutical framework, it appears arbitrary and fideistic. Of course there is a context into which revelation comes and of course this context is the cultural and linguistic source for the articulation of revelation. This is not denied by Barth's approach, but there is more that needs to be said. This "more" is summarized with clarity and precision by Jüngel:

> If, according to Barth, God's being-as-object for the person who knows God can only be perceived and conceived in the objectivity of a medium which

---

[17]Cf. Frank Thielman, *From Plight to Solution: A Jewish Framework for Understanding Paul's View of the Law in Galatians and Romans*, Supplements to Novum Testamentum, vol. 61 (Leiden: E. J. Brill, 1989).

[18]J. Louis Martyn, *Galatians: A New Translation with Introduction and Commentary*, The Anchor Yale Bible, vol. 33A (New Haven: Yale University Press, 1997), 266n163.

[19]N. T. Wright, "Paul in Current Anglophone Scholarship," *The Expository Times* 123, no. 8 (2012): 373. It should be noted that in more recent work on Martyn and apocalyptic in the *Interpreters* volume, Wright is much more favorable to Barth. I suspect there has been a slight shift in his appreciation of Barth that is now registering in these conversations.

witnesses to God's being-as-object, a medium taken from the created reality which surrounds [humanity], then we must follow Barth in making a clear distinction between God's being-as-object as such and the creaturely objectivity which witnesses to God's being-as-object.[20]

The distinction between "God's being-as-object as such" and the creaturely objectivity that witnesses to this being-as-object is of crucial importance. A hermeneutical approach limits the knower to the creaturely objectivity—and rightly so. However, if this hermeneutical perspective is taken to be coextensive with the limits of a theological epistemology, then a confusion is introduced that obscures the priority of God's being-as-object before the creaturely objectivity given to human observation. In all of this what remains determinative is the priority of the act of God to reveal himself. The claim of fideism denies the priority of God's activity, and therefore his reality, focusing instead on the "leap of faith" from the human side.

Furthermore, the context into which revelation comes remains in need of redemption, especially to the extent that this context is known as a history, or any sort of cultural framework or social ideology. Therefore a "solution-plight" structure is a necessary theological structure precisely because of the soteriological dimension of the revelation of God in Jesus Christ. The solution is such that it relativizes all that went before. This relativizing of the historical frame is not its denial, however. Rather, as we will see, it is its recontextualization.

In *Climax of the Covenant*, Wright rejects a "plight-solution" structuring of Paul's thought in favor of a more nuanced plight (1)-solution-plight (2) structure.[21] In this interpretation, Paul's understanding of the problem that needed a solution is reinterpreted in light of the solution. This happens "with eyes now unveiled."[22] This "unveiling" (itself within the family of apocalyptic reference) in Wright's description of Paul's new status as Christian theologian is a result of events (his conversion and subsequent experience) and his reflection on those events as they related to his understanding of God and God's purposes. In Wright's work what we see is an account of Paul's epistemology that might

---

[20]Jüngel, *God's Being Is in Becoming*, 62.

[21]N. T. Wright, *The Climax of the Covenant: Christ and the Law in Pauline Theology* (Minneapolis: Fortress Press, 1993), 261. See also *PFG*, 747-64. Cf. John M. G. Barclay, "Paul, the Gift and the Battle over Gentile Circumcision: Revisiting the Logic of Galatians," *Australian Biblical Review* 58 (2010): 38-39.

[22]Wright, *Climax of the Covenant*, 262.

be interpreted according to the apocalyptic theology being sketched out here,[23] but that retains the hermeneutical perspective characteristic of CRw. Specifically, Wright maintains that, for Paul, there is a "double epistemological shift" that takes both the "One God and . . . the new creation ushered in by the risen Messiah" as the critical transformational points.[24] In the final chapter we will look more closely at these two dimensions in Paul's epistemology. For now it is important to see how Wright's basic critique of apocalyptic theology falls back on a hermeneutical framework, neglecting the priority of the theological, and so apocalyptic, dimension. Wright's objection to the way apocalyptic is used by Martyn's school is grounded in the assumption that there is an apocalyptic worldview, describable by scholars working in that specialized area—most notably Christopher Rowland, John J. Collins and, more recently, Anathea E. Portier-Young—through whose work we know what apocalyptic is, and according to which we can make sense of this aspect of Paul's theology.[25] So, in dialogue with these literary accounts,[26] he has argued against certain unnecessarily dualistic configurations of apocalyptic and offered his own carefully nuanced version in *NTPG*.[27] The problem is that this obscures the epistemological premise that I think is at least implicit in Martyn, among others, that no apocalyptic worldview exists or has existed that makes sense of the apocalypse of Jesus Christ, a priori, since in Jesus all other worldviews are relativized. The perspective no longer follows a historical narrative of forward progression, but rather looks both backward and forward from the central perspective of the unique event of God's revelation in Jesus of Nazareth. Significantly, just such a position is assumed and articulated by Wright's problem (1)-solution-problem (2) schematic, as long as the apocalyptic element of the solution is given the full weight of the reality and freedom of God. Wright's account has the necessary structure, just not the theological depth implied by the nature of the solution itself. The solution cannot be abstracted or idealized apart from the reality that it is God who is at work both in and beyond history.

---

[23]See especially *PFG*, chap. 14.
[24]*PFG*, 1195.
[25]See Wright's depiction of the problem in *Paul*, 41-42.
[26]NB: these are not exclusively literary accounts since part of the question of the biblical scholar looking at a genre like apocalyptic is specifically concerned with the assumed or implicit theology of the genre. Such an approach is, of course, fully consistent with CRw.
[27]*NTPG*, 280-99.

Nor can the solution be so historicized that we no longer find ourselves saved, only reinscribed or renarrated into another way of telling the story.

Now, we need to be absolutely clear at this point. This does not mean that we somehow know Jesus apart from history, or outside of any cultural or linguistic context, or even worldview. And it does not mean that we must somehow speak of Jesus apart from his historical context—as if it makes sense to call Jesus *Christ* apart from the history of Israel.[28] What it does mean is that this history is powerless to provide the context for understanding Jesus apart from the positive act of God unveiling himself *and* providing the condition of reconciled subjectivity to see and to know that unveiling. This is warranted by the fact that, for the reconciled understanding, Jesus is known to be very God and very human, and that God does not give that knowing over to human possession, but remains actively self-revealing in human knowledge of God. Apart from God's act of self-revelation in Jesus Christ, we cannot know him as he truly is, the God-man, because such knowledge cannot be had on the basis of historical or other forms of finite human knowing.

Apocalyptic theology, at this point in our development of this theological approach, simply points out that if we let the hermeneutical perspective take *theological* precedence, then we overdetermine the revelation of God in Jesus Christ and subject him to a human construct.[29] If, however, we prioritize the theological sense of apocalyptic, then we (methodologically?) subject all worldviews and contexts to the freedom of God's sovereignty over his own self-revelation. This event of self-revelation is the apocalypse, in subjectivity and objectivity, of Jesus, Israel's Messiah.

Perhaps the crux of the issue is that *apocalyptic theology*, if it is to be consistent, rejects the very contextualization that the academic study of *apocalyptic literature* assumes—at least from a hermeneutical perspective. So, ac-

---

[28] At key moments in the present text I have tried to alternate between *Christ, Messiah,* and *Jesus of Nazareth* to suggest just this point. Yet it does not mean that the reverse is the case, that the history of Israel is adequate to make sense of Jesus.

[29] Again, the question that is left aside here, but that is of utmost significance not only for my argument but for the important concern of Wright, is the question: What has this apocalyptic perspective to do with the apocalypses from the writing of Daniel up until possibly the fourth century CE? If it has nothing to do with them, then simply call it "revelational" theology and leave it at that. That I do not leave it there is because I think there is some significant value in the association once the first point that I am making about epistemology is made. I will develop this more in depth in the final chapter.

cording to the latter perspective, if Paul is an apocalyptic theologian, that means that he has been shaped by an apocalyptic worldview that stands as the framework within which the apocalypse of Jesus the Messiah makes sense. This worldview, even if it is transformed to some degree by a revelatory experience, nevertheless contextualizes that experience.[30] The apocalyptic theologians, however, see in this the same sort of *Offenbarungsmächtigkeit*, or "capacity for revelation," that Karl Barth rejected so forcefully in his interaction with Emil Brunner.[31] Apocalyptic literature does not give us the proper worldview within which to understand the apocalypse of Jesus Christ.

The confusion between the two is not helped by the fact that those who advocate an apocalyptic theology in this epistemological sense draw for their inspiration, and understanding of apocalyptic, upon biblical scholars and theologians who are also working with the genre of apocalyptic literature.[32] Even with the muddling between these two types of apocalyptic—theological and literary—the biblical scholars being sourced for, and contributing to, an apocalyptic theology can be shown to support an apocalyptic perspective that is not dependent upon their particular and nuanced recreation of an apocalyptic worldview.[33] In fact, the *actuality* of the revelation of God in Jesus the Messiah in the apocalyptic understanding, far from being contextualized by a suitable worldview or appropriate language

---

[30]I am indebted to a conversation with J. Davies that helped me see this distinction.

[31]Brunner and Barth, *Natural Theology.*

[32]Here we think of J. Louis Martyn, Ernst Käsemann, Martinus C. deBoer and Douglas Campbell, among others. Beverly Roberts Gaventa operates according to the distinction I am identifying when she writes, "By using the word 'apocalyptic' . . . I mean not simply that Paul's metaphors of maternity have some parallels in apocalyptic thought. What I mean is that these metaphors are substantively connected to *the apocalyptic nature of Paul's theology.* That relationship may be most obvious in Rom 8, where creation's labor pains anticipate God's final redemption. Yet it also has a bearing on Gal. 4:19, since it is not Paul who will birth the Galatians again but Christ who will be born among them; only Christ's intervention makes this birth possible. And when Paul engages in the subversive act of referring to himself as a nurse caring for children or as a breast-feeding mother, he acts out the epistemology of the 'new creation.'" Beverly Roberts Gaventa, *Our Mother Saint Paul* (Louisville: Westminster John Knox Press, 2007), 79-80, italics added.

[33]Doug Harink's essay "Partakers of the Divine Apocalypse: Hermeneutics, History, and Human Agency After Martyn," in *Apocalyptic and the Future of Theology: With and Beyond J. Louis Martyn,* ed. Joshua B. Davis and Douglas Harink (Eugene, OR: Cascade Books, 2012), 73-95, makes this point regarding Martyn: "Unquestionably, as a commentator Martyn *stands with* Paul in the singular apocalyptic reality in which Paul claims to be standing," 77 (italics in original). Regardless of Martyn's success in reading the Galatian context, a reading that is highly contested, not the least by Wright, his theological approach is self-consciously apocalyptic in the sense of the term I am describing.

game, is what requires the apocalyptic theologians to point out that it is *we* who are contextualized by this apocalypse. If this seems far removed from the account of Wright's historical method we looked at in chapter one, it is nevertheless exactly what he is saying when he reconfigures Paul's plight-solution perspective so that the solution that comes with the Messiah Jesus reinterprets and recontextualizes what Paul had originally thought the plight was in the first place. The problem is learned in light of the solution.

The language of *contextualization* is used in this way by Walter Lowe to address the modern need for an apocalyptic theology: "The accustomed business of the mind is to place or contextualise things, to label and handle them. But occasionally it happens that we ourselves are contextualised—placed in an unfamiliar setting that exceeds and relativises *us*. It is this event that I propose to call contextualisation."[34] Regarding much of the popular-level discourse regarding apocalyptic, Lowe writes, "The problem with many who use the language of apocalyptic is that they seem all too certain of the ground under their feet."[35] This same critique can be argued against those who insist that apocalyptic must be understandable in terms of an already present worldview that gives apocalyptic its contextual ground. It is the *reality* of the unique apocalyptic event as an event that comes from God that transfigures the contexts into which it comes. Donald MacKinnon puts it like this, speaking of the transcendent in such a way as I am speaking of the apocalypse of Jesus Christ:

> I am tempted to suggest that if one is a realist in philosophy of religion, one is not inclined to the view that supposed reference to the transcendent is to be regarded simply as the preliminary condition of the believer's life, and that which gives that life its form. The transcendent is not a notion which emerges in that life nor one that finds in that life its proper context. Rather it is manifested by its intrusive presence as something continually demanding that we transform our understanding of its content more and more rigorously, as if every articulation of that content were precarious and necessarily incomplete, in order that we may begin to grasp what we seek to refer to.[36]

This brings us back to the point that this has to do with the *actuality* of the apocalypse of Jesus Christ, and that it does so reminds us of the realism

---

[34]Walter Lowe, "Why We Need Apocalyptic," *Scottish Journal of Theology* 63, no. 1 (2010): 48.
[35]Ibid., 49.
[36]Donald MacKinnon, *Explorations in Theology* 5 (Eugene, OR: Wipf and Stock, 1979), 157.

that is essential to the epistemological question. The reality in question, if it is the revelation of God in Jesus Christ, brings with it the particular dynamic appropriate to the objectivity of the knowledge of God. To this dynamic, with respect to hermeneutics, we now turn.

Apocalyptic and the Question of Method

If hermeneutical theory is concerned with the way in which humans understand the world or, in the language we have been using, external reality, then theological hermeneutics will ask in what way God can be the reality that is given for humans to understand.[37] Hermeneutics brings the epistemological questions of human knowledge to the applied processes of interpretation and understanding with respect to objects that carry or suggest meaning (even if the meaning is only located in the interpretive communities): texts, cultures, performances, images and so on. By describing apocalyptic theology according to a retrospective hermeneutic and in terms of passive contextualization, I am arguing that an apocalyptic *event* is central for theological hermeneutics.

Therefore the particular significance of apocalyptic for the present discussion is that it articulates the conviction that Christian theology, biblical studies and historiography must each be understood, in Webster's terms, as "a human activity whose substance lies in its reference to and self-renunciation before the presence and action of God."[38] That is, the reality and actuality of God is the determining methodological factor.[39] What might this method look like? When Karl Barth wrote the second edition of his Romans commentary, he wrote against critics "by asking quite simply whether, if the Epistle is to be treated seriously at all, it is reasonable to approach it with any other as-

---

[37]James M. Robinson describes the move from "explanation" to "understanding" as "the first move toward the new hermeneutic." James M. Robinson, "Hermeneutic Since Barth," in *The New Hermeneutic*, ed. James M. Robinson and John B. Cobb Jr., New Frontiers in Theology: Discussions Among Continental and American Theologians (New York: Harper & Row, 1964), 20.

[38]Webster, *Holy Scripture*, 72.

[39]I suspect that this aspect of the relationship between the interpreter and text—namely, the reality and actuality of God—is what is bypassed in Robinson's essay describing the "new hermeneutic" as he passes from Barth to Gadamer. Gadamer is, after all, concerned with the fusion of the twin horizons of interpreter and interpreted. Barth, on the other hand, is concerned also with a *third* horizon, that of the living and active God. Cf. Robinson, "Hermeneutic Since Barth," 22-27.

sumption than that God is God."[40] This statement follows a lengthy polemic against the tendency of modern commentators who neglect to struggle with the subject matter of the text. If, for Paul, the subject matter (and here we think of our arguments regarding the object of knowledge) is the "permanent KRISIS of the relationship between time and eternity,"[41] then such a subject matter is left out of modern commentaries, making them simply prolegomena to the sort of exegesis Barth is talking about.

In Barth's theology, this permanent "KRISIS" is given according to the formula, "God is God."[42] For our purposes this enigmatic statement need not trouble us beyond the point that Barth is making by it—namely, that God's being (and knowledge of his being) is wholly determined by God's act. God cannot be known in reference to anything other than himself. There is no other acceptable predicate of God that does not have this tautology preceding it. If God is the object of Paul's writing, then God may be encountered therein, and the reader confronted with a crisis. Barth goes on to say, "Paul knows of God what most of us do not know; and his Epistles enable us to know what he knew. It is this conviction that Paul 'knows' that my critics choose to name my 'system,' or my 'dogmatic presupposition,' or my 'Alexandrianism,' and so on and so forth. I have, however, found this assumption to be the best presupposition, even from the point of view of historical criticism."[43] It is just this sort of crisis that Martyn identifies in his writings on Paul, and which form the "methodological" basis for apocalyptic theology. Based on his commentary on Galatians, we might say that Martyn, like Barth, assumes that Paul is writing "through Jesus Christ" (διὰ Ἰησοῦ Χριστοῦ, Gal 1:1) vis-à-vis the "apocalypse of Jesus Christ" (δι' ἀποκαλύψεως Ἰησοῦ Χριστοῦ, Gal 1:12) and therefore Paul is to be read with the expectation that the reader might encounter a third horizon: God may, indeed, speak. The reality and actuality of God "in" the text is encountered as the *event* of God's self-disclosure: God's being revealed in God's act.

Douglas Harink has made this point with respect to Martyn and Barth on several occasions, most recently in his contribution to the collection of essays,

---

[40] Karl Barth, *The Epistle to the Romans*, trans. Edwyn C. Hoskyns, 6th ed. (London: Oxford University Press, 1968), 11.
[41] Ibid., 10-11.
[42] Ibid., 11.
[43] Ibid.

Apocalyptic and the Future of Theology. Here his language is especially vivid:

> Martyn presents us not in the first place with an incremental exegetical "advance" toward an apocalyptic "perspective," but rather with a fundamental shift of hermeneutical stance; that is, exegesis is standing in the midst of the theological earthquake of the gospel, of which Paul's letter is a powerful shockwave, giving an account of what is going on while the quake is still happening.[44]

This is what is implied by MacKinnon above when he describes the "intrusive presence" of the transcendent as "something continually demanding that we transform our understanding of its content more and more rigorously, as if every articulation of that content were precarious and necessarily incomplete, in order that we may *begin* to grasp what we seek to refer to." It is the reality of that intrusive presence that determines our exegesis. Harink points out that Martyn, like Barth, works according to the assumption of a self-involving hermeneutical perspective, one that attempts, as far as possible, to come under the authority of the true subject matter of Scripture. This is all to say that apocalyptic names a movement in biblical/theological hermeneutics that gives absolute priority to God as the object of knowledge whose freedom and activity are determinative for the subject's interpretation. Apocalyptic seems a fitting term for a theology that pays attention to this "intrusive presence."

To further clarify this point, consider Donald A. Hagner's summary of exegesis:

> The goal of exegesis is a severely restricted one: to arrive at the meaning of the passage intended by the original author, as that author meant the original readers to understand it. The exegete seeks nothing less, nothing more and nothing other than this. . . . If we are to achieve our goal we must enter into the world of our author and addressees to the fullest possible degree. . . . In short we must do everything we can to recreate the entire situation that confronted writer and readers. Insofar as it is possible, we must stand in their shoes, feel as they felt, think as they thought, perceive as they perceived, dream as they dreamt.[45]

---

[44]Harink, "Partakers of the Divine Apocalypse," 79. This is what is implied by MacKinnon in the quote above.

[45]Donald A. Hagner, *New Testament Exegesis and Research: A Guide for Seminarians* (Pasadena, CA: Fuller Seminary Press, 1999), 29.

The question that apocalyptic theology raises is whether or not this includes an encounter with the living God, who is the subject matter of the Bible. Can we walk in Paul's shoes if we hold an encounter with the risen Jesus at arm's length and not allow it the force of the existential and "epistemological crisis"[46] that it was for Paul? Can we hear what Paul is saying if we limit ourselves to the twin horizons of interpreter and text? God-talk requires that this crisis has taken place with the result that a qualitatively new subjectivity has been given, a subjectivity that no longer knows κατὰ σάρκα (2 Cor 5:16) but that has been given the eyes to see with "doxastic immediacy."[47] Theological reflection is grounded in the immediacy of the event of revelation and only as such becomes God-talk. Without this crisis theology can be no more than God-talk-talk, an inadequate basis for theology since it is not true to its object.[48] This "epistemological crisis," as Martyn calls it, is not only present as Paul's own "worldview," but to the extent that we would read *with* Paul, and understand him, it must, by God's grace, become the theologian's crisis too.[49] Apocalyptic theology, rather than stopping with the hermeneutical question— which would be a way of avoiding true presence with Paul and his subject matter—takes the apocalyptic motif into the realms of theology, ontology, metaphysics, politics and mission. Because the object of knowledge is God, the subject who is made subject in that knowing relationship is entirely determined by the God who has acted and continues to act. The point is to use

---

[46]Cf. Martyn, *Galatians*, 104, 132, 142, and J. Louis Martyn, *Theological Issues in the Letters of Paul*, Studies of the New Testament and Its World (Edinburgh: T&T Clark, 1997), 89-110.

[47]Cf. Alan J. Torrance, "Analytic Theology and the Reconciled Mind: The Significance of History," *Journal of Analytic Theology* 1, no. 1 (2013): 40.

[48]God-talk-talk is not unimportant—much theology is only this—but it must have God-talk as its referent and hope in order to speak of anything at all. Alan E. Lewis points to this when he writes, "Even the second-order [god-talk-talk] makes me queasy: methodology in isolation is the refuge of those with nothing positive to say; and the wish to choose what shall be true for us becomes idolatry if we forget that God first has chosen us and put us in the Truth." "Apocalypse and Parousia: The Anguish of Theology from Now Till Kingdom Come" *Austin Seminary Bulletin* 103, no. 8 (1988): 37.

[49]See Martyn, *Galatians*, 104, 132, 142, and Martyn, *Theological Issues*, 89-110. It is important to point out that for Martyn the "epistemological crisis" is not an existential option open to the inquisitive seeker, but rather it "can be seen only by the new eyes granted at the *juncture* of the ages." In Martyn's work, however, this is not a condition *in abstracto*, but occasioned by the crisis that is presented *kata stauron*, a way of knowing that is occasioned by the in-breaking of the new age. Cf. *Theological Issues*, 108n52. That Martyn emphasizes the externality of this event (the coming of the new age) does not, however, mean that the "eyes to see" are somehow available as an option apart from what I am calling, with Kierkegaard, the "condition." Nor does this mean that we must accept Martyn's account of apocalyptic literature as uniquely distinguished by these two ages.

this dialogue with apocalyptic to further a constructive claim that will show how epistemology and history are mutually determined, providing a way of reading history "apocalyptically" and "covenantally" so that apocalyptic discontinuity is held together with historic continuity, all the while being true to the unique objectivity of God.

APOCALYPTIC AND SOTERIOLOGY: BEGINNING WITH THE NEW BEGINNING

At the beginning of this chapter it was proposed that an irruptive apocalyptic logic would be the appropriate corrective to Wright's type of historical method. Now that the concept of apocalyptic has been introduced, the heart of this logic can be articulated constructively. By using the word *logic*, I simply mean to follow an orderly progression determined by the two subject matters under discussion: the knowledge of God and the practice of historiography. This present section begins this logical progression with the doctrine of reconciliation.

Revelation Is Reconciliation, Reconciliation Is History

The historical nature of the apocalypse of Jesus Christ is inextricably bound up with the doctrine of reconciliation. Apocalyptic, as I am arguing, helpfully names the New Testament understanding of the actuality of the revelation of God in Jesus of Nazareth, an actuality that is present in and for history. By *actuality* I mean to point both to the external reality of the event of Jesus Christ, its unique objectivity, and to the nature of that event as revelatory *in itself*. "Most simply stated," writes Douglas Harink,

> "apocalypse" is shorthand for Jesus Christ. In the New Testament, in particular for Paul, all apocalyptic reflection and hope comes to this, that God has acted critically, decisively, and finally for Israel, all the peoples of the earth, and the entire cosmos, in the life, death, resurrection, and coming again of Jesus, in such a way that God's purpose for Israel, all humanity, and all creation is critically, decisively, and finally disclosed and effected in the history of Jesus Christ.[50]

---

[50]Douglas Harink, *Paul Among the Postliberals: Pauline Theology Beyond Christendom and Modernity* (Grand Rapids: Brazos Press, 2003), 68.

The actuality of apocalyptic is a historical event, bringing together the historical and the theological, conscientiously holding these together in such a way that the nature of the particular apocalyptic event—the apocalypse of Jesus Christ—determines both. The relationship between the unique, singular history of Jesus and the way in which God's action is described are inextricably linked. If God has acted in a unique and decisive way in Jesus of Nazareth, then that event contains within it the revelation of God himself in his act.

What is revealed in this act is not just an object for historical knowledge, but also an active Subject, one who cannot be objectified. By *objectification* is meant the act of constraining an object within one's own categories of understanding and so restricting an object's freedom to be a subject. Abraham Lincoln can be objectified as a historical figure because he ceases to be subject with respect to his own historical existence. Jesus, however, remains subject by virtue of the unique content of his revelation—resurrection and ascension. Jesus remains as active, personal subject. Jesus cannot be objectified, because to do so would negate his subjectivity, a subjectivity that is human but is also, and fully, divine. The two natures of the one Son of God make the question of the knowledge of the apocalypse of Jesus Christ—as a unique, but nevertheless historical, event—epistemologically and theologically complex.

So, if apocalyptic refers to Jesus Christ's history, it also refers to the way in which that history is bound up with soteriology. For if what is revealed in his history is not just a historical figure, but, as Käsemann says, the righteousness of God,[51] then the history of Jesus, in its revelatory mode, is also reconciliatory. As Philip G. Ziegler writes,

> Revelation itself is an event that *initiates,* even as it *discloses,* a new state of affairs; not simply "a making known," revelation is also "a making way for," involving God's conclusive "activity and movement, an invasion of the world below from heaven above." The event in which God is made known as Saviour—the coming of Christ—is the very event that saves. Revelation thus *is* reconciliation.[52]

---

[51]Ernst Käsemann, *Commentary on Romans*, trans. Geoffrey Bromiley, 4th ed. (Grand Rapids: Eerdmans, 1994), 30.

[52]Philip G. Ziegler, "Dietrich Bonhoeffer—an Ethics of God's Apocalypse?," *Modern Theology* 23, no. 4 (2007): 581. Internal quotations are from Martinus C. de Boer, "Paul, Theologian of God's Apocalypse," *Interpretation* 56, no. 1 (2002): 25.

The language of *above* and *below* and its metaphysical implications will be examined below according to a doctrine of creation, but for now it is significant that we understand that the objectivity of God's revelation, the apocalypse of Jesus Christ, is never given over to objectivity except as it comes together with the reconciliation that it effects. God's act in history is inseparable from the actuality of reconciliation. We are again back to Kierkegaard's account of subjectivity. God has acted to make us subjects in his self-revelation as object—this is true in our own subjectivity and in history. Revelation is, therefore, reconciliation. Or, apocalyptic theology, construed from the standpoint of the knowing subject, begins with soteriology. If we begin with the question of revelation and human knowledge of that revelation, then we are obliged by the nature of that revelation to begin with soteriology. More on this needs to be said now with respect to the question of the relationship between soteriology and Christology.

The actuality of reconciliation in the event of revelation is, as we have seen in T. F. Torrance, located in the person of Jesus Christ. An analysis of this actuality belongs to the theological subdisciplines of Christology and soteriology. Because Christology is grounded in the actuality of Jesus of Nazareth, God's self-revelation, both doctrines look for their content in the historical event of atonement, what Karl Barth identifies as the history of Jesus Christ.[53] This christological history decenters both our subjective experience of history and the way we approach the knowledge of history. It forces us to understand history from an altogether new perspective, a perspective that is given to us in the event of reconciliation but that is then located outside of our subjectivity in the subjectivity of Jesus Christ. The relationship between Christology and soteriology is therefore complementary if the epistemological question is raised—in other words, if the knowing subject is to be included in the dogmatic formulation.

In the event of revelation, Christ becomes the new subjective center of history; his subjectivity becomes determinative for human subjectivity. Therefore the person of Jesus Christ is the beginning point for a theology of history on both soteriological and christological grounds. In the actuality of

---

[53]See Karl Barth, *Church Dogmatics*, ed. G. W. Bromiley and T. F. Torrance, trans. G. W. Bromiley et al., 14 vols. (Edinburgh: T&T Clark, 1969), IV.1, 157. Hereafter I will follow the conventional citation form: e.g., *CD* IV.1, 157.

reconciliation, the subject experiences the interruption of the history in which she understands herself and is given the new mind to be able to see history reoriented around the event of God's self-revelation. In this way, history and subjectivity are taken together to make sense of the continuity of both in light of the irruptive nature of revelation.

Revelation Is Irruptive: The Question of the Novum

This christocentric, reconciliatory apocalyptic is articulated by Nathan Kerr as "God's interruption of history" that "precludes any perspective on reality, any worldview, historical system or mythical framework, any principle, or idea, or metaphysic, which evades or abstracts from the concrete flesh-and-blood reality of that crucified Jewish peasant of Nazareth."[54] This section begins the task of reconfiguring *history* in christological terms, but does so by beginning with the knowing subject, and therefore with soteriology.[55] Soteriology is an interruption in two ways: as an interruption of the continuity of the subject who is being saved, and as an interruption of the continuity of history from "without," as it were. In the sense that the event that saves and interrupts comes from "outside"—in other words, it is external to immanent psychological, intellectual, world-historical forces—it can be described as "irruptive." Revelation is, in its salvific and historical dimensions, irruptive. It follows from this that at the heart of Christian theology is an event that is truly new; Christian theology is in response to this *novum*.

Christian theology, for the knowing subject, begins in reconciliation. This reconciliation is accomplished in the person of Jesus of Nazareth, in a real historical event. This event is grounded, however, not in a historical trajectory, but in the freedom of God's act of revelation. This creates a tension between the historical nature of God's revelation and the transcendent

---

[54]Kerr, *Christ, History and Apocalyptic*, 13.

[55]Following from the argument in the previous section, in a brief and preliminary way this ordering can also be defended on historiographical grounds. First, as we have seen, Wright begins his series on the question of God in the New Testament with a methodological discussion that grounds his theological and historical work in a particular epistemological approach. By beginning with soteriology I am attempting to directly engage with his starting point. Second, if historiography is a human discipline that is engaged in interpretation and representation, and if as such it is a subjective discipline (although in a critically realist way), then the question of the subject is where we ought to start when engaging in a dialogue with historiography.

nature of God with respect to the immanence of historical forces. This tension is worked out by Barth in the *Church Dogmatics* (*CD*) IV.1.

Barth begins the section of *CD* titled "The Obedience of the Son of God" with the simple statement, "The atonement is history."[56] Yet, rather than making this claim an entry point for a particular historical way of knowing,[57] the claim is developed further so that Barth goes on to say that "the atonement takes precedence over all other history"[58] because this "is the very special history of God with man, the very special history of man with God. As such it has a particular character and demands particular attention. As such it underlies and includes, not only in principle and virtually but also actually, the most basic history of every man."[59] The history that is the atonement is, then, an absolutely unique history and functions as the historical reference point for all other history.[60]

According to Barth, the New Testament lifts the man Jesus Christ "right out of the list of other men, and as against this list (including Moses and the prophets, not to mention all the rest) it places Him at the side of God."[61] Furthermore, "There is no discernible stratum of the New Testament in which—always presupposing His genuine humanity—Jesus is in practice seen in any other way or—whatever terms may be used—judged in any other way than as the One who is qualitatively different and stands in indissoluble antithesis to His disciples and all other men, indeed to the whole cosmos."[62] Because of this, Barth goes on to say, the human judgment that Jesus is worthy of praise as the one who is equated with the majesty of God is not a judgment that a human being could make on her own, but is only possible because God himself had made such a judgment possible. From the perspective of the continuity of human history, any worldview that makes sense of that continuity is incapable of knowing this one man who is equated

---

[56]*CD* IV.1, 157.
[57]See the interaction between Richard Hays and Wright in which Hays suggests this passage in *CD* to Wright and Wright correctly recognizes that what he and Barth acknowledge as "history," beyond the external reality of the events in question, might very well be different things. *JPPG*, 58-59, 64-65.
[58]*CD* IV.1, 157.
[59]Ibid.
[60]Here is the starting point for a proper, christologically oriented theology of history.
[61]*CD* IV.1, 160.
[62]Ibid., 161.

with the majesty of God. This is because of the epistemological priority of his own history. Because of the immediacy or "contact" required for knowledge of Jesus as very God, that knowledge necessarily involves individual human lives in the history of Jesus of Nazareth.[63] Human judgment separates and judges, dividing the known from the knower. Theological epistemology brings them together, reconciling the knower in the gift of the known. "[The Apostles'] estimation and judgment of Jesus is as such something secondary, a necessary consequence. It is not itself their theme, the subject-matter of their preaching. They are occupied with Jesus Himself. They aim to be His witnesses. They answer His question. They give an account of His existence. He has placed them in this attitude."[64]

What this means is that God gives the human knower the gift of subjectivity and so contextualizes the knower according to Jesus Christ's own history, which becomes the truth of the knower's existence.[65] "The fact that He is [the Word of God] can be known only as He Himself reveals it, only by His Holy Spirit."[66] This is, indeed, a rupture of the continuity of the knower's own existence, which has been reconciled and given a new understanding of the meaning of human existence, "the most basic history of every man."

The context for understanding, for knowing the truth as this history, this event, must come with the event itself. This is what makes the history of Jesus an absolutely new kind of history. Even though we affirm that it occurs "in history," in order to know the theological and existential import of this history, the history of God with us, this history must bring with it the very condition for knowing it for what it is.

In the words of the Gospel of John, the subject must be "born anew" (γεννηθῇ ἄνωθεν, John 3:3). This new birth is understood soteriologically, as the reconciliation of the human with God, in such a way that a new status of subjectivity obtains for the subject that is essential for truly knowing the event of reconciliation. In this section of the *CD*, Barth describes this in relationship to the "particular character" of the history of God together with humanity in the atonement. This particular character has absolute existential

---

[63]See the discussion of the historicity of Jesus in Kerr, *Christ, History and Apocalyptic*, 90-93, 130-33.
[64]*CD* IV.1, 162.
[65]Ibid., 158.
[66]Ibid., 163.

import: "Everyone who knows it as truth knows in it the truth of his own existence."[67] In other words, humans know who they are in and through this event and not as they interpret this event according to a previous knowledge of their existence. The event of truth at once disrupts the context and provides an entirely new condition in the subject so that the event can be seen accordingly. The event *is* the reconciliation of God and humanity.

If this rupture characterizes the human subject that knows Jesus as Lord, apocalyptic theology begins to tell the story of this Lord as a disruptive event. This event is the parousia of God's Son. Truth, for apocalyptic theology, is grounded in this event. The event of God's coming interrupts the subjectivity of the individual as it interrupts the continuity of history.[68] Yet, by describing the revelation of God as an interruption, or through the various cognates of *rupture*, we introduce a variety of conceptual problems.

Problems with the concept of the **novum.** One problem is that when, as an event in history, God's revelation is said to be a rupture to that history, a contradiction appears to be introduced because rupture only makes sense— that is, it can only be interpreted—according to an account of historical continuity in order to provide context to it *as* rupture. How can there be something new that is only known in terms of what is old?[69] One answer to this contradiction involves a description of rupture that makes it perpetual—a perpetual irruption from outside that is never possessed or knowable in terms of the continuity into which it comes. For the subject, this means that the subjective condition in which knowledge of God is obtained is never a possession of the individual subject, but rather continues to depend on the active irruption of God. In this way the event is not dependent upon the existing context, but brings its own context. This is similar to the thought experiment of the *Philosophical Fragments*: "Can the truth be learned?" The contextual challenge to the novelty of the truth event—the apocalyptic event—comes under the same criticism as does the Socratic in the *Fragments*.

For history, this means that the event, while being in and given *to* history, never becomes an event *of* that history as if the history to which it comes

---

[67]Ibid., 158.

[68]This is why subjectivity and history are inextricably bound together.

[69]E.g., Jürgen Moltmann, *The Coming of God: Christian Eschatology*, trans. Margaret Kohl (Minneapolis: Fortress Press, 1996), 22.

already contains the truth, but becomes an event according to its own stability or continuity (from "outside," as it were) that disrupts and destabilizes any other source of the continuity of history. This stability "from outside" is given to history in the atonement, but only seen as such, or known, in the gift of the condition necessary to see it.

For the subject, the irruptive event that disrupts the subject's identity within the context of the continuity of history can be said to be "perpetual" to the extent that the irruptive event is an event of personal engagement. If we were to characterize the event in terms that limited it to simply an event that takes place, a fact of history such as the crucifixion or even the resurrection, such a fact would simply become a part of the past and take its place as a point of reference within history for the subject, but never maintain the continuing irruptive force needed to prevent such an event from being abstracted into a principle or simply a part of history; it would easily become a "possession" of the subject. If, on the other hand, the event is, at its core, *personal,* then the event remains determined by the freedom of the person who acts. For theology this is the freedom of the person of Jesus Christ, and the freedom of Christ is maintained in his person and appropriated to the individual through the gift of the Spirit. The Spirit, like the person of the Son, can never be a possession; rather, he gives himself in his *charismata,* as unpossessed gift. Again, it is by virtue of his personhood that the Spirit cannot be possessed. This perpetuity of the irruptive, clarified according to the reality of the person who interrupts human existence through personal and salvific encounter, Jesus Christ, and appropriated through the charismatic gifting through the person of the Spirit, is actualized in history in the obedience of the subject's response to the personal call to discipleship. This actualization remains bound to the personal initiative of the divine call.

> Discipleship is a commitment to Christ. Because Christ exists, he must be followed. An idea about Christ, a doctrinal system, a general religious recognition of grace or forgiveness of sins does not require discipleship. In truth, it even excludes discipleship; it is inimical to it. . . . Christianity without the living Jesus Christ remains necessarily a Christianity without discipleship; and a Christianity without discipleship is always a Christianity without Jesus Christ.[70]

---

[70]Dietrich Bonhoeffer, *Discipleship,* Dietrich Bonhoeffer Works, vol. 4 (Minneapolis: Fortress Press, 2001), 59.

Another problem with the concept of the *novum* is that the danger of a Marcionite exclusion of the history of Israel lurks in a misappropriation of the language of interruption. How does the language of the *novum* relate to the history of Israel? This question is absolutely central to addressing Wright's concerns with "apocalyptic." Surely there is a history to which the Son of God comes that is hermeneutically significant for the proper understanding of that event. For Wright, if Paul is an apocalyptic thinker—something Wright repeatedly affirms—this "does not rule out, but rather leads us to expect, an emphasis on the long, dark history of Israel, and on the divine purpose at work behind the scenes, not as an immanent process but as part of the sovereignty of the creator God, bringing about the final great moment of judgment and mercy."[71] Ultimately, the question of Israel and Israel's history is important for the sake of avoiding a supersessionist reading of the New Testament. For this we return to Barth.

Barth for and against the novum. There are at least two sections in the *Church Dogmatics* in which Barth uses the term *novum*. That these appear first at the beginning of his project (*CD* I.2) and then toward the end (*CD* IV.1), and that the early use is positive and the latter use is negative, might suggest to some that Barth had changed his early position by the time he had come to the doctrine of reconciliation. In this section I intend to examine both uses of the term and, in good dialectical form, show how both Barth's "for" and his "against" work together to inform the relationship between the irruptive act of God and the continuity needed to make sense of God's acts with and for the world in and through the people of Israel.

For. If the event contextualizes us, rather than being contextualized by us, then we can say that it *is* something new, since its origin is "outside" of us and has the nature of an "event."[72] When Barth, early in the *Church Dogmatics,* uses the term *novum* in a positive manner, he does so to make just this point.

> God's revelation in its objective reality is the person of Jesus Christ. In establishing this we have not explained revelation, or made it obvious, or brought it into the series of the other objects of our knowledge. On the contrary, in establishing this and looking back at it we have described and designate it a

---

[71]N. T. Wright, *Paul and His Recent Interpreters* (Minneapolis: Fortress Press, 2015), 2:92.
[72]This takes us back to the force of Climacus's question, "Can the truth be learned?"; i.e., what does it mean if the truth comes from outside of us?

mystery, and not only a mystery but the prime mystery. In other words, it becomes the object of our knowledge; it finds a way of becoming the content of our experience and our thought; it gives itself to be apprehended by our contemplation and our categories. But it does that beyond the range of what we regard as possible for our contemplation and perception, beyond the confines of our experience and thought. It comes to us as a Novum which, when it becomes an object for us, we cannot incorporate in the series of our other objects, cannot compare with them, cannot deduce from their context, cannot regard as analogous with them. It comes to us as a datum with no point of connexion with any other previous datum.[73]

But this *novum* is operative on us as subjects, not on the context itself. "It comes *to us* as a *Novum*." Given new eyes to see and ears to hear, we see what has always been the case. This is the epistemological effect of God's saving work. The context that we thought would interpret the event turns out to be entirely new—*from the perspective of the one reconciled.* The context as determined according to the logic that is immanent to history is completely incapable of contextualizing the unique event, that history that Barth calls "atonement."

From the vantage point of reconciliation we see that this event is an event that comes from "outside." Now that we have seen with some level of nuance the way in which the attempt to contextualize the event according to any particular worldview fails with respect to this event, the notion of an outside makes sense. Barth describes this as

> the aspect of the grace of God in Jesus Christ in which it comes to man as the (sinful) creature of God freely, without any merit or deserving, and therefore from outside, from above—which is to say, from God's standpoint, the aspect of His grace in which He does something unnecessary and extravagant, binding and limiting and compromising and offering Himself in relation to man by having dealings with him and making Himself his God.[74]

But the condition that makes humans see the event of truth is not the end, for the event itself is the movement of God into the far country. Barth continues,

---

[73]*CD* I.2, 172.
[74]*CD* IV.1, 158.

> In the fact that God is gracious to man, all the limitations of man are God's
> limitations, all his weaknesses, and more, all his perversities are His. In being
> gracious to man in Jesus Christ, God acknowledges man; He accepts respon-
> sibility for his being and nature. He remains himself. He does not cease to be
> God. But He does not hold aloof. In being gracious to man in Jesus Christ, He
> also goes into the far country, into the evil society of this being which is not
> God and against God.[75]

Still speaking in terms of the rupture, the apocalypse of Jesus Christ, we can
see that it is God's movement into the sinful, "evil society" that constitutes
the interruptive nature of the event of truth. But, and here is the surprise, he
does not defeat the evil powers by opposing them with force; rather, God
defeats the evil and blindness of the world by entering it and taking it into
himself so that, as Barth says, "all the limitations of man are God's limitations . . . all his perversities are His." This is where we start to see the *continuity* in the rupture. What we see in Christ is ourselves. He takes into his
own life our fallen, broken selves. He enters our evil society, subjects himself
to the powers, suffers and dies.

Against. Now we turn to the section in the *Dogmatics* titled "The Way of
the Son of God into the Far Country." If this title appears to imply a radical
irruption into history such that the Old Testament is done away with, Barth
definitively rejects this implication.

> The Old Testament, and also the New Testament in its constant implicit and ex-
> plicit connexion with the Old, makes it quite clear that for all its originality and
> uniqueness what took place in Christ is not an accident, not a historical *novum*,
> not the arbitrary action of a *Deus ex machina*, but that it was and is the fulfilment—
> the superabundant fulfilment—of the will revealed in the Old Testament of the
> God who even there was the One who manifested Himself in this one man Jesus
> of Nazareth—the gracious God who as such is able and willing and ready to
> condescend to the lowly and to undertake their case at His own cost.[76]

Here, *against* the claim that Jesus Christ is somehow a historical *novum*,
Barth, much later in *CD*, claims that the coming of the Son was "not the arbitrary action of a *Deus ex machina*, but that it was and is the fulfilment . . . of

---

[75]Ibid.
[76]Ibid., 170. Italics in original.

the will revealed in the Old Testament." This movement of the Son of God into the far country, into the world of sin and death, is an act of grace in continuity with the will of God in the Old Testament and, as such, it is *not* a *novum*. It is not a *novum* precisely because if it were, it would not be a true incarnation; the journey into the far country would be incomplete. The *logic* of incarnation, as it is revealed in the *actuality* of incarnation, works according to the *totality* of the event of incarnation.[77] God enters the world so that he is in history, so that he is "*incognito*,"[78] hidden in the processes of world history. Kierkegaard's Anti-Climacus describes the totality of this incognito as an "omnipotently maintained incognito":

> Only in this way is there in the profoundest sense ernestness concerning his becoming true man; this is also why he suffers through the utmost suffering of feeling himself abandoned by God. He is not, therefore, at any moment beyond suffering but is actually in suffering, and this purely human experience befalls him, that the actuality proves to be even more terrible than the possibility, that he who freely assumed unrecognizability yet actually suffers as if he were trapped or had trapped himself in unrecognizability.[79]

But, in this incognito, he comes into the history of Israel. It is Israel's history in which he hides and in which he reveals himself.

The tension between the initial positive assessment of the *novum* by Barth and his later negative assessment can be seen in the following passage, one that brings together the historical continuity of Jesus vis-à-vis the history of Israel and the fact that with Jesus being God in history, history itself is relativized:

> But where in the Old Testament we find Israel, or the king of Israel, in the New Testament we find the one Israelite Jesus. He is the object of the same electing will of the Creator, the same merciful divine faithfulness. . . . He is the Son of the Father with the same singularity and exclusiveness. Of course,

---

[77]For an important account of the relationship between the incarnation and apocalyptic theology, see Susan Grove Eastman's essay, "Apocalypse and Incarnation: The Participatory Logic of Paul's Gospel," in Davis and Harink, *Apocalyptic and the Future of Theology*, 165-82. In accord with the subtitle of the collection of essays, Eastman goes beyond Martyn's account of the crucifixion to show that the invasive logic of Paul's gospel relies on a strong account of the humanity of Jesus as he fully participates in the human condition; cf. 2 Cor 5:21: "[God] made him to be sin who knew no sin."

[78]Cf. Søren Kierkegaard, *Practice in Christianity*, trans. Howard V. Hong and Edna H. Hong, vol. 20, Kierkegaard's Writings (Princeton, NJ: Princeton University Press, 1991), 127-33.

[79]Ibid., 132.

what is and takes place between Him and the Father is relatively much greater, and as the self-humiliation of God much more singular, than anything indicated by the father-son relationships of the Old Testament. For this one man— it is as if the framework is now filled out and burst through—is the Son of God who is one with God the Father and is Himself God. God is now not only the electing Creator, but the elect creature.[80]

If the history of Israel is the "framework," that is, if Jesus is himself Israel, this framework is "burst through" because Jesus is not just a human standing in for Israel as the Messiah, but he is also God standing in as Israel, an unprecedented event that can only be held together according to the dialectic of the hypostatic union. Discontinuity and continuity, divinity and humanity, *novum* and not *novum*; when Barth commented that we can speak of God's coming as "from outside, from above,"[81] he was drawing attention to the fact that God was doing something from "the aspect of His grace in which He does something unnecessary and extravagant, binding and limiting and compromising." That is, the externality that characterizes the *from* of the divine movement is precisely the freedom of God's electing grace. This is the locus of the continuity that would characterise Barth's apocalyptic theology.

After rejecting the Christ-event as a historical *novum*, Barth turns to the history of Israel as the particular history into which Jesus was born to show that this history is itself evidence that God's action in Jesus is "the conclusion and sum of the history of God with the people of Israel."[82] This history as the history of God's work carries on from the history of God in the Old Testament in which "He is already on the way into the far country to the extent that it is an unfaithful people to whom He gives and maintains His faithfulness."[83] That which characterizes this journey into the far country is, again, grace. "The grace and work and revelation of God has [*sic*] the particular character of election."[84] That which makes up the continuity between the Old and New Testaments is the electing grace of God, who is faithful to a sinful and disobedient people. This is why Barth says it is not a historical *novum*. God has been active. We can affirm that the nature of God's act is

---

[80]*CD* IV.1, 170.
[81]Ibid., 158.
[82]Ibid., 166.
[83]Ibid., 171.
[84]Ibid., 170.

invasive with respect to human sin and the structures of evil that characterize the world in rebellion to God. Barth describes the situation of human rebellion, the situation of the human being elected by God as one who in the contradiction of rebellion "is broken and destroyed by the greater contradiction of God. He cannot stand before Him, and therefore he cannot stand at all. He chooses a freedom which is no freedom. He is therefore a prisoner of the world-process, of chance, of all-powerful natural and historical forces, above all of himself."[85] In this world so enslaved, the only continuity one can point toward in order to make sense of the whole of history is the grace of God in his election to save. This is not a *novum* with respect to God, but it *is* a *novum* with respect to human judgment and the way in which, from an anthropological epistemic base, we tell the human story. In other words, the Christ event is external with respect to the intrahistorical forces of world process, forces that would interpret the direction of history according to an immanent logic.[86] Or, as Paul writes to the Corinthians, "From now on, therefore, we regard no one from a human point of view; even though we once knew Christ from a human point of view, we know him no longer in that way. So if anyone is in Christ, there is a new creation: everything old has passed away; see, everything has become new! All this is from God, who reconciled us to himself through Christ" (2 Cor 5:16-18a).[87]

According to Bonhoeffer, the unity of the individual (the one who, in Paul's words, has, *in Christ*, become a new creation) is to be found "where human beings have been created, or are created anew, and where this creation both

---

[85]Ibid., 173.

[86]Here, Nathan Kerr is especially helpful, pointing out the way in which apocalyptic directly challenges the "presuppositions of modern theological historicism." Specifically, these presuppositions should be understood as the purely immanent forces that direct human politics toward a telos that exists in the future. Kerr, following John Howard Yoder, identifies these forces with the Pauline "principalities and powers." Such an identification cannot, of course, be made except from the perspective of the new in Christ. Kerr, *Christ, History and Apocalyptic*, 137-38.

[87]Cf. Wright's comment in *PFG*: "And with that new creation . . . there went a new mode of knowing. . . . For Paul, the point was that the new creation launched with Jesus' resurrection was the *renewal* of *creation*, not its abolition and replacement; so that the new-creation mode of knowing was a deeper, truer, richer mode of knowing *about the old creation as well*. And with that deeper knowing came all sorts of consequences," 1310. Wright's comment seems to miss the "sense of rupture" in Paul's formulation. We might contrast "everything old has passed away" in Paul with "the new creation . . . was . . . not its abolition and replacement." Surely Wright is concerned to preserve the "this-worldliness" of the Christian faith, but does he also neglect the rupture that seems evident here and elsewhere in Paul?

happens to them and is something in which they participate."[88] The location
of this unity, the continuity of identity that makes an individual an "I,"

> must be sought . . . where human beings must know themselves, without inter-
> pretation, in clarity and reality. This means they must know that their unity and
> that of their existence is founded alone in God's Word. It is this word that lets
> them understand themselves as "being in Adam" or "being in Christ," as "being
> in the community of faith of Christ," in such a way that the foundation of unity
> in the Word becomes identical with the foundation of that unity in the being in
> Adam or in Christ. This . . . is not a datum of experience but is given to faith as
> revelation. Only in faith does the unity, the "being," of the person disclose itself.[89]

If the continuity of history is found in the elective grace of God, the continuity of the subject is found in the one who gives the gift of subjectivity,
the one who creates us anew in Christ. This "in Christ" is a significant aspect
of the apocalyptic logic that is being developed here, and will be explored
with more dogmatic precision in the next chapter.

CONCLUSION

We can now see the way in which we can speak of the enslaved cosmos and
the individual who continues along in its darkness, both of which are in
need of God's irruptive act, his act of entering into human existence himself
and rescuing humanity from slavery to the powers of sin. To the extent that
the act of God in Jesus Christ is a movement into the darkness of the world,
it is irruptive; with respect to the path of history apart from God, it is a
novum. For the present soteriological concern, we can identify continuity
only with respect to the elective grace of God. The doctrine of election is
therefore that which holds together, in continuity, the individual human and
history. But this continuity is only known as the grace of knowledge given
in the discontinuity of God's irruptive and salvific act. In this way, the apocalypse of Jesus Christ demands that we begin with the new beginning, hermeneutically, theologically, epistemologically and historically.

---

[88]Dietrich Bonhoeffer, *Act and Being: Transcendental Philosophy and Ontology in Systematic Theology*, trans. H. Martin Rumscheidt, Dietrich Bonhoeffer Works, vol. 2 (Minneapolis: Fortress
Press, 1996), 102.
[89]Ibid., 102-3.

4

Christology and Creation

FURTHERING THE APOCALYPTIC LOGIC

THE SOTERIOLOGICAL RUPTURE articulated in the previous chapter, according to an account of apocalyptic theology, is grounded in the event of God's revelation in Jesus of Nazareth. Wright's epistemology has been the occasion for this theological critique, and for that reason we began with an examination of the knowing subject, a move that required that we begin with the soteriological rupture of epistemological subjectivity in divine revelation and the consequent conceptual problems this raises for hermeneutics and historical thinking. Now those problems need to be addressed from within a more focused account of Christology. The next step in the sequence, after Christology, will be in the direction of the doctrine of creation. This move toward the doctrine of creation addresses the metaphysical implications of the language of rupture or irruption that apocalyptic theology uses.

CHRISTOLOGY: ANHYPOSTASIA AND ENHYPOSTASIA

In our apocalyptic logic we began with the reconciliation of the knowing subject. The next theological move must be to interpret the one who has revealed himself in his salvific act, who has given himself as object in history for our knowledge and yet who remains subject in relation to that history; the next task will be Christology.

For in him all the fullness of God was pleased to dwell, and through him God was pleased to reconcile to himself all things, whether on earth or in heaven, by making peace through the blood of his cross. (Col 1:19-20)

At the very heart of the theological doctrine of the incarnation is the union of the divine and human natures in Jesus the Messiah. Rather than an abstraction from the biblical witness, the affirmation of the hypostatic union of the divine and human natures in the one *hypostasis* (ἐν δύο φύσεσιν ἀσυγχύτως, ἀτρέπτως, ἀδιαιρέτως, ἀχωρίστως) is a deeper penetration into the logic of what it means to call Jesus *Emmanuel*, "God is with us" (Mt 1:23). But if this is the case, then the move to look closer at this logic will also require that we look closer at what the Gospels actually say with respect to the historical events in which the one who was, and is, God with us is revealed. For Wright this means especially looking at the actual message of Jesus—namely, his proclamation of the kingdom of God.[1] But to reiterate, knowledge *that* this is God with us is not derived from historical reasoning, but from the new birth that comes from God. For now the task is to articulate a Christology according to the apocalyptic logical sequence of reconciliation-Christology-creation, acknowledging that these are not abstract statements, but are rooted in the actual events of God's self-revelation to human history. It is the gospel and the ground of Christian theology that God has freely revealed himself as both subject and object and that this knowledge comes about in a reconciled relationship with God through Jesus Christ. It is this God, revealed in this way, of whom theology must speak, and it cannot do so apart from the sort of confession that Chalcedonian Christology affirms. Apart from this, Jesus is just another "crucifiable first-century Jew."

T. F. Torrance articulates twin doctrines of the hypostatic union, *anhypostasia* and *enhypostasia*, in such a way that we can map them on to the apocalyptic movement described above, that is, God's coming to, or invasion of, the cosmos. This will help further clarify what we are actually saying when we say that the apocalypse of Jesus Christ is an "irruption" into the enslaved cosmos. Torrance emphasizes that "we cannot think of the hypostatic union statically,"[2] which means that the fact of God's unity with the

---

[1]I agree with Wright that if we are to talk about the divinity of Christ—as we must—we must pay just as much attention to what the Gospel writers were trying to say about Jesus—namely, "that he really was inaugurating the kingdom of God—the kingdom of *Israel's* God—on earth as in heaven." *JPPG*, 133.

[2]T. F Torrance, *Incarnation: The Person and Life of Christ* (Downers Grove, IL: IVP Academic, 2008), 85.

man Jesus is only known in the *dynamic* of God's coming, in the *act* of God making himself known, and as such has the nature of an event. Since God is the subject who presents himself to us as object, we cannot say what God is without first saying who God is, and therefore, conversely, what God is, is who God is. Who God is, is God as he acts to reveal himself, and his being cannot be abstracted from this act. God is only known as *"active* subject."[3] The doctrine of the hypostatic union is, therefore, not a doctrine of God's being, and then a doctrine of that being in relation, but it is a doctrine of God's relation in act and, as such, is a doctrine of God's being in act.[4] It follows that the twin doctrines that expound the hypostatic union, *anhypostasia* and *enhypostasia*, are equally dynamic and relational doctrines that describe an event and therefore God's being through this event.

Anhypostasia

In the *anhypostatic* movement, God the Son *comes* to his creation and assumes humanity for himself "in terms of the great divine act of grace in the Incarnation."[5] *Anhypostasia* (an-*hypostasia*) affirms that Jesus of Nazareth is not a person, a hypostasis—or "personal mode of being" (Barth)—apart from his union with the Son. This is expressed by Torrance negatively by the statement, "Apart from the pure act of God in the Incarnation, there would have been no Jesus of Nazareth."[6] Dogmatically, this means that Christ's human nature lacks its own personal subsistence apart from the person of the Son; the subject that we encounter when we encounter Jesus is the subjectivity of the Son.[7] The hypostasis of the Son, *as* Jesus of Nazareth, is, in

---

[3]Eberhard Jüngel, *God's Being Is in Becoming: The Trinitarian Being of God in the Theology of Karl Barth; A Paraphrase*, trans. John Webster (Grand Rapids: Eerdmans, 2001), 78.

[4]Cf. Dietrich Bonhoeffer, *Act and Being: Transcendental Philosophy and Ontology in Systematic Theology*, trans. H. Martin Rumscheidt, Dietrich Bonhoeffer Works, vol. 2 (Minneapolis: Fortress Press, 1996).

[5]Torrance, *Incarnation*, 84.

[6]Ibid.

[7]Ivor Davidson finds this in Cyril of Alexandria, who "famously contended that the Word was united 'hypostatically' (*kath'hypostasin*) with human nature, so that the Word was the subject of all the experiences of the enfleshed Christ. Logically, therefore, for Cyril, the human nature did not have its own hypostasis, but was hypostatised by the Word." Davidson, "Theologizing the Human Jesus: An Ancient (and Modern) Approach to Christology Reassessed," *International Journal of Systematic Theology* 3, no. 2 (2001): 139. Cf. Karl Barth, *The Göttingen Dogmatics: Instruction in the Christian Religion*, trans. Geoffrey W. Bromiley, vol. 1 (Grand Rapids: Eerdmans, 1991), 157.

Barth's words, "that of the Logos, [and] no other. Jesus Christ exists as a man because and as this One exists, because and as He makes human essence His own, adopting and exalting it into unity with Himself."[8] The emphasis on human essence is important for Torrance because it links the incarnation with humanity, not with a particular human person. He assumed that which makes humanity human, and not just one already existing person or hypostasis;[9] so, following the rule laid down by Gregory of Nazianzus ("For that which He has not assumed He has not healed; but that which is united to His Godhead is also saved"),[10] he is the savior of humankind, not just the savior of one man (one human hypostasis). Simply put, the Son does not unite himself with a man (*homo*), but with humanity (*humanitas*). The singularity of Jesus as a man is uniquely subsistent with the divine Logos.[11]

Historically speaking, this means that the Jesus of history is uniquely and exclusively identified with the person, or mode of being, of the Son. Jesus is not a person apart from the personal identity of the Son. On this positive side, then, it is affirmed that "the truly and fully human life of Jesus is grounded in the act of the Son or the Word becoming flesh."[12] Jesus' humanity is true humanity, but it is a humanity in unity with the Son as this one, definite, individual (*in uno certo individuo*).[13] "He is a real man only as the Son of God."[14] So we affirm one hypostasis, fully human and divine. Precisely because of the *anhypostatic* denial (the hypostatic union of God and humanity in the person of Jesus is not separable into two hypostases), the union is dynamic; it is a true *becoming*. God's being is revealed in his act, and this act

---

[8]*CD* IV.2, 49.

[9]Oliver D. Crisp's argument that human nature needs to be understood in this formulation according to a concrete-nature view rather than an abstract-nature view is instructive but, for my purposes here, beyond the needs of the argument. However, Crisp's contribution is important as far as it serves to establish the analytic coherence of the *an-enhypostatic* distinction. Oliver Crisp, *Divinity and Humanity: The Incarnation Reconsidered* (Cambridge: Cambridge University Press, 2007), 72-89.

[10]Gregory Nazianzen, "To Cledonius the Priest Against Apollinarius" in *Cyril of Jerusalem, Gregory Nazianzen*, ed. Philip Schaff and Henry Wace, Nicene and Post-Nicene Fathers, vol. 7 (Peabody, MA: Hendrickson Publishers, 2012), 440.

[11]The language of *subsistence* is used instead of *existence* for the reason that "'existence' might imply accidental being, whereas 'subsistence' suggests necessarily actual being by virtue of—but only by virtue of—assumption by the divine hypostasis of the Logos." Davidson, "Theologizing the Human Jesus," 135.

[12]Torrance, *Incarnation*, 84.

[13]*CD* IV.2, 49.

[14]Ibid.

is not separable from the person of Jesus because the act is a "becoming."[15] "And the Word *became* (ἐγένετο) flesh and lived among us" (Jn 1:14a). If we read this doctrine together with both a doctrine of sin and a doctrine of *creatio ex nihilo*, it becomes an "irruptive" doctrine. God is free with respect to creation, and this freedom is metaphysically displayed in the ontological distinction between God and the world. This ontological distinction can be conceived in terms of distance (as in the early Barth of the second edition of the *Römerbrief*), but rather than spatial it is truly ontological, meaning that God may be absolutely "close" or absolutely "far," but the real difference is the ontological distinction between the Creator and the creation. It is the sin of the world with its fallen state that makes the reconciliatory dynamic, in biblical imagery, invasive (cf. Col 2:15). The parousia of the Son of God, his "journey into the far country" (Barth)—*anhypostasis*—is unprecedented and radically new and, from the perspective of immanence, is a "breaking-in" from the transcendent.[16] Here the *anhypostatic* side of the *an-enhypostatic* distinction is a "movement" from God to humanity in and as the personhood of the Son.[17] The full movement can be seen here in Barth's description:

> If we put the accent on "flesh," we make it a statement about God. We say—and in itself this constitutes the whole of what is said—that without ceasing to be true God, in the full possession and exercise of His true deity, God went into the far country by becoming a man in His second person or mode of being the Son—the far country not only of human creatureliness but also of human corruption and perdition. But if we put the accent on "Word," we make it a statement about man. We say—and again this constitutes the whole of what is said—that without ceasing to be man, but assumed and accepted in his creatureliness and corruption by the Son of God, man—this one Son of Man—returned home to where he belonged, to His place as true man, to fellowship with God, to relationship with his fellows, to the ordering of His

---

[15]Cf. Jüngel, *God's Being Is in Becoming*.

[16]Here, of course, the language of transcendence and immanence is not spatial, but metaphysically based on the ontological distinction between God and the world: ontology being a possibility for the world, but not for God.

[17]Crisp critiques the idea that the *an-enhypostatic* distinction can be read, in Barth and Davidson, to be simply the positive and negative aspect of the hypostatic union. If this is the case, argues Crisp, it is not very informative. Yet Torrance's account—and Barth's—can be understood to be making an important distinction between the "movements" in God's self-revelation. In this way they are understood dynamically, contributing to the apocalyptic picture that I am describing. Crisp, *Divinity and Humanity*, 73-75.

inward and outward existence, to the fullness of His time for which He was made, to the presence and enjoyment of the salvation for which He was destined. The atonement as it took place in Jesus Christ is the one inclusive event of this going out of the Son of God and coming in of the Son of Man.[18]

Enhypostasia

We now turn to this second movement, the return of the Son of Man, the *enhypostatic* dynamic that completes the apocalyptic movement. In dogmatic terms, *enhypostasia* affirms that "the humanity of Jesus had real existence in the person of the eternal Son."[19] This is, as Barth clearly affirms in the above passage, from the perspective of the "flesh" or humanity of Jesus. From this perspective we speak of the "*enhypostasis* of the human being of Jesus Christ, His existence in and with the Son of God."[20] This means that humanity, Christ's human nature, is brought into the Godhead in this particular man, Jesus of Nazareth, by way of God's "taking up" humanity into the trinitarian communion, through the one hypostasis that is the Son of God, *now* fully human and fully divine. Because humanity does not exist apart from the concrete particularity of individual human persons, humanity cannot be assumed apart from its actual *en*-hypostasis. This "movement" of humanity into the being of God is actualized in the one person of Jesus. The second part of Gregory of Nazianzus's axiom—"But that which is united to his Godhead is also saved"—reflects this logic in its soteriological implication. It is important to make clear, as well, that it is humanity in this one person, Jesus, that is taken up. It is not all human persons. Because of this, our salvation must be participation in *his* humanity, a participation given to us through the work of the Spirit. Jesus is the new Adam, the one man in whom humanity is refocused (Rom 5:12-21; 1 Cor 15:20-23, 45-49).

Two things need to be said at this point to advance the argument. First, this takes us back to the account of participation that Torrance offers, in which we see the knowledge relationship between the Father and Son as the fulfillment of the human knowledge of God within a sort of closed polarity.

---

[18]*CD* IV.2, 20-21.
[19]Torrance, *Incarnation*, 105.
[20]*CD* IV.2, 53.

Knowledge of God is realized for humanity only in the knowledge *that the Son has of the Father*. We are given the gift of participation *in* this knowledge by the gift of the Spirit, who, in the act of rebirth, makes us to be subjects, in Christ, of God as object. In this way God remains both object and subject of human knowledge, and humans can know God only through the divine act of the Spirit. The unity of object and subject is therefore described according to the orthodox trinitarian affirmation of the *homoousion*, an affirmation that is preserved in the pneumatological account because the Spirit, too, is affirmed as *homoousion* with the Father and the Son. We know God, therefore, only through God; we know the Father in the Son, through the Spirit.

Second, this allows us to focus on the singularity of the history of Jesus the Messiah as the historical focus of what it means to be a human subject. This is because it is as this one man, Jesus of Nazareth, that the divine Logos, the Son of God, redeems and restores humanity, and so humanity is redeemed *in him*, and is restored to knowledge of the Father. This is the import of the *enhypostatic* movement, in which humanity in essence (*humanitas*) is taken up into the singular hypostasis of the divine Logos. Humanity is now understood as revealed in this singular history of this one man. The universal is narrowed into the particular.

If in the incarnation God gives himself, as the Son, to be known in his subjectivity to humanity, and then restores human knowledge of God in himself, as both subject and object of knowledge, where does that leave us? Where does that leave the humanity that God assumed in the actual event of incarnation, a humanity that is necessarily part of the human community—society, history, culture, and so forth—in which the subjectivity of the Son was an actuality given to history? If the incarnation is, epistemologically, a closed polarity, does it not therefore make Jesus' time here with us incidental? And yet, the doctrine of the incarnation and the hypostatic union are profound precisely because of the unity that is understood between God and humanity. Jesus' is not a truncated humanity; he is not a fleshly shell only to be abandoned, but a real human subject as the one subjectivity of the Son. It is human subjectivity taken up into the subjectivity of the Son as one subjectivity that makes the incarnation such a profound and transformative doctrine for our understanding of what it means to be reconciled to God. The "closed polarity" of the *an-enhypostatic* movement is only closed as it *includes* humanity in the dynamic sweep of God's movement into human history and back, *with* humanity, into the divine life and knowing relationship between the Father and the Son in the Spirit.

But can the Son's subjectivity in history be inadvertently isolated from the world of history by closing the loop and speaking of a closed polarity apart from humanity? What of the effects of this one historical subject in history, given as effects of a theanthropic presence, but nevertheless effects that can be known and studied in the normal methods of historical research? *Anhypostatically*, when one is investigating the person of Jesus Christ—his aims and intentions as well as his acts—one is investigating the one divine subject, the Son of God. Yet *enhypostatically*, when one is doing this, one is also investigating the fully human nature of this one divine subject. How does one investigate, according to the normal methods of the historian, the subjectivity of the Son of God, even as he is given to us in his assumed full humanity?[21] On the other hand, how does one formulate theological dogmas of the one subjectivity that is the Son without paying close attention to the historical contexts that provide the connection of his humanity to humanity at large? Is this connection merely incidental? How are they related, the historical to the divine subject?

These questions will be addressed in due course, but at this point it remains to be seen how the Bible understands the participation of the individual subject in the humanity of Jesus Christ. This participation, rather than being an abstract, spiritual retreat from history, is instead a subjective refiguring of the history of the individual around the personal history of Jesus of Nazareth. This way the historical question begins to be answered by attention to the Christian practice/sacrament of baptism. We began with soteriological arguments regarding human subjectivity, yet these arguments remained somewhat abstract until they could be fleshed out according to a

---

[21]It must be made clear that this way of speaking about the one subjectivity of the Son is not a way of saying that the man Jesus was not a human person. If we were to say that he is not a human person, then we would be denying the incarnation. If we were to affirm that he is two subjects (one human and one divine), that would fail the Chalcedonian test of christological orthodoxy. If he was a human subject given a divine essence, then that would deny the eternal existence of the hypostasis of the Son, since his hypostatic existence would be dependent on the existence of the human, finite hypostasis of Jesus of Nazareth. It remains that we need to affirm the one subjectivity of the fully human, fully divine Jesus of Nazareth that is identical to the one person of the eternal Son.

more robust Christology. Here, as we begin to consider baptism, the soteriological dimension is given rich, christological and ecclesial content.

Baptism: Romans 6:1-11

Human participation in the particular humanity that is Jesus' life is not given to us according to a general participation in humanity, but is given to us as a participation in the life of one man. In this one man is the unity of subject and object, a unity in which the origin and goal of humanity is realized in history and this one man is given so that all may participate in his new humanity. This participation is focused on the Christian baptismal practice, in which the individual human finds his or her humanity redeemed in the one human who died and rose again. Baptism is that central, identity-determining practice in which we find the *anhypostatic/enhypostatic* dynamic proclaimed in such a way that it includes the individual, through the Spirit, in its dynamic, and forms through identification a new humanity determined by the risen and ascended Jesus.

Paul, in Romans 6, asks, "Do you not know that all of us who have been baptized into Christ Jesus were baptized into his death? Therefore we have been buried with him by baptism into death, so that, just as Christ was raised from the dead by the glory of the Father, so we too might walk in newness of life" (Rom 6:3-4). If, as Paul says, Christians are, first, baptized into his death, then the epistemological position that has been articulated herein with reference to Torrance and Kierkegaard begins, *not* with a simple transitional, revelational experience, but with a mortal crisis! Death precedes resurrection. This raises the question of continuity. If the subjectivity required for theological knowledge is given as a requisite condition by God, and this condition is understood in conjunction with the death of Jesus, a death in which the subject participates through baptism, then how is it that the human subject can be understood in continuity? If new creation, or death and resurrection, are the motifs governing this theological grammar, then the issues of continuity and discontinuity are given a certain biblical clarity in baptism.

In baptism the continuity of a disciple's life is identified with the life of Jesus. The significance of this is that the resurrection, an actual event in the life of Jesus, is claimed by Paul to be an actual event that each baptized believer can expect in his or her own future, after death. "For if we have been united with him in a death like his, we will certainly be united with him in a resurrection like his" (Rom 6:5). If Jesus' resurrection was an actual resurrection—a return to physical life from the death of the body—then the resurrection the believer expects is also a physical resurrection. The future holds out the sure hope that there will be resurrection from the dead, that is, an actual, future historical occurrence. What does it mean, then, that the baptized subject is to expect a death like his? Is such a death just as certain as the resurrection is certain? Is water baptism to be understood as that death? My suggestion is that the act of going in (or under) the water, symbolically or actually, rather than being simply a remembrance of Jesus' death, or a sacramentally effectual washing, or a crossing of the Jordan, or an ordeal that must be gone through symbolically,[22] is in fact the pledge that the life the baptized will now live is a life of discipleship lived on the way to the cross. This is the corollary of the equally important point that the life of the baptized, after baptism, is lived in the light of the still-future resurrection. That is, we need to correlate two deaths: the still-future death of the individual and the death of Jesus. So the cross of Jesus, in baptism, has a twofold effect.

First, it is Jesus' act, his death, on behalf of the baptized. The old humanity, in Adam, is judged and killed, taken up by God himself, "the judge judged in our place" (Barth): the *anhypostatic* dynamic in the hypostatic union. For that reason sin no longer has final dominion over humanity. "We know that our old self was crucified with him so that the body of sin might be destroyed, and we might no longer be enslaved to sin" (Rom 6:6). This has been done for humanity in the one God-man, Jesus. Paul continues his argument: "Whoever has died is freed from sin" (Rom 6:7). This means that, because of the resurrection of Christ, death holds no more dominion over him (Rom 6:9). The dominion of death, its logic that subjects every decision to the fear and the finality of death, is broken, and humanity is free; this freedom is claimed and realized in baptism. In baptism, the human individual dies with Christ, participating in his death, and is therefore freed from this logic. The individual is no longer a slave to the tyranny of sin and the force that it plays in determining a life lived according to fear inherent in the ultimate finality of death. But then, in Romans

---

[22]Although it may indeed be all of these things, too.

6:12, Paul exhorts the Roman church, "Therefore, do not let sin exercise dominion in your mortal bodies, to make you obey their passions." Why, if death has happened in baptism, must we still find sin exercising dominion?

The answer to this question, and the second effect of the cross for baptism, is that the cross remains ever before the baptized as the determining factor for an individual life. Christian life is lived toward the cross. The answer must be that just as the resurrection awaits the baptized individual's future (although it is already a reality *in* Christ), so too, death still awaits, so that its logic and dominion remain always before the believer, as a reality that remains determinative for the future. Baptism, however, provides the baptized with a new frame of reference in which to understand this future; namely, the cross—or the death—of Jesus. This means that the life lived *toward each individual's own future death* is to be shaped according to the life Jesus lived toward his own death. Jesus' sinless life, in which he took up humanity in its sinfulness, was lived free from the constraining logic of death and is to be the new model for the life of the disciple, lived toward his or her own still-future death. In this way baptism identifies the individual's future death with Christ's own death, giving life meaning according to that which gave his life meaning. Because life lived toward the cross is not determined by death, but by resurrection—that is, the faithfulness of God—the witness of Christian living is to the resurrection. This patterning in baptism is what C. Kavin Rowe identifies with the missionaries in the book of Acts.

> The life of the missionar[y] . . . is in essence a life of response, an alternative way of being in the world that takes as its pattern the life of the one to whom they bear witness. Differently said, Acts does not construe "witness" mono-thematically as the proclamation of Jesus's resurrection—preaching the word, as it were—but more comprehensively as living out the pattern of life that culminates in resurrection.[23]

Baptism witnesses to the rupture that was Jesus' death and resurrection and identifies that rupture as determinative for the rupture that occurs as humans are made subjects to the knowledge of God. Baptism is the new birth or new creation of humans into a reconciled relationship with God.

---

[23]C. Kavin Rowe, *World Upside Down: Reading Acts in the Graeco-Roman Age* (Oxford: Oxford University Press, 2010), 153.

The fullness of this reconciliation is in Christ, in whom the baptized participate by the Spirit. But for each individual who remains in the time before death, this time is characterized according to the tension between future death and future resurrection. The tension, however, is not dialectical for the very reason that resurrection is more determinative than death. This robs death of its finality and frees human lives from the logic of death, from its determinative "sting." The baptized participate through the Spirit in Christ's life now, but nevertheless remain in this tension: reconciled, yet in a world in which the old Adam remains. On the one hand, the point that all of this makes with respect to history, to the extent that human lives are given meaning in the life of Jesus, is that the *collective* meaning of lives *not* baptized can only be death. That means that human history, even the history of the baptized, plods along its way to death, even the death of the cross. On the other hand, the collective meaning of the lives of those who have been baptized can never be the finality of their own deaths (for they will still die), but they will find collective meaning—history—in the one history of Jesus the Messiah.

CREATION AND APOCALYPTIC

The third movement in what I am calling the logic of apocalyptic theology is that it moves theology from the epistemic base of reconciliation to the dynamic of christological participation through the Spirit, and only then can turn to say something about the creation. The following words from MacKinnon help to describe this movement:

> The doctrine of creation trembles, as it were, on a tight rope between the fields of natural and revealed theology. For, though in the classical natural theology of St. Thomas the quinque viae might be thought to yield us a creator, the whole mystery of creation can only be penetrated (in a manner proportionate to our understanding, be it insisted), when in the Incarnation of His Son God finally and once for all disclosed His love for man. For in and through His own self-imposed act of self-disclosure we are in a measure privileged to scan the being of God Himself and therefore to dare to frame the question—"Why did God create?"[24]

---

[24]Donald MacKinnon, *Philosophy and the Burden of Theological Honesty: A Donald MacKinnon Reader*, ed. John McDowell (London: T&T Clark, 2011), 141.

For MacKinnon the question "Why?" is the key to the metaphysical puzzle, since metaphysics attempts to account for the contingent by appeal to the necessary. But the reason the necessary brings forth the contingent cannot be shown, and so metaphysics remains a problem. In Christian theology this question is thrust back on God, and as such must be focused on the revelation of God's answer to the *why* question. That question, now echoing Bonhoeffer, is directed to the question "Who?"[25] since the revelation of God's being is located in the *person* of Jesus Christ. However, the need for a metaphysical link between the necessary and the contingent is never satisfied for the very same reason that grounds the doctrine of *creatio ex nihilo*: God is a free Creator. No necessity links the contingent and the necessary except the freedom of God, who creates out of nothing.

There are two significant reasons for carrying the logic of apocalyptic to the doctrine of creation. The first is that opposition toward an apocalyptic theology focuses on its assumed metaphysical dualism, implied by spatial metaphors, and supported by invasive language. If God has to invade from outside, where was he? "Invasive" language appears to favor discontinuity at the expense of continuity, thereby disrupting any sense of historical continuity or overarching context, narrative, worldview or ontology that consistently accounts for the whole of life in creation. Second, a doctrine of creation apocalyptically construed counters other formulations of creation theology that undermine the apocalyptic dynamic that I have articulated thus far. Creation is an essential piece of the apocalyptic logic. To make this claim, it will be helpful to look at one alternative account of the relationship between continuity and discontinuity in the doctrine of creation. Although there are far more than just this one, the selection that follows will serve to orient the argument in such a way that the reasons for choosing an apocalyptic approach will become clear.

Creation Order

One common theological approach for the sake of maintaining ontological or conceptual continuity within the created world is through an appeal to an original created order. If the creation itself can be understood to possess,

---

[25]Dietrich Bonhoeffer, "Lectures on Christology," in *Berlin: 1932–1933*, ed. Larry L. Rasmussen, Dietrich Bonhoeffer Works (Minneapolis: Fortress Press), 302.

or be characterized by, an order that is translapsarian and God-given, then the created order of the world itself is the continuity necessary for making sense of temporal life. A path can be traced from the contingency of existence back to the divinely ordained, and therefore necessary, created order. This provides norms for human agency in history. One example of this is the moral theology of Oliver O'Donovan.[26] O'Donovan articulates one way of arriving at a theological account of order that also attempts to affirm a revelational (apocalyptic?) perspective alongside the continuity provided by an appeal to created order:

> We are constantly presented with the unacceptably polarized choice between an ethic that is revealed and has no ontological grounding and an ethic that is based on creation and so is naturally known. This polarization deprives redemption and revelation of their proper theological meaning as the divine reaffirmation of created order. . . . It is the gospel of the resurrection that assures us of the stability and permanence of the world which God has made. . . . In the sphere of revelation, we will conclude, and only there, can we see the natural order as it really is and overcome the epistemological barriers to an ethic that conforms to nature.[27]

For his part, Wright follows O'Donovan and this line of reasoning, especially with respect to the history of the resurrection and its significance for epistemology. In an interesting essay, Wright agrees—tentatively—with the claim that the resurrection is the starting point for a Christian epistemology. Yet an epistemology begun in resurrection turns us back to the created order and naturalistic epistemologies by validating that order, a validation warranted by the assertion that the resurrection affirms the goodness of "God's present creation."[28] The tension between the new (discontinuity) and the constant (continuity) can be seen where Wright recounts the limits of natural epistemologies: "A resurrection-based epistemology, in other words, while being significantly new, might nevertheless affirm the goodness of non-resurrection-based historical knowledge, even while recognizing, as

---

[26]Oliver O'Donovan, *Resurrection and Moral Order: An Outline for Evangelical Ethics*, 2nd ed. (Grand Rapids: Eerdmans, 1994).

[27]Ibid., 19-20.

[28]N. T. Wright, "Resurrection: From Theology to Music and Back Again," in *Sounding the Depths: Theology Through the Arts*, ed. Jeremy Begbie (London: SCM Press, 2002), 208.

such knowledge itself sometimes insists, that it cannot reach beyond the naturalistic and even reductionistic account such as we find in Troeltsch."[29]

Appeals like O'Donovan's or Wright's use the resurrection as a means of turning us back to the ontology of the created order as the source for either moral norms or as a validation of natural epistemologies.[30] Even if those norms are learned through the revelational act of God in Jesus Christ, the "rupture" nevertheless affirms a prior and more basic creation order, turning us to a doctrine of creation that can be constructed apart from the resurrection. It can be construed this way because the resurrection is only a validation or affirmation of an already existing order; the resurrection is valued in this way according to its importance as a signifier. The order itself *does not change* in any fundamental way based on the ontological reality of the resurrection.

Apocalyptic theology offers a dual critique. First, the biblical witness to the revelation of God in Jesus Christ points us to a *new* creation rather than to a restored old creation. Even if God's work of new creation is considered more of a transfiguration rather than a complete destruction and re-creation, it nevertheless maintains its focus on the revelation of that order in the resurrected Lord, and not in the creation itself—a creation, it should be noted, that has *not* been resurrected (see Rom 8:18-25).[31] Second, the apocalypse of Jesus Christ invites our participation in the new creation by way of baptism, of death and resurrection into Christ's life, not into a renewed creation now (see, e.g., 2 Cor 5:1-5; 1 Pet 1:3-5). For now it is enough that O'Donovan and Wright show us one way that continuity and discontinuity can be related differently than in an apocalyptic theology. This difference can be identified with clarity if the question is focused on the ontological locus of continuity. For the creation-order account, continuity is guaranteed by the ontological unity of the creation itself (even if guaranteed by God). For the apocalyptic account, continuity is guaranteed by God's action of raising Jesus from the dead, an ontologically unique and novel event.

---

[29]Ibid.

[30]Based on this essay, Wright would want to say more than just this since the point he is making is that the resurrection is the valid starting point for a Christian epistemology. Regardless, the effect is seen in the shortcomings of his CRw—namely, that it does not allow for the reality of God and God's continuing activity to inform the interpretive method.

[31]The argument in Romans that the creation waits to be set free from its bondage to decay is not a look back to the created order, but a look to the "freedom of the glory of the children of God," arguably a reference to the glory that we have in the (resurrected) Messiah (cf. Rom 8:17).

The importance of thinking about soteriology and the doctrine of creation together can be seen in the contrast between the creation-order approach and the apocalyptic. O'Donovan emphasizes the continuity and stability of a normative created order, validated by the resurrection. Salvation is understood in this view in restorative terms, even if the attempt is made to describe it eschatologically.[32] The apocalyptic approach emphasizes the discontinuity of the soteriological event and deemphasizes any positive gain from an appeal to creation order (unless that order is christologically determined).

Creation, Soteriology and the Apocalyptic Imagination: Clarifying Tensions

There are several important strands in the apocalyptic imagination that are not operative in the creation-order schema and that create difficulty communicating between the two positions: (1) the opposition, in spatial terms, of God and the world; (2) the Marcionite possibility of an opposition between a distant (alien) God and the God of creation, who is known according to the world; (3) the revolutionary character and pathos of the alien God; and (4) the eschatological character of this God who "promises new things." The first two characteristics bring to our attention the relationship between God and creation. How God is said to relate to creation determines to a great extent the way in which we articulate our knowledge of his acts and the way in which we understand the continuity of those acts. Is God in the world? Is he part of the world? Does he exist away from the world, outside of it? Assuming that there is no real temptation to affirm two oppositional deities as did Marcion, is there nevertheless a tension between the God of apocalyptic theology and a Creator God, so that Marcion's ghost must always haunt apocalyptic theology? Is there a possibility of an apocalyptic doctrine of creation?

The second two questions address, loosely, the question of soteriology. For the apocalyptic theologians, how does God save? The use of metaphors like *irruption, invasion* and so on suggest a particular spatial relationship to the world, but they also suggest a soteriological orientation, one characterized by movement, force, action and even violence. The question that this raises for our overall question of theological epistemology and its relationship with his-

---

[32]O'Donovan, *Resurrection and Moral Order*, 53-75.

torical method, given that theological epistemology is rightly located within a doctrine of reconciliation, is whether the apocalyptic proposal is adequate to the metaphysical dimensions of the question (the question of God's relationship to the world; creation and spatial questions) and the soteriological dimensions (the question of problem and solution; history and theology).

Our concern throughout this chapter has been an interaction with apocalyptic theology, tracing its dogmatic implications from soteriology to Christology and now to creation, with an eye toward its implications for the epistemological relationship between history and theology. Martyn's work, as a key genealogical source for this new apocalyptic, is illustrative of the way in which the soteriological and creation dimensions interact. With respect to the creational question of space, we can, with clarity, see the way spatial metaphors operate in Martyn's apocalyptic in his assumption of the designation *cosmological apocalyptic eschatology*, drawing on the work of his student Martinus C. de Boer.[33] Martyn proposes to read Pauline apocalyptic (in Galatians) according to an image of cosmic liberation: "Specifically, both God's sending of Christ to suffer death on behalf of humanity (the cross) and Christ's future coming (the *parousia*) are *invasive* acts of God. And their being invasive acts—into space that has temporarily fallen out of God's hands—points to the liberating war that is crucial to Paul's apocalyptic theology."[34] In the notes on Galatians 4:4,[35] he writes, "Redemption has occurred in the human orb via an invasion that had its origins outside that orb." The language of invasion is distinctive of Martyn's work and, when combined with the extensive use of *apocalypse* and *apocalyptic*, creates a powerful imagery that, of itself, contributes to the way his theological claims are read. A further comment on Galatians 4:3-5, a text Martyn sees as "the theological center of the entire epistle,"[36] reveals, again, language that relies upon metaphors of spatial distance and active invasive movement: "In short, the Son's sending is an invasion

---

[33]Cf. J. Louis Martyn, *Galatians: A New Translation with Introduction and Commentary*, The Anchor Yale Bible, vol. 33A (New Haven: Yale University Press, 1997), 97n51; and most recently, Martinus C. de Boer, *Galatians: A Commentary*, The New Testament Library (Louisville: Westminster John Knox Press, 2011), 31-35.

[34]Martyn, *Galatians*, 105.

[35]"But when the fullness of time had come, God sent his Son, born of a woman, born under the law, in order to redeem those who were under the law, so that we might receive adoption as children."

[36]Martyn, *Galatians*, 406.

of cosmic scope, reflecting the apocalyptic certainty that redemption has come from outside, changing the very world in which human beings live, so that it can no longer be identified simply as 'the present evil age' (1:4). In this sense the Son is a distinctly other-worldly figure who has his origin in God."[37] Martyn's language is decidedly spatial and mythological.

This spatial imagery contributes to the way in which the soteriological dimensions of Martyn's apocalyptic are worked out. The plight that Martyn sees from Paul's letter to the Galatian church is cosmic in scope, larger than the unique plight of Israel (although inclusive of it[38]), and describable in terms that go beyond modern notions of sin as personal guilt (although inclusive of this as well).[39]

> God has invaded the world in order to bring it under his liberating control. From that deed of God a conclusion is to be drawn, and the conclusion is decidedly apocalyptic: God would not have to carry out an invasion in order merely to forgive erring human beings. The root trouble lies deeper than human guilt, and it is more sinister. The whole of humanity—indeed, the whole of creation (3:22)—is, in fact, trapped, enslaved under the power of the present evil age. That is the background of God's invasive action in his sending of Christ, in his declaration of war, and in his striking the decisive and liberating blow against the power of the present evil age.[40]

From the perspective of plight, we see that Martyn's interpretation is cosmic and spatial in scope, whereas in Wright's articulation of the plight, located in Israel's self-understanding as a nation called into existence by their God, the plight is existential and historical, having to do with their existence as a people in history.[41] For Wright, God is there, in history, with his people, bringing their history to a climax. For Martyn, God is presumed distant from a world given over to evil powers, and this distance necessitates nothing less than an invasion.

These two aspects of the plight that salvation addresses, its cosmic dimension and historical context in the history of Israel, can be reconciled if we

---

[37]Ibid., 408. Cf. ibid., 105.
[38]Ibid., 390. Here, "inclusive of it" can be read rather as if it had been subsumed under the larger, more determined category of "cosmic element."
[39]Ibid., 97.
[40]Ibid., 105.
[41]This, of course, has a bearing on the cosmos as well, but the differences in emphasis should be clear.

look back to the previous chapter and reiterate Barth's account, "The Way of the Son of God into the Far Country."[42] In this section, as we have seen, the metaphor of movement from one place to another is given its proper apocalyptic emphasis with respect to the "invasive" nature of a particular event, the relationship of that event to the plight that is both cosmic in scope and historic in nature, and a consistently maintained commitment to the epistemological priority of the Christ event. All of these are held together in Barth's theology by the doctrine of election. Election grounds the continuity of history and the subject but preserves the apocalyptic dynamic. By looking at Barth we can see how the main concerns of this section—namely, the relationship between soteriology and a doctrine of creation—are addressed as the tensions inherent in the "apocalyptic" continuity-discontinuity are given a dogmatic resolution. Nevertheless, if the soteriological problems are addressed in Barth, what about the creational question? Is there a material continuity, derived from the doctrine of creation, that contradicts the apocalyptic perspective?

Creatio ex Nihilo: *The Metaphysics of God's Freedom*

The doctrine of creation, as we have seen, can function as a stabilizing doctrine, using the language of order to establish ontological continuity. The way order functions is to give both material reality and social reality a stability and normativity that grounds human epistemological enterprises, enterprises such as history, sociology and the natural sciences. So, for example, if we know God through history, that means that he has a relationship with human history in which he is given to be known according to the norms of human knowledge of past events. However, if God's relationship to history is other than this, if the continuity, the stability that makes knowledge of anything possible, is grounded in God's elective grace—if it is apocalyptic— then the doctrine of creation must be articulated so that creation order is understood with respect to this contingency, rather than as an epistemological ground in its own right. If the continuity that makes knowledge of God possible is the elective (and therefore active) grace of God, seen supremely in the resurrection, then the appropriate way to describe the metaphysical relationship between God and creation is through the doctrine of

---

[42]*CD* IV.1, 157-210.

creatio ex nihilo. The doctrine of *creatio ex nihilo* maintains two key affirmations essential to an apocalyptic account of creation: (a) the absolute distinction between God and the world, and (b) the freedom of the Creator. But before considering these two affirmations in detail, it must be seen in what way the doctrine relates to Christology since Jesus the Messiah is the person and event that centers our epistemological project.

"The world exists in the midst of nothing, which means in the beginning. This means nothing else than that it exists wholly by God's freedom."[43] Bonhoeffer's articulation of creation from nothing in his lectures on Genesis 1–3 is instructive because he grounds our knowledge of the doctrine in the resurrection. This gives a christological priority to the doctrine of creation and locates our knowledge of God's creative act definitively in the revelation of God in Jesus. "The world exists in the beginning in the sign of the resurrection of Christ from the dead."[44] The editor of Bonhoeffer's lectures references at this point a quotation from Willhelm Vischer: "As absurd as it may seem to base the exposition of the first book of Moses on the Easter faith, so much does it make sense and so pertinent and essential is it to do so. For the Easter message is the verification of the message of the creation story, and the message of the creation story is the presupposition of the Easter message."[45] This is, of course, similar to the argument advanced by O'Donovan and affirmed by Wright. Yet with Bonhoeffer we have, rather than a validation of the created order, the validation of the freedom of God in the creation of the world, known in the resurrection of Jesus from the dead. The affirmation is theological, rooted in God and God's act, not creational, that is, rooted in our knowledge of the created world. Does this mean that creation is not affirmed in the resurrection? Not at all! Creation is affirmed, but it does not become epistemologically central. The resurrection affirms the value and goodness of creation, but because this affirmation comes from the freedom of God, God is the only epistemological ground for knowledge of the relationship between the Creator and the creation. There is no necessity in the resur-

---

[43]Dietrich Bonhoeffer, *Creation and Fall: A Theological Exposition of Genesis 1–3*, trans. Douglas Stephen Bax, Dietrich Bonhoeffer Works, vol. 3 (Minneapolis: Fortress Press, 2004), 34.
[44]Ibid., 34-35.
[45]Ibid., 35n[32].

rection or in the creation, but God's freedom to bring into being that which is not (Rom 4:17).[46] Furthermore, the resurrection points to its own *new* ontological quality and not to the existing (groaning) creation. Of course, the doctrine of creation out of nothing is not a novelty unique to the Christian faith,[47] but with the Christian faith it is reoriented hermeneutically to the resurrection. Reoriented accordingly, the two doctrines— *creatio ex nihilo* and resurrection—mutually inform each other. So Bonhoeffer writes, "There is absolutely no transition, no continuum between the dead Christ and the resurrected Christ, but the freedom of God that in the beginning created God's work out of nothing."[48]

There is also no reason to think that the emphasis here on creation out of nothing nullifies any account of creation *order*, for surely God's creation is ordered. To think otherwise would be verging on nonsense, since any act of communication presumes order. And if the Genesis creation account affirms anything, it is that God brought order out of chaos.[49] Rather, given what is revealed in the resurrection—the new life of Jesus, the firstborn of creation and the firstborn from the dead (Col 1:15-18)[50]—Christian theology looks to the resurrected Lord for knowledge of creation and the created order. Furthermore, the classical doctrine of *creatio ex nihilo* does not reject, nor replace, the concept of a created order. As Eric Osborn points out with respect to Irenaeus's formulation of the doctrine, God as architect and king are held together in the doctrine of creation out of nothing: "*Creation of matter and the shaping of the world are two aspects of a single act by God who is both supreme king and wise architect.*"[51] That is, both God's lordship and his act of creating order are grounded in the free act of God, according to his will, rather than according to his being.[52]

---

[46]Rom 4:17 brings together the resurrection and creation in the context of God's act of calling the people of Israel into existence out of Abraham. In each of these cases it is the freedom of God's elective grace that is at work.

[47]Cf. David B. Burrell, CSC, "*Creatio Ex Nihilo* Recovered," *Modern Theology* 29, no. 2 (2013): 5-21.

[48]Bonhoeffer, *Creation and Fall*, 35.

[49]Cf. *CD* III.1, 123.

[50]I take this to be the point in Colossians, not to point us to a creation order, or affirm such an order, but to show that the creation is known in its relationship to and dependence upon Jesus.

[51]Eric Osborn, *Irenaeus of Lyons* (Cambridge: Cambridge University Press, 2001), 69. Italics in original.

[52]See the helpful discussion in Alan J. Torrance, "*Creatio Ex Nihilo* and the Spatio-Temporal Dimensions, with Special Reference to Jürgen Moltmann and D. C. Williams," in *The Doctrine of Creation: Essays in Dogmatics, History and Philosophy*, ed. Colin E. Gunton (London: T&T Clark, 2004).

But this means that the doctrine of creation articulated in terms of *creatio ex nihilo* is not first of all a doctrine about temporal origins, one that teaches the first cause in a causal chain, but rather it is a doctrine that articulates particular nuances of the ontological and metaphysical relationship of God to creation. If approached from the direction of soteriology, it does this according to the reality of the incarnation, the presence of God *as* and *in* the person of Jesus the Messiah. God's presence as this man is not the presence of a higher form of being made into a lower form of being, but is, rather, the unprecedented entrance of the Creator of all things into the creation that he has made (see Jn 1:3; Col 1:15-20). It is the dynamic of entrance in the incarnation that introduces the need for an account of the metaphysical distinction implied in that dynamic. If the distinction between the Creator and the creation, "transgressed" in the incarnation, is pressed, we find that it is the doctrine of creation out of nothing that most satisfactorily answers the questions and articulates the distinction between God and creation that we see in the one man Jesus the Messiah.

Because we are beginning with soteriology, the distinction between God and the world appears first and foremost as a relation. The nature of that relation, revealed in the person of Jesus, is elucidated in its distinctive form for creation theology by the absolute distinction between God and the world. God is absolutely other than the created world, an otherness that is dogmatically grounded in the affirmation that he created the world out of nothing, by divine *fiat*; God spoke, and the world came into existence. *Nothing* in this sense is not another way of saying God created out of "something" that is cleverly being called nothing. Rather, nothing truly is nothing (or, nothing truly *isn't*). The key to articulating the distinction between God and the world is to take great care with any implied either-or logic or dualism in our talk about God and the world. First, this means that we do not say, "God and the world are one." God is ontologically distinct from the world. But second, we must also be careful about the way we say that "God and the world are two." This especially is the case if by *two* we are implying two realities subsumed under one ontological category. It is imperative to recognize that when we speak of the reality of God and the world we distinguish between God as a *necessary* being and the world as a *contingent* being. Indeed, God and the world are both real, although, as should be clear from the above, God and the world do not compete for ontological space: God's way of being and the world's way of being are absolutely distinct. "God is not an oppositional reality . . . not *a* being among beings, not *a* power among powers."[53] Because of this there is no reason to say that the absolute distinction between God and the world carries the implication that God is far removed or far away from the world. Just the opposite is true. It means that there is no ontological barrier, however large or small, that would introduce a competitive barrier to God's presence. Robinette clarifies this point:

> Although on our "side" of this qualitative distinction we might conventionally speak of transcendence as "beyond" the world and immanence "within" it, a more consistent way of putting the matter is that the self-bestowal of the wholly transcendent God is "the most immanent factor in the creature." God is nearer to me that I am to myself, as Augustine declares.[54]

But his absolute distinction from the world *is* a barrier for those created, since we are made in contingency, dependent upon God's own freedom to reveal, to make himself known. His closeness to us is just that—*his*.

The doctrine of *creatio ex nihilo* teaches us that God is absolutely distinct from the world so that his transcendence is unlimited, as well as his immanence. We can chase down the trail of contingency toward some metaphysical resolution, but in the end all we end up with is more contingency, not the necessity and universality we are looking for. If we peer beyond this from where we stand to speak in protological terms on the basis of what has been made, we necessarily err. Irenaeus corrects our attempts to say more in this regard:

> Moreover we shall go wrong if we affirm the same thing concerning the origin of matter, namely that God produced it, for we have learned from the scriptures that God holds primacy over all things. But whence did he produce it and how? That, scripture nowhere explains, and we have no right, with our own opinions, to launch ourselves into an unending sea of fantasy concerning God; we must leave such knowledge to God.[55]

---

[53]Brian D. Robinette, "The Difference Nothing Makes: *Creatio Ex Nihilo*, Resurrection, and Divine Gratuity," *Theological Studies* 72 (2011): 533.

[54]Ibid., 534. Internal quote is from Karl Rahner, "Immanent and Transcendent Consummation of the World," in *Theological Investigations* (New York: Seabury, 1978), 10:281.

[55]Quoted in Osborn, *Irenaeus of Lyons*, 72-73.

What we know in Scripture is that God created, he acted and there is no more that we know regarding the *how* of that act other than metaphors and anthropomorphisms. Neither are we given the *why* of that except in the perspective gained by God's act of redemption. *Creatio ex nihilo*, as a metaphysical corollary of soteriology and Christology, serves to emphasize the limits to what we can say about creation from the basis of the creation itself. But these limits tell us something important. Were we to look for an answer to the question *why* God created in the doctrine of *creatio ex nihilo*, we would come up empty. On its own, *that* there is a creation, even that a god created, gives us nothing to say with respect to divine rationale. In other words, we are not given the divine deliberation "behind the scenes," as it were, regarding God's decision to create. But this is *not* to affirm that the creation of the world was an arbitrary act. Eberhard Jüngel argues that to claim such arbitrariness is to reject theology itself, since if it were the case that God created for no reason, then theology would have nothing to say, for there would be no order to theology. He writes that "[humanity] can be thought of only as the creature of a creator who is not conceived of as arbitrary when the being of this [person] who is to be created moves the being of the creating God inwardly."[56] In other words, there is something that orders the relationship between God and the world, and this is not an order that is exerted from the side of the creature, for then the act of creation would still be left in question. Rather, there must be some reason that makes sense of God's act of creation. If that act is affirmed to be a free act, then it is moved by something that is not ontological, but relational. Christian theology looks to the revelation of Jesus Christ for the answer, where we are told that because he loved us we are given the gift of his Son (Jn 3:16). Jüngel, again, states:

> That God creates as his counterpart man is the execution of his self-determination, according to which God does not desire to come to himself without man. This self-determination, if it really is a decision of love which desires to come to itself with another one and only with that one, implies the freedom of God and man as opposites of each other. If God has created man as the one

---

[56]Eberhard Jüngel, *God as the Mystery of the World: On the Foundation of the Theology of the Crucified One in the Dispute Between Theism and Atheism*, trans. Darrell L. Guder (Grand Rapids: Eerdmans, 1983), 38.

elected for love, then man is what he is for his own sake. For one is loved only for his own sake or not at all.[57]

God is revealed in his free movement to us, and not in the being of the world. This is expressed in the doctrine of *creatio ex nihilo* since the world is not created out of God's being, but out of nothing. There is no ontological link, no path back from the contingent to the necessary that we can follow to have our questions answered. Because he remains distinct from the world and because that distinction is absolute ontologically, we cannot work backwards from the creation or its order and derive at some knowledge of the God who made the world. Instead we come back against nothing, the nothing out of which the world was created.[58] But this nothing means that if we are to know God, we must gain such knowledge according to the same basis on which God created and relates to the world, that is, according to his divine freedom (in love). That freedom is what we see in his electing to save the world. Therefore the doctrine of *creatio ex nihilo* turns us back on the God who is absolutely free with respect to creation, and who is related in continuity with it, not in his being, but in his freedom, in his electing and reconciling grace. The movement of God to us is definitively known in the incarnation and the events of the life, death, resurrection and ascension of Jesus of Nazareth. God is revealed in the freedom of his acts, in the "dynamic" of his coming to us, in the apocalypse of his Son, and not in the "static" being of the cosmos. Karl Barth's tautology, "God is God," implies this dynamic, since God is known as God only in his act of coming to us, and this is known decisively and finally in the *anhypostatic/enhypostatic* dynamic of God the Son.

The doctrine of *creatio ex nihilo*, therefore, separates the being of the cosmos from the being of God, but links God's creation to God ultimately according to the free act of divine self-giving love in which the Creator takes into himself the very being of the creature. The tautology *God is God* is therefore an apocalyptic movement of God that includes "movement" of God into the world and his return to himself, bringing humanity (and the cosmos; see Rom 8:18-25) along with him. The doctrine of creation out of nothing implies an ontological discontinuity that is contrasted with a continuity lo-

---

[57]Ibid.
[58]This is the metaphysical counterpart to what is going on when Jüngel talks of "the worldly non-necessity of God." Ibid., 14-35.

cated in the freedom of God's elective love, known in Jesus Christ. "If then man is the one elected for love, he is what he is in a relationship to God which is determined by freedom. This relationship could only be diminished by any talk of the necessity of God for man. Love bursts apart the relationship of necessity by surpassing it."[59] The similarity to Kierkegaard's Climacus is evident: "Out of love, therefore, the god must be eternally resolved in this way, but just as his love is the basis, so also must love be the goal."[60]

To be clear, the issue at hand remains the implications of the sheer reality of God for theological knowledge. This has been discussed in terms of God's objectivity and what that means for human subjectivity—namely, that human subjectivity vis-à-vis God has its source in God. The doctrine of creation helps us see how the metaphysics of the God/world distinction, essential for understanding the objectivity of God, imply an absolute distance from God from the human perspective, but an equally absolute closeness to God from the theological perspective. This closeness, however, is only metaphorically spatial; God's closeness is based on his freedom, our distance on our creatureliness and our sin. Where this distance is overcome, from our perspective—the perspective of the creature—is in the incarnation. And, as such, it is irruptive—necessarily so as seen from within the contingencies of creation. The question that remains is that of history, if there is, indeed, an unbridgeable gap between the world of creational—and therefore, historical—being, and the God who created the world and the place and time for history. To paraphrase Lessing, to what extent can the contingent, the historical, deliver the necessary truths of theology?

N. T. WRIGHT AND APOCALYPTIC RECONSIDERED

Again, this theological conversation has perhaps become too abstract and has found dogmatic and theological doctrines to be the definitive sources for understanding apocalyptic and its theological import. Continuity has been described in terms of God's electing love and gracious salvation; discontinuity is seen in terms of sin and the powers of evil and also in terms of

---

[59]Ibid., 38.
[60]Søren Kierkegaard, *Philosophical Fragments*, in *Philosophical Fragments/Johannes Climacus*, ed. and trans. Howard V. Hong and Edna H. Hong, Kierkegaard's Writings, vol. 7 (Princeton, NJ: Princeton University Press, 1985), 25.

the absolute ontological distinction between God and the world. At this point Wright might join in and point to the overarching narratives that make sense of the whole, stories that have their sources in the history of Israel's interaction with the God who called them out of Ur, from Egypt, into Canaan and to Mount Zion. In *Paul and the Faithfulness of God*, Wright identifies three interrelated stories that make up Paul's worldview: the story of God and the cosmos, the story of God and humans, and the story of God and Israel.[61] Where is this narrative in the account I have provided and, conversely, how might sense be made within the biblical narratives of terms like *creatio ex nihilo* or *the nonnecessity of God*?

Apocalyptic, in Wright's theology, belongs within the overarching narrative of God's covenant faithfulness. For Wright, apocalyptic is not a theological movement or motif, but rather a particular worldview, or set of conditions that make possible the reading of apocalyptic literature. This does not mean that he rejects the sort of apocalyptic perspective for which I have been arguing, but it does mean that the conversation can get confusing. At this point in my analysis, I want to argue that Wright's perspective on apocalyptic fundamentally agrees with the account I have provided. This leads to a particular narration of Israel's history vis-à-vis the Messiah that suggests a particular theology of history. But this theology of history undermines his methodological commitment in *NTPG*.

Wright rejects the apocalyptic direction taken by Schweizer, Bultmann, Käsemann and others.[62] This program was characterized, as we have seen, by the imminent expectation of the return of Christ and, in Wright's interpretation, the end of the space-time world. In Wright's account of apocalyptic, rather than a radically dualist and gnostic interpretation of early Christian expectation, apocalyptic is interpreted according to "classical prophecy: complex, many-layered and often biblical imagery is used and re-used to invest the space-time events of Israel's past, present and future with their full theological significance."[63] First, the difference between what I have described as apocalyptic and what Wright is interpreting as apocalyptic should be clearer. Wright is concerned with the hermeneutical con-

---

[61]*PFG*, 478.
[62]*NTPG*, 285.
[63]Ibid., 286.

texts for making sense of a body of literature given the name *apocalyptic*. Schweitzer, Bultmann, Käsemann and Martyn (to follow the genealogy) are also interpreting apocalyptic literature, or, at least, apocalyptic tendencies in the biblical literature. But the apocalyptic theology I have been describing, and that is equally present (although not at all uniform) in Bultmann, Käsemann and Martyn, is not exclusively tied to a literary genre (although it is attentive to the genre). Rather it is attentive to the theological implications of God's self-revelation as free, dynamic and resurrecting. Käsemann, who certainly defined *apocalyptic* as imminent expectation (even in a personal letter to Wright),[64] also uses it in the manner I am describing: "But where Protestant theology conceives apocalyptic *as the message of God's kingdom revealed in Christ* and as the worldwide liberation of the children of God, world anxiety may not be derived from it."[65] The point here is that apocalyptic is turned back on Jesus Christ, as the one "apocalypsed," and, as such, he is imminent expectation realized.

> At Easter is repeated that apocalyptic event which the Gospel reports Jesus himself underwent in the Jordan baptism. At Easter the Son, proclaimed as such by the divine voice and equipped with the Holy Spirit for his mission, creates sons and daughters of the heavenly Father who follow him in his mission throughout the world and to whom he gives the Spirit as the power for their earthly service. What he defined as his task in his inaugural sermon at Nazareth they must pursue in discipleship, that is, set on the way with him under the sign of the cross, in the transport of the Spirit bringing the promise of freedom to those captive to demons.[66]

To the extent that Käsemann is turning to the messianic events as the arrival of what was "imminently expected," his use of *apocalyptic* is consistent with what Wright claims, writing about Paul: the realized apocalypse "*has already come about* in and through the events concerning the Messiah, Jesus, particularly through his death and resurrection."[67]

---

[64]Ibid., 286n19: "'*Apocalyptic ist bei mir stets als Naherwartung verstanden*' ('for me, apocalyptic always means imminent-expectation')."
[65]Ernst Käsemann, *On Being a Disciple of the Crucified Nazarene: Unpublished Lectures and Sermons*, ed. Rudolf Landau and Wolfgang Kraus, trans. Roy A. Harrisville (Grand Rapids: Eerdmans, 2010), 14. Italics added.
[66]Ibid., 13.
[67]Wright, *Paul*, 52.

In his interpretation, Wright describes Paul as "playing the part of the angel" as he describes "how these strange events actually unveil God's mysteries, and how the whole picture now works out."[68] This identifies an interesting transition between the literary genre and apocalyptic theology. Even if the literature that we now identify as apocalyptic was forming Paul's worldview, it was the apocalypse of Jesus the Messiah that became the event around which apocalyptic themes were interpreted. The actual event of apocalypse became the hermeneutical center. What seems to be the crux of the issue for Wright is that apocalyptic is not about the end of the space-time world, but rather about the faithfulness of God to his covenant. Wright's position on apocalyptic is laid out in a clear way in the following passage, making it worth quoting at length.

> [For] Paul, "apocalyptic," the sudden, dramatic and shocking unveiling of secret truths, the sudden shining of bright heavenly light on a dark and unsuspecting world, is after all what God had always intended. One of the central tensions in Paul's thought, giving it again and again its creative edge, is the clash between the fact that God always intended what has in fact happened and the fact that not even the most devout Israelite had dreamed that it would happen like this. We cannot expound Paul's covenant theology in such a way as to make it a smooth, steady progress of historical fulfilment; but nor can we propose a kind of "apocalyptic" view in which nothing that happened before Jesus is of any value even as preparation. In the messianic events of Jesus' death and resurrection Paul believes both that the covenant promises were at last fulfilled and that this constituted a massive and dramatic irruption into the process of world history unlike anything before or since. And at the heart of both parts of this tension stands the cross of the Messiah, at once the long-awaited fulfilment and the slap in the face for all human pride. Unless we hold on to both parts we are missing something absolutely central to Paul.[69]

We will return to this tension between apocalypse and covenant in the final chapter—there is still much to be said. Nevertheless, at this point in our examination of Wright's articulation of apocalyptic we can see that he has opened the door to the sort of language that Martyn uses (e.g., "irruption"),

---

[68]Ibid.
[69]Ibid., 54.

and it is this opening that might anticipate a certain rapprochement between apocalyptic theology and Wright's project. Or, perhaps it is just the opening for an apocalyptic Trojan horse to infiltrate and dismantle aspects of Wright's Pauline defenses!

To anticipate arguments yet to be made in full, the faithfulness of God to his covenant, rather than implying a rejection of apocalyptic theology, actually affirms one of its key tenets—namely, that the continuity of history is located in God's act, in his relationship to creation in self-revelation. For covenant, revealed in Jesus Christ as "new covenant" (1 Cor 11:25; Jer 31:31-34), is entirely dependent upon God's graciousness and his faithfulness. Just as we have seen that Jesus is the one who knows the Father and so fulfills the telos of human existence, so also Jesus fulfills the requirements of the covenant in such a way that his messianic vocation is to represent the people of Israel in covenant faithfulness. Wright makes this point in reference to Galatians 2:19-20, where Paul says that he has "been crucified with Christ" and that it is no longer he who lives, but "Christ who lives in me." The identity of the people of the Messiah is now found in the Messiah, "in terms of the Messiah's own new life."[70] Here the similarity between Wright and Barth is clear. Both articulate an interpretation of Jesus as the embodiment in one man of the identity of the entire people of Israel:

> We have seen that according to the Old Testament Israel is the son who is pledged to obedience and service to God as its Father and Creator, and that according to the New Jesus accepted this obligation in its place. . . . The place taken by the one Israelite Jesus according to the New Testament is, according to the Old Testament, the place of this disobedient son, this faithless people and its faithless priests and kings.[71]

And, just as we have seen in the forgoing discussion of creation, "the energy driving this redefinition is nothing other than the love of the Messiah himself, just as in Deuteronomy the reason for election was simply the love of YHWH for Israel."[72] The continuity, revealed in the Messiah, is the continuity of the love of God for the world, and nothing else.

The question remains, however, as to the value of what came before the

---

[70]Ibid., 113.
[71]CD IV.1, 171.
[72]Wright, Paul, 113.

Messiah as preparation. Whatever sudden break apocalyptic writers imagine, the Bible is the source in which the break makes sense. When Philip is called by Jesus, he finds his friend Nathanael and tells him, "We have found him about whom Moses in the law and also the prophets wrote, Jesus son of Joseph from Nazareth" (Jn 1:45b). Clearly, the Hebrew Scriptures are the source from which to make sense of what has happened—what was being revealed to Philip and Nathanael (Jn 1:50-51). How does the history that went before, and, more specifically, our ways of knowing history, interact with the revelation that comes to history as unprecedented, new and irruptive? In short, how does apocalyptic theology understand historical knowledge? That question is the task for the next chapter.

CONCLUSION

This chapter and the previous one have been articulating an apocalyptic theology in both its genealogical trajectory (Käsemann to Martyn and even Wright) and its theological commitments. Apocalyptic theology is committed to the reality of God for theology—not God's reality as an idea or concept, but as both subject and object. In theological, biblical terms, this means that God is a reality in the past, present and future history of Jesus the Messiah, the Son of God, God with us. Theology can therefore be structured according to a "soteriology-christology-creation" sequence.[73] At the heart of this sequence, from the human side of things, there is a determinative rupture, a break with the old and a start of something new. This rupture is the human experience of God coming to us from "beyond" as one who is transcendent, although in a noncompetitive way with our existence. This rupture is also the human experience of God's invasive act with respect to human sin and the evil powers that hold the cosmos enslaved. Yet, in theological perspective, there is no rupture, for God's resolve to love and to redeem, out of which we learn that he has created the world and everything in it, is given the most assured continuity that there could be: God's free, electing grace. In the history of world events, this electing grace is clearly seen in the covenants he has made with his people, Israel, and then with the world in the atonement made by Jesus the Messiah. For the individual

---

[73]That soteriology comes first simply affirms the subjective starting point; i.e., the question of human knowing is the question that drove this sequence. In actuality, Christology comes first.

knowing subject who would know God, the reality of God is only given to us as true knowledge as we participate in Christ's knowledge, his humanity and his history, in and through the Spirit; and this can all be seen and known in terms of the Christian act of baptism.

5

History According to the Theologians

FROM A THEOLOGY OF HISTORY TO A THEOLOGY OF HISTORIOGRAPHY

BY NOW TURNING OUR ATTENTION toward a theology of history and a theology of historiography, we can bring together the epistemological concerns with which we began: the reality and objectivity of God, his relation in movement toward the creation (described apocalyptically) and the way in which we ascribe meaning to the temporal events that originate in this divine movement. After a first section preparing the conceptual ground, the following section will present a theology of history and the final section will make some suggestions for a theology of historiography.

TOWARD A THEOLOGY OF HISTORY AND HISTORIOGRAPHY

Understood at the most basic level, a theology of history is history subject to the criterion of theological knowledge. That is, in order for anything to be a "theology of," it must be determined by the unique object of theological knowledge—namely, God. Only then can the object of the preposition, in this case history, be understood to be properly qualified theologically. Because this is so, history must remain a general conceptuality that is only given definitive content in light of the priority of the proper object of theology.

At this basic and elementary level of general conceptuality, before the theological work is applied to it, we can define history with R. G. Colling-

wood's help: "History is knowledge of the past."[1] We can differentiate between *history* and *historiography* at this point simply by distinguishing historiography as the methodological dimension of the larger field of discourse
that is designated *history*. The relationship is similar to the relationship between means and ends; historiography is the means by which one achieves
the end that is history. If history is *knowledge* of the past, then it is rightly to
be considered an epistemological discipline.

A *theology* of history locates the epistemological question that is central
to historiography, the "science" of history (knowledge of the past), in the
epistemological question germane to theological science (knowledge of
God). Only after this has been articulated can the object of history (history
as "the past") find its place within a theology of history and be understood
with respect to this proper but secondary object (secondary because it is
primarily grounded in theology).

In order to delve deeper into the way in which theology conditions both
the study of history and the object of history, it will be helpful to review the
historical paradigm within which Wright works and offer a constructive,
theological critique. First we will review Wright's historical method, and
then we will turn to consider two sets of distinctions that condition the work
of Wright's historiography, the past/present distinction and the real/ideal
distinction. This will be followed by a theological, trinitarian corrective.

N. T. Wright's Historical Method Revisited

Following the general consensus of contemporary historiography, Wright
claims that "all history is interpreted history."[2] The proper object of
history, being in one sense knowledge of the past, is never simply presented as the knowledge of bare facts about "the past," whatever those
would be, but rather as past events that belong within complex webs of
meaning. It is in these complexes that events of the past can be known
according to the unique way in which past events can be known.[3] These

---

[1]R. G. Collingwood, *The Idea of History with Lectures 1926–1928*, rev. ed. (Oxford: Oxford University
  Press, 1994), 363.
[2]*NTPG*, 88.
[3]Collingwood points out that knowledge of the past is not like knowledge of the actual, the present,
  but is properly considered to be "ideal." Collingwood, *Idea of History*, 364.

webs of meaning are found to condition both the events of the past in their contexts and the epistemological situation of the historian. From within her own worldview, the historian directs questions of meaning to the events of history. These are appropriate questions of meaning, inquiring into aims, intentions and motivations of historical subjects. These questions and their answers guide the historian to hypothesize, to formulate meaningful stories about events and then to verify those meaningful stories, testing them against the historical data. So the object of the historian's research is not simply bare facts about the past, but rather the meaning of those facts or events.

To get at the meaning of an event or series of events, the historian must look at both the "outside" of the event and its "inside."[4] This inside of an event is known by investigating the aims, intentions and motivations of individuals and societies as these are knowable to the historical method.[5] This is in part because, as Collingwood argues, history as a discipline is interested in thought.[6] Bare facts are unimportant except as they reveal or relate to human thoughts and intentions. The goal of historical knowledge is both to get at the event that happened—what actually took place—and, more importantly, to understand how that event reveals and informs human thinking, both then and now. The historian "is only concerned with those events which are the outward expression of thoughts."[7] To say that history is knowledge of the past therefore must be expanded to qualify the past as the past of human intentionality. If historians simply wanted to get at events qua events, they would be more akin to natural scientists than historians.[8]

---

[4]*NTPG*, 110.

[5]Ibid., 110-12. Wright limits this investigation to that which can be known through historical methods but excludes psychological investigation.

[6]Collingwood, *Idea of History*, 215-31.

[7]Ibid., 217.

[8]This distinction points the longstanding distinction within German theology between *Historie* and *Geschichte*. It is important in light of the conversation partners chosen for this project that the difference between these two German words be clarified so as to acknowledge this broader theological conversation. According to Karl Barth, "'*Historie*' is something that can be proved by general historical science, whereas '*Geschichte*,' is something that really takes place in time and space, but may or may not be proved. The creation story has to do with '*Geschichte*,' for instance. It has to do with something that happened and therefore something historical, but something that is not open to historiographical investigation" (John D. Godsey, ed., *Karl Barth's Table Talk* [Richmond, VA: John Knox, 1963], 45). For Barth, *Historie* and *Geschichte* can be simply distinguished along the lines of the difference between "history as event and history as

"The task of the historian is thus to address the question 'Why?' at all possible levels, down to its roots in the way the people under investigation perceived the world as a whole."[9] Wright's own particular definition of history in *NTPG* reflects this understanding of history and is a good baseline from which to begin our consideration of a theology of history. According to Wright, "History is . . . neither 'bare facts' nor 'subjective interpretations,' but is rather the *meaningful narrative of events and intentions.*"[10]

The Past/Present Distinction

In an analysis of the general norms of historiography from its ascendence within the political upheavals of the Renaissance and Reformation, Constantin Fasolt identifies "absence" and "immutability" as two character-

---

record," respectively (Geoffrey W. Bromiley, *An Introduction to the Theology of Karl Barth* [Grand Rapids: Eerdmans, 1979], 112).

This simple understanding is different from the understanding that permeated theological discourse with the work of theologians such as Paul Tillich and Rudolf Bultmann. It is not clear that Bultmann truly follows this dichotomy, although T. F. Torrance assumes that he does. Cf. Anthony Le Donne, *The Historiographical Jesus: Memory, Typology, and the Son of David* (Waco, TX: Baylor University Press, 2009), 34. Torrance describes the way in which these two words came to stand for a "fateful disjunction between two kinds of history"(Torrance, *God and Rationality* [Edinburgh: T&T Clark, 1997]), 51. *Historie* came to be used as a way to describe the "closed continuum of cause and effect," while *Geschichte* was used to describe "the way the Early Church creatively expressed its orientation to 'other-worldly' reality" (*God and Rationality*, 109, for this and the following quotations). *Geschichte* was not, in Torrance's interpretation, an account of reality except that reality was located in "man's understanding of himself cut off alike from his conceptual relation to God and from his conceptual relation to nature." This movement of theology toward *Geschichte* thus understood is, as an approach to Jesus, one that "thrusts man back through encounter with himself upon his own mental structures divorced from objective and explanatory control from beyond himself" and "is the antithesis of the unremitting attack of Jesus upon every form of human self-centredness."

The division represented here by these two "types" of history, while coming under attack from Torrance, nevertheless emerged as a response to the recognition that external reality is always subjectively experienced. All events, in order for them to have meaning, come to us from people who have experienced them subjectively, and thus they come to us always already interpreted; our reception of these events as others' interpretations involves us in further interpretation. Contact with the actual event, even for the eyewitness, is to engage in interpretation. *Historie*, if much is to be made of it, may be said to subject the historical event to the "acceptable" standards or methods for historical science. *Geschichte* may be said to be the interpretation of those events beyond the simpler question of "Did it happen?" to the more complex question, "What does it mean?" Regardless, the two types are not easily separated without doing violence to more recent developments in hermeneutical theory (Cf. the discussion in Le Donne, *Historiographical Jesus*, 17-39).

[9]*NTPG*, 112.

[10]Ibid., 82. Italics in original.

istics that determine the object of historical investigation, if that object is understood to be knowledge of the past. Any given event in the past is, in the modern historian's perspective, absent; and in its chronological absence it is fixed and unchanging, therefore immutable.[11] The truth about history, about the past, is that it is a fixed reality, it is distant from us and it cannot be changed. If this is the case, then one cannot really have contact with events of the past, but only with objects in the present that tell us, in various mediums, about the past. Because of the *absence* of history's object signified by historical evidence, that is, because it points to something that is not here, the evidential nature of history undergirds the distinction that is fundamental to modern historiography: the distinction between the past and the present.

> We said that history was founded on the distinction between past and present. Quite so. But we failed to add that this is not a distinction given, but a distinction made. Reality may be impossible to know. (In order to avoid skeptical mis-interpretations, I hasten to add that this is different from saying that reality does not exist. The opposite is closer to the truth: reality does exist, which is why it is difficult to know. . . .) But history is not the study of reality, much less the study of the reality of time. History is the study of evidence . . . and evidence is not reality. Evidence is a sign, as different from reality as letters are from meaning and as numerals are from numbers.[12]

Rather than the events themselves, the direct object of historical research—the past—turns out to be only available through evidence,[13] sources that contain accounts of, or clues to, the actual events (whether the "inside" or "outside" of these events). But the distinction that evidence relies on points to and reinforces the distance between the present and the past. The very method of the historian that enables access to the past in fact creates the distance between the past and present that, in turn, is basic to the paradigm within which the historian works. One example Fasolt uses in this regard is the example of anachronism. Anachronism imposes the present view of things on the past and thereby transgresses the boundary between past and present.

---

[11]Constantin Fasolt, *The Limits of History* (Chicago: University of Chicago Press, 2004), 5.
[12]Ibid., 12.
[13]Ibid.

Have previous historians fallen into anachronism? Of course they have, as all historians must. Is that a reason to turn back? Quite the opposite, it is a reason to go on. It is a signal that the line between past and present has been breached. Alarms are sounded and historians rush to the defense in order to prevent the past from making its presence felt again.[14]

It may very well be that the approach to history that Wright defends and articulates, for all its effort at admitting the subjective factor in the historical endeavor and, in this, rejecting the hard and fast distinction between subject and object,[15] nevertheless remains a modern exercise in historiography precisely because he continually asserts the "normal" methods of hypothesis and verification conditioned within worldviews. Worldviews, although usually hidden, "can themselves in principle be dug out and inspected"[16] in a spiraling process of hypothesis and verification that gradually objectifies and knows, with increasing certainty and clarity, the object, the historical fact, event, aim or intention. By specifically focusing on worldviews, Wright acknowledges the subjective aspect of the historian's task, but makes this subjectivity, finally, into an object, isolated in the historiographical task, and determined by the distance between the present and past. If CRw acknowledges that we know reality by our contact with it, then for the historian, contact is with evidence and texts that function as signs to the past, *but not the past itself.* This method, as Fasolt has shown, not only *assumes* the nature of the reality under investigation, but it goes further: it conceptually *determines* the nature of that reality. This is done as a determination of the distinction between past and present in such a way that the past is gone, absent and immutable. If Fasolt is right, then in this way, "history is a form of self-assertion."[17] By that he means that history asserts the autonomous position of the historian with respect to history and the question of the reality of history. This is a distinctly political reading of history. Not only is it political in the sense that the historicism that emerged in the seventeenth century emerged as a radical break from the narratives that located power in

---

[14]Ibid., 14.
[15]*NTPG*, 44.
[16]Ibid., 117.
[17]Fasolt, *The Limits of History*, 230.

monarchies and institutions,[18] but it is political in the sense that it locates power in the present vis-á-vis the past, in the hands of the historian— even if the historian makes allowances for the worldview or subjective element in the process. Modern historiography, almost regardless of method, assumes and reinforces the distinction between the past and the present, and in so doing affirms the place of the present independent of the past—except as the past is admitted on the terms of the present. The historian sets the terms.

The point here is not to critique historiography, but to examine its assumptions and methods so that its relationship with theology can be understood. If the distinction between past and present exerts the sort of pressure Fasolt describes, then the impact of this distinction upon theology needs further examination. Before moving to that, however, there is one more distinction that needs to be made—the distinction between the particular and the universal.

The Concrete and Contingent (the Real); The Necessary and Universal (the Ideal)

Wright's definition, that history is the *"meaningful narrative of events and intentions,"*[19] points to the causal relationship between events and human intentions so that those events can be related by the historian in a meaningful narrative. Meaning and intention point to the subjectivity of the actors within history, their worldviews and whatever those things are to which they point in order to make ultimate sense out of their lives. This can also be the meaning that the historian gives to the narrative that is told. At this point we might observe, with Hans Urs von Balthasar, that history involves the relationship between "the factual, singular, sensible, concrete and contingent; and the necessary and universal (and, because universal, abstract), which has the

---

[18]E.g., Fasolt writes, "By exploding the temporal unity of the period from ancient times to the present, the humanists changed truths that had enjoyed apparently unshakeable permanence into mere antiquities. They transformed things that seemed self-evidently true into things of the past that were henceforth impossible to know without a special effort. They demoted the universal power of pope and emperor from present experience to an aspect of history that had to be judged by means of evidence." Ibid., 20.

[19]*NTPG*, 82. Italics in original.

validity of law rising above the individual case and determining it."[20] That is
to say, history lives within the tension of the contingent and the universal, an
ever-moving fluctuation between one and the other as the quest for meaning
influences the historian's understanding of events and, in an opposite
movement, the events themselves, or the impressions events have left on
human memory and historical evidence, serve as checks upon the universal
interpretation of meaning. There is a circularity to this, as von Balthasar
claims: "The whole of history [is] the world of ideas which gives [history] its
norms and meanings."[21] Without wandering too far afield into the dynamics
of various accounts of the hermeneutical circle, it is important at least to
recognize this feedback loop at work in the historian's enterprise. The commitment required by such a loop is that human interpretation is, to some
degree, checked by a reality external to it, whether a past reality whose effects
remain in the present through historical evidence (memory, artifacts, texts
and the like), or a present objective reality. This latter reality can be the ideo-
logical commitments of the knower or at least the conscious/subconscious
worldview brought to bear upon the reality in question.

A *theology* of history, according to this view of history, will interpret the
historical sources in light of theological claims, doctrines and dogmas; the
"universal" claims of theological knowledge provide the interpretive
framework for understanding the unique particular events of the past. It is
also possible for a theology of history to be articulated according to the
theological beliefs and commitments of historical figures (so, in Wright, this
is what we find when he articulates the theology of the apostle Paul), but
these still remain past artifacts, concrete particulars in the form of beliefs,
which remain removed (to the extent that they can be) from the normative
claims of the universal hermeneutical commitments of the historian: those
commitments that order the historian's work of storytelling. Here, again,
Lessing's ditch reappears. How can the particular history (including beliefs
and events) of Jesus and the apostles be the source (as history) for the theological norms that, in turn, make sense of that history?

---

[20]Hans Urs von Balthasar, *A Theology of History* (San Francisco: Ignatius Press, 1994), 9. Here von
Balthasar is describing the basic tension in Western philosophy, a tension that plays itself out in
the philosophy of history no less than in other areas of philosophical inquiry. This, of course, is
also the basic model that provides the backdrop for Lessing's "ugly ditch."
[21]Ibid., 64.

Again, the split between idealism and realism appears. To review, Wright's work overcomes this tension through his critical realism that essentially lowers the bar for knowledge. Lessing's ditch is an unreal construct that exists only if our standards of knowing are too high—higher than the nature of actual knowledge. Actual knowledge implies contact, which implies the reality of the thing known; but it also acknowledges that the standards for knowing laid out by the Enlightenment do not reflect this reality. Theology enters this mode of knowing according to the standard ways of knowing, a knowing that takes place within the critical examination of worldviews.

A Trinitarian Corrective

In contrast to Wright's position—or in furtherance of it—I have articulated a theological epistemology that assumes God as an active revealing and knowing subject, as both subject and object in the knowing relationship. This relationship is realized in fulfillment of all human knowing in Jesus of Nazareth, where God the Son as the new Adam, in full humanity, knows God the Father. In Torrance's theology, we participate in this knowing relationship through the agency and gift of the Spirit. This way the relationship between idealism and realism is overcome by the perfection of knowledge in the trinitarian relations and as humanity is brought into that relation through the movement of the Son in the hypostatic union and through the work of the Spirit, who gives the gift of participation in those relations to the human knower. Wright's move to lower the bar is the correct move with respect to the development of historiography since its ascendency, but the very epistemological paradigm changes when the trinitarian dynamic is recognized. The paradigm within which Wright is working is the same basic paradigm that has determined historiography since the rise of humanism in Europe, the main distinction being that Wright allows a critical corrective to his method that undercuts idealism with an appeal to an external reality. Yet this paradigm that is at work is still the paradigm of the historian as subject who would know the object on his or her own terms, and who is methodologically committed to a metaphysically basic distinction between past and present. The past, understood as a reality to be known according to the usual methods of hypothesis and verification, held in critical check by evidence that signifies the past, is nevertheless a distant, immutable conceptuality held at that distance by the historian's autonomy over it.

The theological paradigm for history, understood according to a trinitarian paradigm, undercuts this precisely at the distinction between past and present. "And remember, I am with you always, to the end of the age" (Mt 28:20b). When Matthew closes his Gospel with these words of Jesus in commissioning his disciples, or when Jesus tells his disciples, "You will receive power when the Holy Spirit has come upon you; and you will be my witnesses" (Acts 1:8a), what is being claimed is that the ongoing presence of God is the continuity by which the church lives. For a theology of history this ongoing presence and reality is precisely that which changes the historical paradigm. Instead of there being a gulf between the past and the present, there is a theological continuity—theological because it is grounded in the ongoing presence of God with his people. Theological epistemology is a pneumatic event for the human knower, since the actual knowledge relationship is realized outside of the knower in the relationship between the Father and the Son. Theological knowledge is true knowledge, but it is an actively mediated knowledge according to the category of gift. The question that remains is how this changed paradigm relates to the practice of historiography.

The purpose of raising the question of the distinction between past and present and the ideal/real dichotomy is not to claim that there is another way of understanding the past, nor that historiography has been wrong about how it has approached historical knowledge, especially not Wright's critical realism. Rather, the point is both to recognize the way in which these difficulties influence the historian's task, specifically in setting up the historian's position as almost unavoidably autonomous with respect to the past, and to show that theological knowledge, even knowledge seemingly grounded in past events, is *not* subject to these same problems. Wright is simply wrong to say that theological knowledge, that is, knowledge of God and God's involvement in the contingent order, is like knowledge of anything else. The uniqueness of theological knowledge is what necessitates the adoption by theology of the term *apocalyptic*. Apocalyptic bridges the conceptual gap between the past and absent contingencies of history and the present reality of the one revealed in the ongoing contingency of the apocalypse of Jesus the Messiah. The apocalypse of Jesus is the actuality of that which literary apocalyptic can only imagine. It is the irruptive actuality of the living Messiah present to the world in and through the Spirit of God.

The first move toward this trinitarian understanding of historical knowledge is to move in the direction of a theology of history, rather than a theology of historiography. This is so partly because one cannot develop a historiography without acknowledging the metaphysical commitments one makes as one poses historical questions.[22] A theology of history articulates a perspective on the meaning of history as a whole, as, perhaps, a grand narrative that makes sense of all happenings in time and space, but does so according to the presently active reality of God. Again, this reality is not a reality obtained and possessed as universal knowledge in the way described above, but rather is a reality that demands that the meaning of history be placed in the hands of the one who gives history meaning *and who remains, in his freedom, determinative of that meaning.* This is apocalyptic. A theological epistemology, grounded in the trinitarian way of knowing, suggests that a theology of history would determine a theological account of historiography because a theology of history changes the hermeneutical position of the historian with respect to the past. In other words, the shape of history determines how we give it meaning in our historiography since historiography is concerned with the inseparability of events and their meanings.

A Theology of History

What then can be said of a theology of history? Where are we given to look for such a meaning? How can we speak of meaning if we have given up the place of interpretation to God himself? It remains that the only place where we can dare to speak of ascribing theological meaning to world events is at the place where God himself has entered into these events and has given himself to historical knowledge. But now we are in a dizzying circle: God has given himself to human historical knowledge, but in that givenness he remains a present and free active subject with respect to whom knowledge remains contingent. What has been given is not ours to possess. Historical knowledge of God's self-revelation is always a gift, contingent on the giver to sustain the gift. The same epistemological event that determines theo-

---

[22]Cf. R. G. Collingwood, *An Essay on Metaphysics* (Oxford: Clarendon Press, 1940), 49-57.

THE REALITY OF GOD AND HISTORICAL METHOD

logical knowledge, the knowledge of the Father by the Son, given to history in the incarnation, appears to determine historical knowledge, the knowledge of the meaning of history by the singular man Jesus of Nazareth. In order to see how this works more clearly, consider this description by Anthony Le Donne of Friedrich Schleiermacher's (1768–1834) hermeneutical circle with reference to his discussion of *Vorverständnis*:

> Schleiermacher argued that in order for something to be understood, it must be associated with an already understood category. He gives the example of a child learning a new word through the process of comparison. In his view, children are only able to understand a new word by relating the meaning of that word with a previously established category of meaning. He thus concluded that "every Child arrives at the meaning of a word only through hermeneutics." Gadamer further unpacks this concept by explaining that, when a word is learned, one must assimilate an alien category into a limited sphere of significance, and this process initially alters the word's "original vitality." The process becomes circular because one's grammar . . . is in constant interaction with the acquisition of new words.[23]

Here we ought to be reminded of the Kierkegaardian critique of the Socratic. In order for the truth to be learned, that truth must come from outside; that is, it does not comport with any preunderstanding (*Vorverständnis* in Schleiermacher). To confess that Jesus is Emmanuel, God with us, is to confess something that comes as knowledge given by God in the condition, and therefore soteriologically. If this is the case, the circularity of hermeneutics is broken into (irruption) by the gift of this condition so that Jesus can be recognized as the one in history who is the absolute norm of all history. This means that what the believer brings to the historical task is the confession and preunderstanding that Jesus is the absolutely unique event in history in which God has entered the reality of space and time at an ontological level (transgressing the "infinite qualitative difference") and given it ultimate meaning in his very life, death and resurrection. Such a confession only comes to us as a gift from outside—apocalyptically, as it were—and according to the soteriological act of God.

---

[23]Anthony Le Donne, *Historiographical Jesus*, 29. Internal quotes are from F. D. E. Schleiermacher, *Hermeneutik, Nach den Handschriften neu herausgegeben und eingeleitet von Heinz Kimmerle* (Heidelberg: Karl Winter Universitätverlag, 1959), 40; and H. G. Gadamer, "The Problem of Language in Schleiermacher's Hermeneutic," *Journal for Theology and the Church* 7 (1970): 72.

It is important to acknowledge that what comes to us as knowledge is not given apart from history, but rather given to history. Jesus does not come as an otherworldly messenger to give secret knowledge and therefore free us from the contingencies and the meanings that are present to us as creatures within a created world of time, space and therefore meaning. Jesus is the incarnation of the Son of God in and for history to give this history meaning, and therefore redeem us in this particular time and place. History is not rejected in the incarnation, but rather it is embraced—embraced to be judged, to be sure, but embraced nonetheless.

This can be described according to the model of knowledge as contact. If a theology of history/historiography is determined by contact with the reality that determines the meaning of history, then that means that a theology of history would precede a theology of historiography. Historiography is a reflection on what that contact means according to the method of the historian. The method is determined by the nature of the object known. In other words, the historian's method is determined by the metaphysical commitments that are grounded apocalyptically in a theology of history, a theology that determines the interpretive framework of the historian. As Barth says in his *Table Talk*, "Historical research will never be an *approach* to the Word of God,"[24] but rather, as I am arguing here, it is a particular type of methodological reflection on the Word of God with which the believer has already come into contact. The interpretive framework that is basic for a theological historiography is the content of the theology of history. Therefore, theology of history comes first.

My argument in the present section is this: the knowledge given to us in Jesus' history, expressed in the confession of who he is, is a knowledge of the end of human history and the beginning of a new kind of history. In Barth's words, "What took place on the cross of Golgotha is the last word of an old history and the first word of a new."[25] This is an argument about the large sweep of human events and their ultimate meaning. The new history that comes after the history of the Messiah, which ends at the cross, is pointed in two directions: the first, back to the end of history, which is Jesus' death; and the second, to the history of the new covenant given and received in faith and remaining pneumatically determined according to the gift of the

---

[24]Godsey, *Karl Barth's Table Talk*, 69.
[25]*CD* IV.1, 176.

Father, through the Son, in the power of the Spirit. In other words, the meaning of world history, given to human knowledge, is determined by the crucifixion of Emmanuel, God with us.

Jesus Is the Norm of History

In order to make the claim that Jesus is the norm of history, we will turn our attention back to Kierkegaard and then introduce another voice into the conversation, Hans Urs von Balthasar, especially his short book, *A Theology of History.* Von Balthasar will give us the option to move in one direction from an affirmation that Jesus is the norm of history, but I will part ways with him and move in another. If history is the meaningful narrative of human events and intentions, then to say that Jesus is the norm of history is simply to say that he is the source of meaning for history.

Kierkegaard and the unique place of Jesus in history. Having already worked through Climacus's take on the condition required for knowledge of God,[26] it makes sense to build on that discussion at this point with a further examination of its relevance for the question of historical knowledge. Very simply, the idea that knowledge of God is found in historical investigation is a contradiction to the very affirmation of faith that God came in Jesus incognito. If God came to be among us in the very form of a servant, then this move would be imperfect, and radically so, were he to be discoverable as God through historical method. That means that the deliverances of historical method apart from the condition given in the gift and reception of faith are adequate only to hide who Jesus is, and not to reveal him to us.[27] The modern quest for the historical Jesus, whatever it reveals, does not reveal that this is God with us. For Kierkegaard, all it reveals is the offense: "Jesus Christ is the object of faith; one must either believe in him or be offended;

---

[26]See chap. 2 above.

[27]This raises all sorts of christological questions. Can we know through historical method the thoughts, aims and intentions of Jesus? If so, does this mean that what we find are the thoughts, aims and intentions of the divine Logos, the second person of the Trinity? Or are these thoughts, aims and intentions only part of the incognito of the Son in human form? Are his thoughts, aims and intentions available to us as his humanity—and his words—are available to us? To answer with Kierkegaard, i.e., to affirm that these would be part of his incognito and therefore not helpful through historical method, is not to present a docetic Christology, but rather to *affirm* his full humanity in its theological meaning as God *incognito.* Cf. Barth's discussion of the veiling and unveiling of the Word of God in *CD* I.1.4.

for to 'know' simply means that it is not about him. Thus history can indeed richly communicate knowledge, but knowledge annihilates Jesus Christ."[28]

Kierkegaard would have us remember the reason God entered history incognito. What faith in the incarnate God reveals is that the love that God desires is a love between equals. He wishes to establish an understanding between us that is grounded in the humility and actuality of his becoming human. "Only in equality or unity can there be an understanding."[29] Yet the knowledge of him gained through this abasement comes not as something that we have achieved, but rather as a gift, being given the eyes to see. The perceptual shift that comes with this gift allows us to see that this one who comes incognito is God with us, and yet it is him, incognito, humbled, human, whom we see.

History cannot reveal to us who this is, but nevertheless it is this one who, in history, must reveal to us what history is. What is found in Kierkegaard's rejection of history—and especially the historical perspective of his age that wants to know Jesus on its terms, from its historical vantage point—is that because Jesus cannot be known this way, we are thrust back on his life, not the results of his life, and on faith, to see and know history from this perspective. This is what gives Kierkegaard his polemical edge in *Practice in Christianity* (and elsewhere); he sees history from the vantage of the one who chose to be abased and to judge history from this position of abasement.[30] In this way Jesus, God incognito, becomes the norm from which to understand history, but on faith's terms, not history's.

Hans Urs von Balthasar's A Theology of History. Hans Urs von Balthasar's *A Theology of History* offers an account of history that is very similar to the sort of account offered here but with at least one major difference; because of this it is necessary to take a brief look at his account and where the divergence lies. As we isolate that divergence, the distinction of my account should come into sharp relief.

---

[28]Søren Kierkegaard, *Practice in Christianity*, trans. Howard V. Hong and Edna H. Hong, Kierkegaard's Writings, vol. 20 (Princeton, NJ: Princeton University Press, 1991), 33.

[29]Søren Kierkegaard, *Philosophical Fragments*, in Kierkegaard, *Philosophical Fragments/Johannes Climacus*, ed. and trans. Howard V. Hong and Edna H. Hong, Kierkegaard's Writings, vol. 7 (Princeton, NJ: Princeton University Press, 1985), 25.

[30]There is much to be said here regarding this position of abasement. For further discussion of what this might mean, I would defer to the important work of James Cone.

There is much to recommend in von Balthasar's short book, but the most significant for our purposes here is his account of the normative nature of Jesus for history. To begin, von Balthasar recognizes the "methodological demands" of the subject matter of theology, making theology unique with respect to other disciplines, including historiography. In this sense, "Christ is the absolute" since "he remains incommensurate with the norms of this world."[31] According to the circularity we saw above,[32] the particularity of Jesus' historicity is the concrete norm that determines the abstract norm of history. This is tied to a theology of the divine Logos. "In Jesus Christ, the Logos is no longer tied to the realm of ideas, values and laws which governs and gives meaning to history, but is himself history."[33] The abstraction of the Logos in history in the ideality of general laws and values became particularized in the incarnation of the Logos in Jesus Christ. How the Logos personally acts in history is the source for understanding a transpositioning of this once abstract ideality into the particular instantiation that is the particularity of a human life. What this looks like in action is a unique mode of time determined not by Christ's self-assertiveness within history, but rather by his receptiveness to the Father's will, his obedience in renouncing sovereignty over his own existence.[34] "By directly and freely obeying the Father in heaven, the Son fulfils and includes in his task the whole historical dimension, conferring upon it its ultimate meaning."[35] This affirms the proposition that began von Balthasar's essay: "Namely that the life of the Son is related to the whole of history as the world of ideas which gives it its norms and its meaning."[36]

Appealing to a reading of this history in which the Christ-event is seen in terms of recapitulation and predestination, von Balthasar interprets the cross as the "condition for the possibility not only of sin but of existence and predestination itself."[37] The cross holds together the rupture that would separate the old from the new: it makes continuous that which has been made discontinuous.

---

[31]Von Balthasar, *Theology of History*, 19.
[32]See nn. 20 and 21 above.
[33]Von Balthasar, *Theology of History*, 24.
[34]Ibid., 40, 51.
[35]Ibid., 55.
[36]Ibid., 64.
[37]Ibid., 66.

There is an old homily, in the style of Hippolytus, which pictures him thus, as the one who, on the Cross, renews and holds together all things between heaven and earth:

> The tree, which is as wide as the heaven, stretches up from earth to heaven, and he takes his stand—an immortal growth—halfway between heaven and earth. He is the fulcrum of all things, the foundation of the universe, the bond of the cosmos, which encompasses the world and man, riveted to the Cross by the unseen Spirit, so that, made like God, he may never tear himself loose. His head touching the heavens, his feet holding the earth fast, his immeasurable hands embracing the spirit of the atmosphere between: he is the totality of all things throughout all.[38]

Von Balthasar rightly sees the incarnation as central to an understanding of history and focuses that understanding on the particularity of the life of the Son. He brings to the fore the two doctrines of recapitulation and predestination, in which we can see a proper emphasis on the way election grounds the relationship between God and history; and by emphasizing the obedience of Jesus he retains the priority of God's freedom in command over his relationship to the world. That this plays itself out in human obedience to God's will, rather than in idealistic formulations of human morality, has much in common with the ethical perspectives developed in Protestant thought by Kierkegaard, Barth and Bonhoeffer. Yet here, in this account of the cross, von Balthasar makes the cross the source of historical *continuity*, that which would "[hold] together the rupture." In the apocalyptic account I am arguing here, and contrary at this point to von Balthasar,[39] the cross is the location of the rupture, the absolute barrier between the old and the new that cannot be overcome in any way except in the free act of God *ex nihilo*, in resurrection. The cross is not the link between heaven and earth, but just the opposite: it is the rupture, the discontinuity.

Consider, in stark contrast to von Balthasar, this from Alan Lewis:

> Then the grave of Jesus becomes a boundary preventing forward movement until one has first looked back, without the light of Easter, at the cross and

---

[38]Ibid., 69. Internal block quote cited by von Balthasar from *Eis ton Hagion Pascha*, ed. Nautin, in *Sources Chrétiennes* 27, ed. and trans. Pierre Nautin (Paris: Éditions du Cerf, 1950), 177-79.
[39]Von Balthasar is also described, for good reason, as an apocalyptic theologian by Cyril O'Regan, but that discussion is beyond the scope of the present argument. See O'Regan, *Theology and the Spaces of Apocalyptic* (Milwaukee: Marquette University Press, 2009).

seen its cataclysmic extinguishing of every light. In fact, there is no boundary, only a no man's land. With no remarkable tomorrow on the horizon to give that sabbath special identity and form as an interruption between old and new, the interment of Jesus is shapeless and anti-climactic. It is simply the day after terminal rupture. This is the end of a man, a mission and a message; the end of the God of whom the message spoke, from whom the mission came, and to whom the man was Son; and the end of the world for all whose future hung with the coming of the Father's kingdom.[40]

The Cross as the End of History

If Jesus is the norm of history, and his life is the particular instantiation of this norm, a recapitulation of humanity in and as this one, particular life, then what do we make of his death? It is the posing of this question, the question of the death of Christ as the "cataclysmic extinguishing of every light" in Lewis's terms, that leads us away from the conceptual continuity evident in the intended cruciformity of von Balthasar's articulation of history, and toward a more sustained look at the cross as a disruption of historical continuity, as a rupture in history.

Bonhoeffer: from the end of history to the resurrection. In his lectures on Genesis, Dietrich Bonhoeffer turns our attention to the beginning of history, the beginning of human thought that leads toward the movement of culture and community. This beginning is not at the Garden of Eden, where God begins the history of humanity with himself, but instead it begins "on the ground that is *cursed.* It is with Cain that history begins, the history of death."[41] Bonhoeffer's exegesis here is not grounded of necessity in the Genesis text, but is determined hermeneutically from the perspective of the cross of Christ. It is because the judgment that occurs at the cross is the judgment against Adam's usurpation of God's place to judge (good from evil)[42] that one can

---

[40]Alan Lewis, "The Burial of God: Rupture and Resumption as the Story of Salvation," *Scottish Journal of Theology* 40, no. 3 (1987): 345-46.

[41]Dietrich Bonhoeffer, *Creation and Fall: A Theological Exposition of Genesis 1-3*, trans. Douglas Stephen Bax, Dietrich Bonhoeffer Works, vol. 3 (Minneapolis: Fortress Press, 2004), 145. Italics in original.

[42]Cf. Dietrich Bonhoeffer, *Ethics*, trans. Reinhard Krauss et al., Dietrich Bonhoeffer Works, vol. 6 (Minneapolis: Fortress Press, 2005), 313-21. Here Bonhoeffer discusses Jesus' command not to judge in Mt 7:1, which he links to the Genesis story of the fall, "because judging is itself the apostasy from God" (315).

look back and see that which ends at the cross is that which had its beginning with the sin of Adam and Eve. This sin is exemplified by the birth of the first one to murder, Cain, whose place, *sicut deus,* is the final and ultimate extension of the original sin, that is, to be the judge over good and evil in place of God. Abel, in the Genesis account (Gen 4:1-16), is the first human to die, the first human to undergo the curse that, in God's judgment, accompanies the sin of Adam and Eve. The violence of murder begins the history of death. For Bonhoeffer, this interpretation is grounded in the cross of Jesus and is made explicit in his line of reasoning: "The end of Cain's history, and so the end of all history [*das Ende der Geschichte überhaupt*], is Christ on the cross, the murdered Son of God. That is the last desperate assault on the gate of paradise. And under the whirling sword, under the cross, the human race dies."[43] It is clear, then, that at this point in Bonhoeffer's understanding, the historical trajectory that determines the human story is brought to a decisive end with the death of the Messiah.

There is an interesting correspondence here to an apocalyptic perspective on history. In some apocalypses, the relationship between the present age and the age to come is characterized by a significant discontinuity. It is important to note that the dualism evident here is not a distinguishing factor of all apocalypses, nor do all apocalypses assume a radical discontinuity between the present age and the age to come.[44] Nevertheless, many at least participate in an interpretation of history that is illustrative of the discontinuity that Bonhoeffer is describing. History, if it is a history of Cain (Bonhoeffer), is a history in which the waters of chaos, even if symbolically stilled before the throne of God, are, in the present age, battling against the people of God. Surely this is what we find in Revelation, but it is also what we find in multiple other apocalypses. The interpretation of Nebuchadnezzar's dream in Daniel 2:31-45 can be understood along these lines as the progression of kingdoms, and thus of history, that is finally not transferred to a new kingdom, but is shattered by

---

[43]Bonhoeffer, *Creation and Fall*, 145-46. German in brackets as in original.
[44]I am taking under advisement the work Wright has done in *NTPG* to catalog at least ten varieties of dualisms, and his arguments in *Paul and His Recent Interpreters* (Minneapolis: Fortress Press, 2015) that the distinction between the ages is also a common rabbinical belief during the Second Temple period, even though the rabbis were decidedly not advocates of apocalyptic. See *NTPG*, 252-54, and *Interpreters*, 2:9.

the kingdom that is cut "not by human hands" (Dan 2:34).[45] With the new kingdom, history ends and a new history from "outside" begins. Wright, in his engagement with the apocalyptic interpretation of Paul by Martyn and de Boer, points out that the end of the present age, evil as it is, is not to be understood exegetically or otherwise as a "clean break" with history.

> Yes, of course, the redemptive action has rescued people from "the present evil age"; yes, indeed, it has launched the "new creation." But however hard this phrase might try, *to plyroma to chronou* cannot mean "a clean break with the past." It cannot mean it either linguistically or theologically. . . . But God's promise . . . always envisaged a particular time, even though that time always remained under God's own sovereign command. Of course, when you reach "the fullness of time" you reach, in a sense, the end of the journey; but it is "end" as goal, not "end" as "thankful termination."[46]

In contrast to Wright's interpretation, William R. Murdock's study of the understanding of history in Jewish apocalypticism suggests that the "clean break with the past" is part of the hope of the future for the elect of God. This world is a difficult place where the wicked prosper and the moral order that ought to prevail is skewed toward evil. Apocalyptic serves to right this wrong, not by forcing moral order on the present, but by the promise of the limitation of the present age.[47] He writes,

> Although in both apocalypticism and the Iranian parallels this present aeon was created by God, it was the sphere of the conflict between the divine and the demonic. For the apocalypticists, it was the sphere of the "corruptible," an "age full of sorrow and impotence," an "age of ills," "defiled with evils." As such, it was "unable to bear the things promised in their season to the righteous," and for this reason hope was eventually placed in the future eternal aeon. As this present aeon grew older, it would fall progressively under the dominion

---

[45]See William R. Murdock, "History and Revelation in Jewish Apocalypticism," *Interpretation*, 21 (1967): 174n28. According to Murdock, the statue is an "aeon image" borrowed from other sources and so should be taken to represent the totality of history from a certain point. See ibid., n. 15.

[46]*Interpreters*, 2:54.

[47]Such a limitation is consistent with Anathea E. Portier-Young's work that shows how Daniel and 1 Enoch are written as texts of resistance to empire. That the empire's time is limited is a source of vision for those suffering under its unjust rule. One is also reminded here of Psalm 73 in which the crux vision of the end of the wicked is given in the temple (an apocalyptic place if ever there was one!): "But when I thought how to understand this, it seemed to me a wearisome task, until I went into the sanctuary of God; then I perceived their end" (vv. 16-17, NRSV).

of Beliar, "who is the ruler of this world." However, this tragic situation would not exist forever, because this aeon as the sphere of conflict between the divine and the demonic is itself limited in duration. In apocalypticism as well as in the Iranian sources, the function of the eschaton was precisely to conquer the demonic by limiting the duration of its sphere of influence, this present evil aeon.[48]

The eschaton, in this interpretation (it is, of course, a developing perspective, not a static, unified apocalyptic vision), is not the hoped-for future kingdom, but it is, rather, the day of judgment when God will act in sovereignty to judge history. "The eschaton marks the shift from this present aeon to the future aeon. Theologically, it marks the shift from historical dualism to eternal monotheism."[49] Murdock's summation of this interpretation of apocalyptic is worth quoting because he describes just the sort of thing Bonhoeffer appears to be describing:

> Just as the eschaton cannot be construed as the last link in the causal nexus of history, so the eschatological revelation cannot be interpreted as the final brilliant burst of light when the last candle is lit at the end of a history-long candle lighting service. That is to say, the eschaton was understood in apocalypticism not as the goal of history, but as the impingement of eternity that destroys history; and the eschatological revelation was understood, not as the sum of all historical revelations, but as the *doxa* of God bursting in upon this aeon of darkness from the aeon of light.[50]

If these accounts of the "end of history" are on point, then what Wright refers to as "thankful termination" at the telos of history is, in this particular apocalyptic tradition, the judgment of God against the wicked, where the transference from one age to the next is a transition not unlike death and resurrection. It is a transference from a dualistic history in which good and evil oppose each other in tragic, deathly interplay, to a monistic eternity in which the one God has put an end to the old dualistic, historical aeon. Martyn's interpretation of Paul's apocalyptic gospel in Galatians 6:14 displays this

---

[48]Murdock, "History and Revelation in Jewish Apocalypticism," 177. Internal quotes refer to the following texts respectively: *2 Bar.* 74:2; *4 Ezr.* 4:27; *2 En.* 66:6; *2 Bar.* 44:8-9; *4 Ezr.* 4:27; *Slavonic Vita Adae et Evae* (33-34). See nn. 39-45 in Murdock's article.

[49]Murdock, "History and Revelation in Jewish Apocalypticism," 179.

[50]Ibid., 187.

same transitionary distinctive.[51] By the crucifixion of Christ, Paul has been crucified to the cosmos, the world that is distinguished by the foundational elements, "Law/the Not Law."[52] This cosmos, too, has been crucified to Paul, and what remains is neither circumcision nor uncircumcision ("Law/the Not Law") but new creation. This new creation is not a furtherance of the dualistic, tragic world where the righteous suffer, but it is the new creation free from the antagonizing moral duality of history. This apocalyptic reading of historical discontinuity as hope, while not a totalizing perspective that attempts to interpret all apocalypses, is consistent with the account of history Bonhoeffer reads into a doctrine of creation that has been articulated around the cross and resurrection of Jesus.

To understand how this conception of the end of history functions for theology, particularly a theology of history, it is important to be reminded of the fact that the human race, and along with it the creation itself, still experiences the finality of death as a horizon that lies in the future. This point is almost too obvious to warrant mention; nevertheless, if it were not mentioned, we might run the risk of ignoring the importance that death still plays in the way we conceptualize history. Whatever victory Christians proclaim, there is no escaping the finality of death; we live in a history where good and evil are seemingly gripped in a perpetual struggle and where the resurrection is only a promise, sometimes nothing more than a sigh and a whisper preserved in the drudgery of the church's liturgical faithfulness. Whether the death of individuals, genocide, war, the death of nonhuman species or the feared death of the life-supporting ecosystems of the planet due to ecological ruin (human-caused or natural in origin), the reality of death remains determinative and limiting for human self-understanding and for any attempt at human historical progress. "The last enemy to be destroyed is death" (1 Cor 15:26).

Baptism. Baptism is a dwelling at the cross, a confrontation of the finality of death. It is part of a movement of grace that exposes one to the knowledge of the depths of the grave of the Son of God, but does so within the context of the promise of a new life. In baptism one finds one's own death—future

---

[51]J. Louis Martyn, *Galatians: A New Translation with Introduction and Commentary*, The Anchor Yale Bible, vol. 33A (New Haven: Yale Universty Press, 1997), 564.
[52]Ibid.

death—in the one death of the Son of God. "To be conformed to the crucified—that means to be a human being judged by God. People carry before them everyday God's death sentence, that they must die before God because of sin."[53] That fact that death is the reality facing all human life as an end and as a judgment on sin is also the basis for the command to die to sin: "Human beings bear all suffering laid upon them, knowing that it serves them to die to their own will, and to let the justice of God prevail over them. Only by acknowledging that God is in the right over them and against them are they right before God."[54] The good news of the gospel is that the judgment that humans have brought on themselves is, at the cross, taken up by the judge himself.[55] That is how baptism comes to play such a central role in the life of the disciple, for it is in baptism that the believer identifies her life with the life of Jesus on the way to the cross, and so is buried with him in the waters of death. The act of identification is the act of faith that Jesus' death is now our death and the believer is free to live apart from the final, limiting logic of death. In the same way, history, with its end still out before it, is found to be taken up in the cross of Christ. The believing historian who would narrate the meaning of world events, of world history, must see that the only possible end for the world, on the world's terms, is the cross of Christ. But to say "on the world's terms" signals another possibility, as does the association with baptism: What other terms are there? What comes on the other side of baptism?

History, Resurrection and New Creation

In his *Ethics*, Bonhoeffer progresses from the disciple's conformation to the crucified one to the disciple's conformation to the risen one:

> To be conformed to the risen one—that means to be a new human being before God. We live in the midst of death; we are righteous in the midst of sin; we are new in the midst of the old. Our mystery remains hidden from the world. We live because Christ lives, and in Christ alone. "Christ is my life." As long as the glory of Christ is hidden, so the glory of the new life also is "hidden with Christ in God" (Col. 3:2).[56]

---

[53]Bonhoeffer, *Ethics*, 94.
[54]Ibid., 95.
[55]He is "The Judge Judged in Our Place," *CD* IV.1, sect. 59.2.
[56]Bonhoeffer, *Ethics*, 95.

As seen already in the previous discussion of *creatio ex nihilo*, Bonhoeffer relates the transition from death to life as analogous to the transition from nothing to being in the divine act of creation. This is why resurrection is not Hegelian synthesis, not *Aufhebung*, but is, indeed, a *novum*. It is, like the creation, a free act of God that is not contingent on anything but his will. Here we can bring to mind the Kierkegaardian infinite qualitative distinction. It is infinite, not according to a continuum of being stretched between two poles, one finite and one infinite, but it is infinite as a way of saying that it is not ontologically comparable; thus it is a qualitative distinction rather than a quantitative one. The distance between cross and resurrection is equally infinite and qualitative because it is grounded in the freedom of God who is wholly other. The resurrection, therefore, is not a historical event in the sense that history is a continuous narrative that finds its common thread in immanent processes of cause and effect—or even in a deity ontologically bound in whatever hierarchy we imagine to be a part of that process. To assert, as Bonhoeffer does, the relationship between *creatio ex nihilo* and the resurrection is to make the freedom of God apocalyptically related to the history of creation,[57] even if God is intimately involved within history. He is never bound to a process of that trajectory, but free with respect to it. He is never to be discovered within history except as he freely reveals himself in it. This is what it means to affirm that history ends at the cross. What begins at the resurrection is not a new history given to humanity to forge according to a new understanding, but—and this is seen clearly in baptism—a new "history" *in Christ*. This new history is not a history in the "old" sense, in the sense that the old dualisms still remain locked in perpetual struggle. Rather, as a new history this history is eternal life, grounded in the lordship over life and death that is the actuality of human life in the resurrected Lord. Yet this new life, this eternal life in Christ, is lived in the midst of the ongoing tension between life and death in which the history of sin and death—the history of Cain—continues to play itself out. Bonhoeffer states this clearly when he says that "we are righteous in the midst of sin; we are new in the midst of the old. Our mystery remains hidden from the world."

---

[57]Here *apocalyptically* refers to the freedom of God with respect to the immanent processes of history. This corresponds to God's lordship over history, a lordship on vivid display in the Apocalypse of John.

But again, we must qualify this theological reflection on God's aseity and freedom with respect to the contingent, historical order. This is because there is an important christological element that must be identified so as not to lose sight of the fact that the issue is not an escape from history, from the temporal world of time and space, but is rather a unique way of being present in time and space. The Christian way of living within history is a living toward the cross/death, but because death has been redefined by the cross, the person who has claimed the Yes of faith lives free from the constraining logic of death that directs the immanent forces of history.[58] Again, Alan Lewis helps with an important corrective:

> On first hearing, the Easter story confirmed beyond all question God's Yes to Jesus, and revealed him as the irruption of transcendent grace into a godless world. But hearing thereafter the extended story of his passion reinforces the unheard-of immanence: God's presence, incarnate and unseen, in that godless world, among its criminals and cripples, its villains and victims, beside whom and as whom Jesus lived and died and was interred. Mark has a Roman officer penetrate the incognito at the point of maximum ungodlikeness (15.39). . . . To ease the awkwardness, a temporary suspension has in effect been postulated for the Incarnation. At the point of Jesus' godforsakenness and death, the Word withdraws or lapses into quietude, that he should perish in his humanness alone. Yet if the resurrection has confirmed that this is God's humanity, and has been all along, is he less so hanging in the garden or growing in the womb?[59]

There is an "unheard-of immanence" with the incarnation that forces our theological constructs to make room for the essential affirmation that the end of history and the new creation, *ex nihilo*, belong to the world. Preceding Bonhoeffer's discussion of being conformed to the crucified, he writes that we are

> to be conformed to the one who has become human—that is what being human really means. The human being should and may be human. All superhumanity [Übermenschentum], all efforts to outgrow one's nature as human, all struggle to be heroic or a demigod, all fall away from a person here, be-

---

[58]By *forces of history* I do not mean ontological forces, but interpretive forces: whatever narrative continuity makes sense of the movement of history and continues to direct that movement toward the future (e.g., the myth of American exceptionalism, the *Pax Romana*).
[59]Lewis, "The Burial of God," 351.

cause they are untrue. . . . The real human being is allowed to be in freedom the creature of the Creator. To be conformed to the one who became human means that we may be the human beings that we really are. . . . God loves the real human being. God became a real human being.[60]

Shortly after this passage Bonhoeffer goes on to turn on its head Athanasius's claim that God became human that humans might become divine (θεοποιηθῶμεν).[61] Rather, "Human beings become human because God became human. But human beings do not become God. They could not and do not accomplish a change in form; God changes form into human form in order that human beings can become, not God, but human before God."[62] The christological affirmation of the hypostatic union does not allow for the abandonment of history in favor of a nonworldly divine existence after the "end of history." Rather it affirms that the end of history is good news for the world, a news that is given to the world for the sake of the world (but not of the world). Those who have been baptized into this ending live the new life after baptism, in a new history.

The End of History in Christological Terms

All human history is properly understood from the center who is Jesus Christ. If Jesus is the one of whom the confession affirms that he is truly God and truly human, then he must reveal to us, as no one else can, what it means to be human. This is affirmed in what T. F. Torrance refers to as the *anhypostatic* movement of God the Son who became a human by taking into his person (hypostasis) humanity, but *not* a preexisting particular human person, a second hypostasis. This singular hypostasis of the Son in human form, Jesus of Nazareth, not only takes up "humanity," but in taking it up becomes the focal point for what it means to be human in truth. Paul's Adam Christology assumes this close identification between normative (redeemed) humanity and Jesus by associating him directly as the last or second Adam as well as the prototype of resurrected humanity (1 Cor 15:45-49). In this way the meaning of humanity is disclosed in this unique event,

---

[60]Bonhoeffer, *Ethics*, 94.
[61]St. Athanasius, *On the Incarnation*, 54.
[62]Bonhoeffer, *Ethics*, 96.

and therefore human history, to the extent that it is a search for human meaning, is also disclosed in this unique event.

At this point it becomes helpful to say that when God enters history, he enters it "an-historically" in the same way that he takes up humanity *anhypostatically*. This proposal would affirm that he takes up the meaning of all human history as he takes up humanity, and in that act he locates it in the one "en-historical" (because *enhypostatic*) person of Jesus, the Messiah of Israel. Furthermore, it is *anhistorical* in the same sense that the *anhypostatic* union is not determined by an existing person but rather determines the humanity to which he comes according to the preexisting person of the Son. The *anhistorical* movement means that the coming of God is not determined by a history in such a way that the history to which he comes would determine his own history, but he comes freely to history as the ground and meaning—the norm—of all human history in himself.

To be clear, the language of *anhistorical* does not function here in analogical correspondence to the language of *anhypostatic*. It is not in reference to *another* movement, but rather signals a *deeper* movement into the logic of what it means for the Son to take humanity to himself, and not a particular, preexisting human person. In our ontological descriptions of humanity, however we conceive of the physical/spiritual/psychic composition of the human person, we must include in that description the aspect of temporality. But to include the consideration of the unity of the human being in temporal endurance means that we enter the realm of the historical, the meaning that can be given to a person as that person endures through time. Human nature can never be abstracted from the historical dimension, but to the extent that Jesus takes up humanity, he necessarily takes up its historical dimension. So, to speak of the *anhypostatic* movement is also, at a more specific level, and in analytic continuity, to speak of an *anhistorical* movement.

It should also be clear that in this formulation the concept of history is not an ontological concept that refers to history as an existence of the sort found in Hegel's philosophy of history. Rather, history is the meaningful interpretation of events and the identification of that meaning in narrative form, or in shorthand narrative referents (e.g., "The Reformation," or "The Roman Empire"). Therefore, if the Son takes humanity to himself and recapitulates it in his own existence as the God-man, then we must say that our

search for meaning in human history necessarily looks to the God-man as
well. In other words, to ask about humanity is to ask about history. Jesus of
Nazareth is the theological ground for anthropology and, therefore, history.

This move does not negate the *enhistorical* movement; when the Son becomes human he does so by becoming a particular human person. So too,
when the Son becomes the human Jesus, he "becomes" a particular history.
This movement to "become" a particular history is a significant part of what
it means to become human. However, there is a slight but significant difference between the way we speak of him being human and the way we
speak of him having a history of his own. Without the historical piece it is
easy to think of his becoming human apart from the addition of a human
hypostasis to his being, but it is difficult to think of his movement into
history in the same way. This is because we imagine history in such a way
that it is an ongoing process into which a human enters simply by being
born. By entering the world as the person of Jesus, the Son enters a history,
namely, the history of Israel. The problem with this sort of thinking is that
Jesus as the Son is not determined by this history, but rather he determines
that history. This is the same dynamic that occurs when his personhood
comes to determine the identity of the person of Jesus of Nazareth. Because
he is the norm of history, history is entirely determined by his own life
history. In the *enhistorical* dynamic the history of Israel is elected again as
the location for the ground of the meaning of history, but it is done so according to the new messianic norm for Israel revealed in Jesus. In other
words, the incarnation is the divine electing, once again, to be in covenant
with people, through Israel, for the world.[63] God, therefore, centers the
meaning of all human history in this one particular history, just as the *enhypostatic* movement of the Son centers all of human identity in the one
person, the Son of Israel, Jesus of Nazareth.

Nevertheless, if we follow Kierkegaard's reasoning, we must affirm that
in this *anhistoric-enhistoric* movement of the Son he remains incognito as
the Son of God. His history is knowable as a human history. He is a crucifiable, first-century Jew. It is inconceivable that in this one man and this one

---

[63]See Rom 11:17-24. I take this text and the whole thrust of Romans 9–11 to be affirming the
priority of Israel through God's gracious election, in continuity with the prior covenant, but now
revealed in Jesus.

history all of humanity and the entire history of the world is gathered up and taken to its judgment. This is for the very reason that it is a *particular* human being's history. Such a thing is inconceivable unless this is God with us. But that it is God with us is the scandal, the offense, and this means that in Jesus of Nazareth and his history is the whole of history incognito.

That Jesus of Nazareth is God with us is the *enhistorical* event that reveals to us the meaning of human history. History, according to the logic of the incarnation, is not an abstract, universal history, just as humanity in Christ's *enhypostatic* movement is not an abstract, universalized humanity. In Jesus, the Jew, we see the truth of humanity inseparable from the particularity of human existence. Jesus is not humanity in abstract, universal form. History, revealed in Jesus, is covenantal history. So Willie Jennings is right when he writes that

> Israel presents a reorientation of truth for Gentiles. Israel's life was not simply an example of human life but the very ground on which God inscribed the nature of our lives. At the threshold of Israel's land, in the presence of Israel's God, the story of every people ruptures, cracks open, revealing a second layer, an underlying layer of reality bound to this God. This second layer of reality was there all the time, yet it remained hidden apart from the revelation in Israel of the Creator who made covenant and whose character was slowly being exposed over the vast landscape of Israel's odyssey.[64]

Jesus, the Messiah of Israel, is the apocalyptic event that reveals to all humanity that this history that is *enhistorically* present in Jesus's singular Jewish life is the opening to that layer of reality that is the meaning of all history. But, and this is the point Jennings makes, that opening is a deeper penetration into the covenant God has made with his people Israel, and not an abstraction away from it. This way of narrating the apocalyptic historicity of Jesus is in deep agreement with Wright's reading of Paul's apocalyptic gospel. Wright is careful not to allow the apocalyptic dimension of Pauline theology to divorce itself from the covenant history of Israel. Responding to reviews of *PFG*, he writes that "in Paul's case, the fact that he now believed Israel's God *had* now done a radically new thing—was not set over against either the covenant or

---

[64]Willie James Jennings, *The Christian Imagination: Theology and the Origins of Race* (New Haven: Yale University Press, 2010), 258.

the long, dark, and confused narrative of promise and failure, of rebellion and restoration and rebellion again, of which the texts speak."[65]

The cross stands at the end of Jesus' history and so it also stands as the end of human history. The cross is the telos toward which all things move. All human events that might find meaning or be given meaning through human practices of storytelling or narration—the work of the historian or the work of the preacher—move toward the cross. The theological move here should be evident: the same identification that is at work in baptism, where the individual identifies her life with the life of Christ and so dies with Christ, is also at work in the believer for whom perception has been shaped by the gift of the Spirit, that is, given the condition to see. This new perception must see history according to the humanity taken up by the Son, particularized in the Messiah of Israel and ended at the cross. The identification of the individual in baptism is simply extrapolated to the identification of the collective history of all people. There is no telos, no teleology that can escape the gravitational pull of the cross of Christ.

What then of the question of continuity? Is there any sense left to speaking of historical continuity between the time before the crucifixion and the time after? For world history, continuity is not an issue since time and its sequential events, grounded in human intentions, continue along the same trajectory, toward the same end, the end revealed in crucifixion. History remains condemned by its own judgment when it judged the one who is the norm of history, which was epitomized in the cry of the crowd, "Crucify him!" and in the indifference or political expediency of the court of Pilate. But what of history redeemed, history considered in the light of the victory of the Messiah over death, on the other side of the cross? Is there a continuity that can be affirmed there? Yes. But the continuity is preserved according to the *enhistoric* and *enhypostatic* union; history is preserved in continuity only in the divine hypostasis who is the Son of God. Historical continuity is only preserved this way in the person of the Son because he remains as he has

[65]N. T. Wright, "Right Standing, Right Understanding, and Wright Misunderstanding: A Response," *Journal for the Study of Paul and His Letters* 4, no. 1 (2014): 87-103, at 91. It is interesting to note that in later writings Wright is referring to Israel's history as a dark history. I take this to be a way of warding off criticism that is based in a misreading of his account of history, one that has interpreted him to be arguing for a progressive account of history culminating in the arrival of the Messiah.

become, human. But, as Bonhoeffer rightly claimed, the continuity of human history in the risen Son of God is grounded not in humanity qua humanity, but in the freedom of God who created the world *ex nihilo*.[66] This same freedom is the freedom of God to bring life out of death—to bring into existence things that were not, to bring life into the void where death has worked its victory. History is, in this view, out of the hands of the various world-historical forces—economies, nations, corporations, regimes, ecclesial bodies and so on—and is in the hands of the Lamb who was slain.

> Then I saw in the right hand of the one seated on the throne a scroll written on the inside and on the back, sealed with seven seals; and I saw a mighty angel proclaiming with a loud voice, "Who is worthy to open the scroll and break its seals?" And no one in heaven or on earth or under the earth was able to open the scroll or to look into it. . . . Then I saw between the throne and the four living creatures and among the elders a Lamb standing as if it had been slaughtered. . . . He went and took the scroll from the right hand of the one who was seated on the throne. When he had taken the scroll, the four living creatures and the twenty-four elders fell before the Lamb, each holding a harp and golden bowls full of incense, which are the prayers of the saints. They sing a new song: "You are worthy to take the scroll and to open its seals, for you were slaughtered and by your blood you ransomed for God saints from every tribe and language and people and nation; you have made them to be a kingdom and priests serving our God, and they will reign on earth." (Rev 5:1-3, 6-10)

If the scroll in this text from the book of Revelation is taken to be the outcome or the future of human history, it supports the case being made here that Jesus is the one to whom we look for the meaning of history since he is the only one able to open the scroll.[67] Furthermore, the end of history appears to be death and destruction as each of the seven seals is opened. Yet in the midst of the opening of the seals the reader of the apocalypse sees in the fifth seal "the souls of those who had been slaughtered for the word of God" (Rev 6:9). They cry out to God for vengeance on the inhabitants of the earth. In the final seal, whose opening begins in Revelation 8, there is silence

---

[66]See chap. 4 above. Bonhoeffer, *Creation and Fall*, 35.

[67]See, for example the discussion in G. K. Beale, *The Book of Revelation: A Commentary on the Greek Text*, The New International Greek Testament Commentary (Grand Rapids: Eerdmans, 1999), 337-42.

in heaven for half an hour. Then we see a great quantity of incense offered, the smoke of which rose "with the prayers of all the saints" (Rev 8:3). Once this is done the censer is filled with fire from the altar and thrown to the earth in a great show of thunder, lightning and an earthquake.

The point of this excursus into the vision of John is to show that the history of the world, depicted in the definitive Christian apocalyptic text, is thoroughly consistent with the dogmatic account that I am providing. It is grounded in the person of Jesus, and its end is consistent with the end revealed in the crucifixion. For the saints who wait and pray, their hope for history, their sense of continuity, is revealed by their prayers, their hope in the one who holds history in his hands because he entered history, and entered into the judgment of history.

The implication of this for the relationship between theology and the other "scientific" disciplines is stated with clarity by Hans Urs von Balthasar:

> There are three things we cannot do: we cannot carry on with natural metaphysics, natural ethics, natural jurisprudence, natural study of history, acting as though Christ were not, in the concrete, the norm of everything. Nor can we lay down an unrelated "double truth," with the secular scholar and scientist on the one hand and the theologian on the other studying the same object without any encounter or intersection between their two methods. Nor, finally, can we allow the secular disciplines to be absorbed by theology as though it alone were competent in all cases because Christ alone is the norm. Precisely because Christ is the absolute he remains incommensurate with the norms of this world; and no final accord between theology and the other disciplines is possible within the limits of this world.[68]

If Christ is the norm of everything, his cross stands central as that which spells out the limits of both the human qua human, and of the totality of human history.

Historiography According to Theology: Three Theses

The question now arises, What has all this to do with the historian? To be clear, the issue before us is not the issue of secular historiography. Whatever the metaphysical commitments of the secular historian, the arguments pre-

---

[68]Von Balthasar, *Theology of History*, 18-19.

sented thus far have only to do with the historian who understands herself to be working from *within* the Christian tradition. In order to focus the discussion, I have taken the work of N. T. Wright as an example of the sort of historian/believer that I have in mind. That Wright has undertaken to think through and articulate carefully and repeatedly his historical and theological method makes his work especially suited to be examined with the purpose of furthering a theological understanding of historiography. Indeed, Wright himself has on several occasions hinted that the conversation on method is either lacking or needs more reflection.

> It is history as well as faith which enables us to say "he loved me and gave himself for me." It will not do to shun history, to declare it off limits, just because there is such a thing as skeptical historiography—any more than we should shun the use of money because there is a god called Mammon. . . . There is a proper history and there is an improper history, and though they may sometimes look alike they need to be distinguished, and the former not rejected because of the existence of the latter. There is a large task still waiting here, namely, the fresh articulation of a historical method which will not be dictated to from within the shrunken world of post-Enlightenment epistemology but rather be open to genuine knowledge of the past. . . . When faith says, "he loved me and gave himself for me," it can properly look to history to back it up. Otherwise we lay ourselves open once more to the obvious charge of fantasy.[69]

Wright has given us an account of historiography that can engage serious history in a variety of forums, from the seminar rooms of academia to the fellowship halls of almost every Christian denomination. What Wright calls "skeptical historiography" is that historiography that rules a priori that the world of historical events is a world closed to the agency of God so that the biblical narratives must be examined methodologically to explain, based on immanent relations of cause and effect, events that would otherwise be understood by the biblical writers to be "miraculous" or "supernatural." Wright takes the biblical writers on their own terms, attempting to enter their thinking as the sort of thing Collingwood articulated, "to 'rethink' or inwardly re-enact the deliberations of past agents, thereby rendering their behavior intelligible."[70] Collingwood puts it like this: "But how does the

---

[69]*JPPG*, 155-56.
[70]Cf. Wright, "In Grateful Dialogue," 250.

historian discern the thoughts which he is trying to discover? There is only one way in which it can be done: by rethinking them in his own mind. . . . The history of thought, and therefore all history, is the re-enactment of past thought in the historian's own mind."[71] The importance of this way of doing history, of thinking the thoughts of the past, is that it comes as close as possible to giving us a genuine encounter with the past:[72] we come into a certain type of contact with it and thus can benefit from it.

> If these systems [of thought] remain valuable to posterity, that is not in spite of their strictly historical character but because of it. To us, the ideas expressed in them are ideas belonging to the past; but it is not a dead past; by understanding it historically we incorporate it into our present thought, and enable ourselves by developing and criticizing it to use that heritage for our own advancement.[73]

Wright is unashamedly attempting to rethink the thoughts and intentions of the people and world of the Bible. The question with respect to Wright is simply this: Is his method adequate to the question of God? For Christian historiography in general the question of God as an object of inquiry remains the significant question.

The conclusion of this chapter will be developed according to three basic theses:

1. The limitation of theology to worldviews is a form of methodological naturalism, even if it allows for theological questions.

2. For a Christian theological epistemology, Christian theology determines epistemology, and not the other way around.

3. Theological historiography will be shaped by a theology of history for which the cross is the hermeneutical center.

To the above theses more could be added by way of a positive development of a Christian historiography, but at this point this work is intended only as a theological corrective to Wright's historical and theological method and not as a development of an entirely new historiographical method. The

---

[71]Collingwood, *Idea of History*, 215.

[72]This is similar to Rudolf Bultmann, *Jesus and the Word*, trans. Louise Pettibone Smith and Erminie Huntress Lantero (London: Charles Scribner's Son's, 1958), 13.

[73]Collingwood, *Idea of History*, 230.

following chapter will develop the implication of these theses toward a rapprochement between literary apocalyptic studies and apocalyptic theology.

The Limitation of Theology to Worldviews Is a Form of Methodological Naturalism: Critical Realism Reconsidered

In an essay written in response to Wright's second volume, *Jesus and the Victory of God*, C. Stephen Evans questions whether or not Wright's method is a form of "methodological naturalism."[74] Evans introduces methodological naturalism as the approach to history, advocated by Troeltsch, that can be articulated according to three principles: the principle of criticism, the principle of analogy and the principle of correlation.[75] In very brief form, the principle of criticism commits the historian to a reliance on evidence, and that evidence is always regarded with suspicion and therefore conclusions are always open to revision. The second principle is a commitment to the "uniformity of natural causes"[76] such that the only causes that are allowed to be considered are the sorts of causes known to be operative in the natural world. Third, the principle of correlation is similar to the second in that it is a causal principle, but this one places the event in question within a "causal nexus," that is, a closed continuum of cause and effect in which are not allowed any causes that transcend the closed system.[77] "The sole task of history in its specifically theoretical aspect is to explain every movement, process, state, and nexus of things by reference to its web of its causal relations."[78] Evans makes the further distinction between two types of methodological naturalism, one being characterized by a commitment to it as obligatory for doing history, and the other that sees it simply as a tool of the historian, one of several possible methodological approaches. Evans makes the claim that Wright is this second type of methodological naturalist.[79] For

[74]C. Stephen Evans, "Methodological Naturalism in Historical Biblical Scholarship," in *JRI*, 180-205. See Wright's brief response in the same volume, 248-52.
[75]Ibid., 183. Evans is here following the three principles attributed to Troeltsch laid out in Van Austin Harvey, *The Historian and the Believer: The Morality of Historical Knowledge and Christian Belief* (London: SCM Press, 1967), 14-15. The page numbers in Evans's citation are incorrect.
[76]Evans, "Methodological Naturalism in Historical Biblical Scholarship," 183.
[77]Ibid.
[78]Ernst Troeltsch, "Historiography," in *Encyclopedia of Religion and Ethics*, ed. James Hastings (New York: Charles Scribner's Sons, 1914), 718.
[79]Evans, "Methodological Naturalism in Historical Biblical Scholarship," 188.

Evans, this is not a problem as long as it is not seen as the only possibility for the good historian. The problem with what Wright does, in this view, is that he does not acknowledge the limits of his naturalistic approach.

Evans finds evidence of this in Wright's rejection of a "'supernaturalist' worldview" in *JVG*.[80] The difference for Wright is that when an appeal is made to a supernaturalist worldview, a sort of methodological trump card is played, making the work of the historian irrelevant because it is unregulated by any but the most permissive or abstract standard. The effect of this for Jesus studies is that attention is directed away from the actual message of Jesus (e.g., Jesus's proclamation of the kingdom) and onto the apologetic question of whether or not we ought to believe the Bible. Evans's critique of Wright is to show that the supernaturalist worldview (and here the conversation is regarding miracles) is in fact the Christian worldview with respect to the question of the nature of the agency of God. But this is not to be oversimplified as a Deist worldview, since the Christian framework affirms at the same time both the transcendence of God and his immanence. Evans clarifies that "Wright . . . does not wish to be committed to a *metaphysical* naturalism. However, one can reject a dogmatic form of metaphysical naturalism and still be committed in practice to a methodological naturalism as the proper stance for historians to take."[81]

Wright's brief response to Evans's critique, found in the same volume, focuses on the accusation that his method appears to be committed to a "causal nexus" limited to natural events.[82] In response, Wright appeals to the fact that his work has attempted to follow, with Ben F. Meyer, Collingwood's method, described above, that is, to enter into the thoughts and intentions of past agents. This approach opens the door to the "supernatural" since the worldviews of past agents are open to the "supernatural." Wright affirms a metaphysical commitment to the active agency of God, but wants to see such agency occurring within and according to the observable within

---

[80]Ibid., 189. Cf. *JVG*, 187.

[81]Evans, "Methodological Naturalism in Historical Biblical Scholarship," 190. Wright's response, "In Grateful Dialogue," in *JRI*, 264, agrees with Evans, yet he wants to distance himself from the language of *supernatural* for the reason that this language in contemporary usage is too closely associated with a Deistic worldview. New ways of speaking of the relation between God and the world need to be developed to avoid confusion. I will continue to use the language of *supernatural* but will include the word in scare quotes to signal this nuance.

[82]For Wright's response see *JRI*, 250-52, 263-64.

history, "that it is in the 'ordinary' events of Jesus' life, just as much as the 'extraordinary' events, that we should recognise the presence of the true God."[83] The question is whether or not Wright allows knowledge of the "extraordinary" to enter the historian's consideration outside of the consideration of the various worldviews of past agents. The difference that Wright sees between methodological naturalism and his own method is that he allows the "supernatural" as part of the worldview of the people who claim such an event to have happened. Was it likely that Jesus could have predicted his second coming? Is that something that could have been part of his worldview? Could Paul have believed such and such? If methodological naturalism limits the possibilities of history to the worldview of the Enlightenment, Wright's version limits the possibilities of history to that which was allowed by the worldviews of the people experiencing the events in question. This is a leap forward in gaining the meaning of a text since it genuinely asks and thinks in the framework of the subject matter. Yet, allowing the "supernatural" or "extraordinary" to be considered within the worldview of objects of study, nevertheless still subjects the historian's method to a sociology of knowledge, and therefore maintains a naturalistic framework. It might be a departure from the Enlightenment framework, but it also might be seen only as an expansion of that framework—a development but *not* a departure.

If Wright's method remains within a naturalistic frame, then here is the heart of the question. Did something *new* happen in the arrival of Jesus the Messiah that, although present enough in time and space to be interpreted in terms of first-century Judaism, nevertheless required an acceptance of something, or the gift of perception, that challenged that worldview from outside *any* conceivable worldview? And if so, how does such an event enter into the work of the historian? In the terms that Kierkegaard's Climacus gave us, can the truth be *learned*?

The entire thrust of the argument in this book has been to press the question of the reality of God—both in divine immanence and transcendence. If Wright's critical realism is committed to external reality, and if that reality is encountered in contact, then the Christian faith is committed to an encounter with the reality of God as its epistemological ground. This

---

[83]Wright in ibid., 264.

does not mean, however, that God is part of the world, the reality that we describe when we speak ontologically, except as he has made himself known through his words and acts and, in a special and qualitatively unique way, in the person of Jesus of Nazareth. Wright certainly recognizes this point: "There is of course no commonly agreed upon conceptuality, still less is there language to express it, to talk about the ways in which the God we know in Jesus Christ and by the Spirit does act in relation to the world to which he is in so many senses always present and from which he nevertheless remains mysteriously distinct."[84] Yet this is the crucial question! How does God relate to this world? How can we know when and where he does? It is how this question is answered with respect to Wright's work that makes the difference for understanding my particular critique of his historical method—and for understanding a theological approach to historiography in general.

The way that I have gone about answering these questions can be focused in the following two points. First, God's act is primary in his self-revelation. There is no way to move from contact with reality (i.e., reality that might be said to be ontologically immanent to the cosmos) and through that epistemological contact to transcend to the knowledge of God on our own. The distance between us and God is, from our standpoint, qualitatively infinite. Again, this is not according to a continuum of being that moves along the same ontological scale from finite to infinite, but the difference is qualitatively absolute; God is wholly other. The account that I have given of theological epistemology rules out any transcendental method that would move along a path of being to the reality of God. Nevertheless, God acts and God reveals himself. Any critical realism that would investigate God, or the things of God, must take into account this as theologically basic. That must at least mean, for Wright's work, that the *question* of God that frames his entire project is open to the *self-revelatory act of God*. Put more directly, Wright's historiography needs to show that it is methodologically committed to the reality of the priority of God's act to reveal himself. Wright himself moves to articulate just this epistemological commitment when he writes of theology, as envisioned by Paul, to

---

[84]Ibid.

be a discipline of the church "rooted in the very being and self-revelation-in-action of the one God."[85]

If this is so, then to bracket out the question of Jesus' divinity at the outset of *JVG* is problematic. On the one hand, it can be a genuinely legitimate move if we are asking the question of the purely immanent perspective of the people around Jesus who would have him crucified. Wright's commitment to work within the limits of worldviews, and to make the epistemological grounding of theology limited to a sociological account of knowing within worldviews, allows for a thorough and holistic approach to the way humans know things. What were those who crucified Jesus thinking, how did they interpret his life and ministry, and what would they lose and gain were they to let him live or have him killed? In what sense was he, in their eyes, a crucifiable first-century Jew?[86] Yet the question about how Jesus saw himself is, from the perspective of Christian theology, a complex theological question that cannot be definitively answered according to a method grounded in naturalism. That is, if we limit the investigation of Jesus to purely naturalistic criteria (by holding aside the question of his divinity), our result may not be docetic,[87] but it is doubtful if it will be useful for an understanding of who Jesus is. In fact, docetism is an incoherent charge in this case since the theological assumption is bracketed out. No one is worried about docetism when the object in question is simply a human being. At the extreme end it might be said to be *methodologically* Arian.[88] Another way of saying this is to say that a naturalistic portrayal of Jesus helps us understand the context of his life, the world into which he came and the questions that people were addressing to him, and so forth. These are of course key aspects

---

[85]N. T. Wright, "Right Standing, Right Understanding, Wright Misunderstanding," 93. To the extent that this is a description of Paul's worldview, it still could be possible to interpret Wright's account of Paul's epistemology within the naturalistic framework described by Evans. My project is aimed at furthering just this account to bear upon the methodological assumptions that guide Wright's own work.

[86]Admittedly there are theological questions here, too, but for the moment it seems such questions are valid on one level for one purpose—namely, understanding the purely human reactions to Jesus' ministry. In Kierkegaard's perspective this might be said to be an examination of the nature of the offense. But of course, to say that implies the theological side of the picture, which I am arguing is completely legitimate.

[87]See *JVG*, 653.

[88]Whether or not this is equally as damaging as being fully Arian remains to be seen, but I am only here putting the emphasis on the qualifier *methodologically*. I am not saying that Wright is a heretic! Nevertheless it is the appropriate corollary to his somewhat frequent appeals to "docetism."

of doing exegesis. But the distinction can be seen if we recall the comment by Barth in his *Table Talk*: "I do not like books trying to prove the rightness of the Bible by archaeological research, but the results of this research are an important help in understanding the biblical witness to Christ. However, no historical research can help us *prove* God's revelation as reality. Historical research will never be an *approach* to the Word of God."[89] I think Wright would agree, but I also want to argue that Wright's method still does not provide us with an "approach" to the Word of God. Evans's simple argument that Christians have for two thousand years claimed to know God in and through history apart from the work of critical historiography suggests that, for faith, there is an approach that is legitimate and useful for the church and that can be claimed as knowledge—even historical knowledge.

Perhaps it would be helpful to picture the act of God in self-revelation through the Spirit as a direct line moving forward, perhaps as a sort of river of God's revelatory act. As the believer is caught up in that movement through the gift of faith, there are moments where it is useful and helpful, even necessary, to look sideways and understand a cross section of that movement, to compare it with the world around, and to take stock of where one is relative to the landscape. Such a move helps to understand the flow of the river and is essential in providing necessary perspective—both for those inside and those outside of the moving river. Nevertheless, such glances are not an approach to the movement of the river, but only a helpful understanding of where one is in the flow. One might even attempt to see the river from the perspective of someone on its bank by methodologically blocking one's own view from consideration. But such an exercise will only be an exercise from the perspective of those in the river, one of not seeing clearly, that is, if the view from the river is the definitive view on all the world. The metaphor, of course, breaks down pressed too far, but it might help to express the distinction Barth is making with respect to historical research, that it is not an *"approach* to the Word of God." The approach always happens *within* the movement and event of the Word of God.

The second point that needs to be made is that if one is trying to be critically realist and brackets out one aspect of that reality for methodological reasons,

---

[89]Godsey, *Karl Barth's Table Talk*, 69.

those reasons need to be explicit and they need to be justified by the reality that is being set aside. Otherwise, the method is not realistic. The critical realist necessarily is bound to the phenomena that presents itself in reality. For the believer this is the act of God in Jesus Christ, known through the work of the Spirit. I have already suggested some reasons for approaching history from a perspective outside of faith, but these reasons are all determined by faith and find their ultimate grounding in faith. This leads us to the next of our theses—namely, that Christian theology determines epistemology.

For a Christian Theological Epistemology, Christian Theology Is Determinative

I have attempted to show that Christian theology stakes out a distinct epistemological position determined by its unique object of knowledge: God revealed to us in Jesus Christ and God active in that knowledge. Through appeal to the "theological science" of T. F. Torrance, the reality of this revelatory event and its continuing reality through God's own self-presentation has been demonstrated in such a way so as to show how it is determinative for theological knowledge. If this account is correct, then the particular dogmatic content of theology determines a systematic account of epistemology. In such an account, our attention should be directed to the continuing agency in freedom of the living and acting God for the Christian way of knowing. This is a corrective to the epistemology of Wright for whom Christian theology, to which he turns in *NTPG* after providing a more general account of theology and worldviews, operates according to his "analysis . . . of worldviews and how they work. . . . Christian theology only does what all other worldviews and their ancillary belief-systems do: it claims to be talking about reality as a whole."[90] This is a corrective to Wright's epistemology, not a wholesale rejection of it. His account of worldviews, to the extent that it reflects accurately the way in which humans know things, is exactly right as far as it goes. The corrective becomes necessary when he wants to speak of God. The reality of God simply will not fit into our conceptions, whatever they are, of "reality as a whole."

The core of this critique then is grounded in the actuality of the relationship between our words about God and God's self-revelation, his acting

---

[90]*NTPG*, 131-32; cf. 471.

in and through those words. At the heart of the church's proclamation, a proclamation out of which the Christian Scriptures emerged, is the actual relation between the event of God's self-revelation in and as[91] the person of Jesus and the church's witness to this event. Or, we might say the ground of Christian knowledge is the personal relationship between Jesus and the disciple who bears witness to him, a relationship grounded in the work of the Spirit. Of crucial importance here is the fact that this relationship is not an abstraction away from the actual relation, but is rather the relation itself, and theological reflection on it is a *deeper* penetration into its concrete particularity. The actual knowing relation can be modeled on Peter's confession of Jesus (Mt 16:13-17) or in the personal call of Jesus for Peter to follow him (Mk 1:17; Jn 21:22). This latter example is given in Bonhoeffer's *Discipleship* and locates the disciple's obedience in the *personal* call to follow given by Jesus.[92] These two examples directly apply to the present subject since the grounding of the disciple's knowledge about who Jesus is and the obedient call to follow him are not rooted in Peter's worldview (although the events could certainly be *interpreted* that way) but rather in the personal reality of the questioner and the call. This is because the relation introduces something new, brought to it from the outside, as it were, by the one who is God with us. A sociology of knowledge could explain these texts, but it could only do so if it refused to believe them, subjecting them to the precondition of an existent or possible worldview. By *possible* I mean all those worldviews that are so just because they are grounded in available perceptions of reality. The incarnation is not one of these possibilities. In a way analogous to Bonhoeffer's analysis of the difference between grace and works, that which unites the past event of God's revelation and the knowledge of that event—whether for the contemporary of Jesus or the present-day believer[93]—is the personal relationship between the knower and the known. Where is this continuing personal presence of Jesus in Wright's historiography?

Torrance locates the place of theological knowledge in the doxological event of the church's communion in which it interprets the Scriptures "in

---

[91]Wright correctly notes this important *as* in ibid., 474.

[92]Dietrich Bonhoeffer, *Discipleship*, Dietrich Bonhoeffer Works, vol. 4 (Minneapolis: Fortress Press, 2001), 46.

[93]Cf. Kierkegaard, *Philosophical Fragments*.

accordance with their inner and real meaning." The inner and real meaning of the Scriptures is determined by the actual relation between God and the church in Jesus Christ through the work of the Spirit. This actual relation has its center in the theological affirmation of the *homoousion*. The story that makes sense of this follows the church's refusal of the Valentinian and Arian insistence that there is a category of being between humanity and God that serves as a bridge or mediating presence. The refusal that grounded orthodoxy in the *homoousion* was not a speculative abstraction, but a faithful insistence that the church's encounter with Jesus was an encounter with God himself. In this way, Nicene orthodoxy centered theological knowledge at this precise point, where the "mysteriously distinct"[94] God, the God who is qualitatively other, has definitively transgressed the onto-logical "distance" and bound himself to his creation in a new and surprising way. It is the church's insistence on its encounter with Jesus as the normative point of reference that allows it to navigate and faithfully refuse the "possi-bilities" that resolve this central paradox of the God-man.[95] This insistence is not an abstraction but a pressing into the very heart of the church's con-fession. This means that the incarnation—in all its theological significance— is the hard core of Christian theological epistemology.

> The epistemological significance of the [*homoousion*] lies in the rejection of the Valentinian and Arian dichotomy that made the Logos in the last resort a creature of God and so recast theological statements into statements with only this-worldly reference, and lies in the insistence that in Jesus Christ we have a Logos that is not of man's devising but One who goes back into the eternal Being of God for he proceeded from the eternal Being of God.[96]

The central epistemological event, the incarnation of the Logos, the Son of God, is the revelation, the apocalypse, of Jesus the Messiah. That he is the Messiah, a word that Wright has taught us is loaded with religious, cultural and theological significance, hermeneutically grounded in a specific time

---

[94]Wright, "In Grateful Dialogue," 264.

[95]"Knowledge of new realities or events calls for correspondingly new ways of thinking and speaking, in which new concepts and terms need to be coined, or in which ordinary forms of thought and speech have to be stretched adapted and refined to make them appropriate to the realities to which they are intended to refer." T. F. Torrance, *The Christian Doctrine of God: One Being Three Persons* (London: T&T Clark, 1996), 20.

[96]T. F. Torrance, *Theology in Reconstruction* (London: SCM Press, 1965), 36.

and place, is not rejected or diminished in this insistence, but is affirmed precisely because it is God himself who takes on this identity. But that this is God with us is precisely *not* to limit the identity of Jesus to the available pre-understandings and possibilities that this concept carried. Wright is exactly right to insist that what was being reworked and reimagined in the proclamation of Jesus the Messiah is the very conception of God himself. But this conception of God that is being reworked is, in the incarnation, given over to God himself in the knowledge that the Son has of the Father, and into which, through the Spirit, we are given to participate.

> As we learn in the gospels, this is what had already happened to the disciples and apostles of Christ as he became disclosed to them in his revealing and saving activity and they were enabled through the gift of his Spirit, by whom God bears witness to himself, to be opened to his intrinsic truth and believe in him. The mighty acts of God in the astonishingly new and utterly unique events of the birth, life, death and resurrection of Christ staked out the ground on which alone they were to be approached, apprehended and understood. No one ever spoke and acted as Jesus did with his divine self-authenticating authority. What he said and did brought about a radically new conception of God and a complete inversion and transformation of man's outlook in terms of the new divine order, the Kingdom of God that had suddenly irrupted into history with the coming and presence of Jesus Christ, and established itself finally in human existence and destiny through his cross and resurrection.[97]

It is telling that when Wright does appeal to theological reasons to ground his epistemology, he turns to the created order. This move is not a strong move within the development of his epistemology, so care should be taken not to make more of this than is warranted. However, it is still theologically significant. In concluding the second chapter of *NTPG*, in which he introduces his variation of critical realism, Wright pauses to "assum[e] for the moment a Christian worldview."[98] In this brief paragraph Wright argues that "the interrelation of humans and the created world" and the belief that humans are created in the image of the Creator obligates them to be stewards of that order through their activity of knowing. This move is important and makes a genuine stride toward overcoming the radical bifurcation of the

---

[97]Torrance, *Christian Doctrine of God*, 20.
[98]*NTPG*, 45.

subject and object in modern epistemology. Furthermore, it makes sense to the extent that Wright is speaking about historical knowledge and not theological knowledge. The worry comes when the move is made from the created order and its implied epistemology to theological knowledge. Theological knowledge is not grounded in the nature of knowledge in the created world, but rather in the reconciling act of God toward that order.

At this point it will be helpful to return to a consideration of some brief comments Wright made with respect to the place of the resurrection as the basis for a Christian epistemology. In the previous chapter I briefly showed how Wright, even while appealing to the epistemic significance of the resurrection, nevertheless uses it to turn back to an argument for naturalistic epistemologies based on the creation order, referencing the work of Oliver O'Donovan. Yet in this particular essay Wright still leaves room for the resurrection to be the unique, central, epistemological event for the Christian faith; in fact, he seems to prefer it:

> I thus cautiously agree with those theologians who have insisted that the resurrection, if true, must become not only the corner-stone of what we now know but also the key to how we know things, the foundation of all our knowing, the starting point for a Christian epistemology. . . . Precisely because it is the resurrection of the crucified Jesus that might now form the staring-point for our thinking and knowing, it will affirm the proper place and power of other epistemologies, as the resurrection affirms the goodness of . . . God's present creation.[99]

The second half of this quotation turns back to affirm naturalistic epistemologies, even though the resurrection still has the place of priority. It would be interesting if Wright then went on to address the way the resurrection might change the methodological considerations of historical knowledge, but unfortunately he does not. What we are given is the following scenario:

> History raises the question, "Granted that only an empty tomb and appearances of Jesus will explain the rise of Christian faith, what will in turn explain these two satisfactorily?" When Christian faith, arising from the whole gospel story, says, "the bodily resurrection of Jesus from the dead," history may reply, "Well, I couldn't have come up with that myself; but now that you say it, it

---

[99]N. T. Wright, "Resurrection: From Theology to Music and Back Again," in *Sounding the Depths: Theology Through the Arts*, ed. J. Begbie (London: SCM Press, 2002), 208.

makes a lot of sense." And perhaps at that point history itself—the mode of our knowing—undergoes some kind of redemptive transformation.[100]

It would be helpful at this point were Wright to go on and explain how the mode of our knowing—history itself—undergoes a redemptive transformation. However, this transformation turns out to be, by the end of the essay, little more than an affirmation of Thomas's classic formulation of grace perfecting nature: "As grace does not destroy but perfects nature, it is right that natural reason should serve faith just as the natural loving tendency of the will serves charity."[101] In Wright's discussion, the affirmation of the resurrection is likened to the observation of two ancient columns, available for all to see, and the missing arch that they suggest is that which faith brings—in this case, the resurrection. Now Wright's entire project comes into view. Wright is doing the work of reason, limited as it is, but nevertheless a reason that gets us just to the point where the picture is almost complete, but not quite. At this point, what is left is for faith to fill in the picture, close the gaps and do so in such a way that we see the result and are validated all the way along as the hard, steady work of the historian is affirmed by the final capstone of faith.

There are many problems with the grace perfecting nature paradigm, as well as many defenders, not the least of which is the great Thomistic tradition in Roman Catholicism. To enter the fray at this point would be a dangerous venture and might risk overextension. Rather, what I want to do is show how the christological affirmation of the *anhypostatic/enhypostatic* movement will challenge Wright's use of this argument.

I take it that Wright has methodologically limited his rational exploration of the resurrection to those arguments that reason alone, unaided by faith, can deliver. This includes his consideration of worldviews, even as they include theological beliefs. As argued above, his historical method, even if it takes theological beliefs into account, nevertheless does not avail itself of theological arguments, but limits itself to those arguments that reason can deliver (and these may be reasons *about* theological beliefs).[102]

---

[100]Ibid.

[101]Ibid., 210. See St. Thomas Aquinas, *Summa Theologica*, I, Q. I. art. 8, ad.2.

[102]John M. G. Barclay, in a review of *PFG*, points out that Wright "fails to tell us where *he* is reading from, and for what goal." In the note that accompanies this claim, Barclay says, "There is a hint of [Wright's goal] in the claim that 'the principal and ultimate goal of all historical work on the New Testament ought to be a more sensitive and intelligent practice of Christian mission and

One way of addressing this is to press the question of what would change if the resurrection were admitted—would the epistemological situation change?[103] It appears that, for Wright, it would not, even though he seems to admit that it would. All it seems to do is turn us back and affirm the deliverances of reason that led us up to the point where faith was needed to bridge the gap, as it were. What really changes, with our way of knowing, with the resurrection? At first it would seem that if we were to reject the "grace perfects nature" paradigm, we are left with the rejection of human reason, or the reasoning ability of humanity to know true things about the world. At a very basic level this would seem to be absurd: humans use their reasoning ability successfully in every area of life. If the resurrection is the starting point for Christian epistemology, it must not be a rejection of human reason, but must allow human reason a place within the purview of an epistemological situation determined by the historical event of the resurrection of Jesus from the dead. I propose that the model of the *anhypostatic/enhypostatic* movement of the incarnation is a helpful way to orient this discussion christologically and is fully consistent with the sort of epistemology I have been articulating throughout this book. Let me explain.

If the gift of faith convinces us of the resurrection, then we have, at once, the reality of a situation where the full import of the incarnation is granted for epistemology. Here, again, T. F. Torrance is helpful:

> We must approach Jesus Christ simultaneously on both the empirical and theoretical levels in the space-time field in which he and we encounter each other. From the very start of our theological interpretation, therefore, we must learn to think conjunctively of him as God and man in the one indivisible fact of Jesus Christ. It is only as we treat the historical events in Jesus' life as empirical correlates of divine acts in an inter-level synthesis, that we can do

---

discipleship' (1484). That is, of course, one possible purpose for historical scholarship. But then one should clarify how commitment to such a goal has influenced this project from the start and all along the way." John M. G. Barclay, review of *Paul and the Faithfulness of God*, by N. T. Wright, *Scottish Journal of Theology* 68, no. 2 (May 2015): 243n18. Wright's methodology would, for theological reasons grounded in a creation order, simply turn back on the discipline of history. This theological reason given toward the end of *PFG* that Barclay quotes is grounded in the resurrection, which, in Wright's interpretation, turns us back to naturalistic epistemologies.

[103]This is Hays's question to Wright in Richard B. Hays, "Story, History and the Question of Truth," in *JPPG*, 61. Wright's response seems to back away from the implications of the resurrection for epistemology, or at least from any perceivable difference in method (64).

justice to their intrinsic organisation and their inner form even as empirical and historical realities, that is, without the artificial manipulation of the observationalist and phenomenalist approach.[104]

If we grant the resurrection epistemic priority, it seems that we would at least be forced to consider the reality that we are confronted with in Jesus Christ "conjunctively" as "God and man." This would certainly influence the way in which we approach our knowledge of him, not the least of which would be the credibility we would give to the possibility—even probability— of the miraculous. For Torrance this is simply determining the method of investigation according to the nature of that which is being investigated. If the resurrection is the key, then the method necessarily changes into conformity with the reality of the resurrection. The old naturalistic methods of reasoning are subject to revision and even rejection according to not only the form (the miraculous) of the resurrection, but also the content and meaning of that event (theology).

The resurrection is integral for the theological event of the self-revelation of God in Jesus of Nazareth. If, as I have argued, the Son comes to all humanity in his *anhypostatic* movement and in the same way, with the same movement, takes all history to himself, then we can also say, by virtue of the fact that human reason is part of what it means to be human, that in this movement he takes human reason to himself. Because the *enhypostatic* movement is not separable from the cross, death and burial of Jesus, the Messiah of Israel, we can make the further dogmatic claim that all of these things are judged and ended, "put to death" in and through Jesus' willing movement to the cross. Yet what is *enhypostasized* in the humanity of Jesus of Nazareth (including the history of Israel and the reasoning ability of humanity) are together redeemed and restored through his faithfulness with them to the point of death, and they are given back to him as his life is given back in the resurrection. These things—humanity, history, reason—are given new life and new purpose *in Christ*. Human reason is grounded in the reality of the resurrection, but not without first being judged at the cross. What returns to us in affirmation, that is, the affirmation that our reason is

[104]Thomas F. Torrance, *Transformation and Convergence in the Frame of Knowledge: Explorations in the Interrelations of Scientific and Theological Enterprise* (Belfast: Christian Journals Limited, 1984), 93.

good and true, remains to be so only to the extent that it is found *in Christ*. Reason has been wrested from us and relocated in Christ.

If, with Bonhoeffer, we affirm that the continuity between the dead Christ and the resurrected Lord is only found in God who creates *ex nihilo*, then the resurrection, as the ground of our Christian epistemology, would introduce a discontinuity into the functioning of human reason. This does not mean that reality changes, or that those things to which our words refer change, but rather that the human capacity to reason, to see the world truthfully, is restructured, dead and raised, in Christ. This is why in our thinking about Christ we must first come under the corrective of the mind of Christ. Only after we have given ourselves to the priority of his mind, his thought, can we, as a matter of *thinking with* fallen human reason, think with the nonbelieving historian. Yet to know the truth and to see Christ as he is is only to see him according to the unity of who he is as God and a man, consubstantial, *homoousion*. In this unity is the reconciliation of our minds, a reconciliation we are not yet given to possess except in the Spirit. So to see with reconciled minds the truth of the world is to see in the Spirit—to perceive the world as a gift, grounded in the reconciliation of the world with God in Jesus (Col 1:15-23). This is seeing the world, as an object of knowledge, according to its nature as judged and reconciled in Christ. To see it truly is to see it through the mind of Christ. I think this is just the sort of thing that Wright describes when he brings Paul into dialogue with the philosophers in *PFG*:

> The problem of true knowledge is not merely that appearances deceive, or that people make wrong inferences, but rather that human rebellion against the one god has resulted in a distortion and a darkening of the knowledge that humans have, or still ought to have. Paul would want to say to the philosophers that wisdom is not simply a matter of learning to see, like the owls, in ordinary darkness. It is a matter of the one God piercing the darkness and bringing new light, the light of new creation, and at the same time opening the eyes that have been blinded by the "god of this world" so that they can see that light.[105]

This, I think, is in full agreement with what I have been arguing. Reason is affirmed in the resurrection as the renewing of our minds in Christ, but it is not affirmed except as renewed in Christ. Rather, human reason is

---

[105]*PFG*, 1363.

judged at the cross—perhaps not for reason's ability to refer, but for its direction away from God, which is, in a sense, the mind turned in on itself (the intellectual corollary of *cor curvum in se*). That Wright uses the language of new creation here hints that the human mind and human knowing are redeemed in the new and fresh act of God, thereby making resurrection, *the* resurrection, the beginning point for a new epistemology.

But this would then mean that we would indeed look back at the life of Christ, from the vantage point of the resurrection, in a new way, with new minds (in Christ), and see him not as simply a crucifiable first-century Jew, but a crucifiable first-century Jew who was, and indeed, still is, God with us.

Theological Historiography Will Be Shaped by a Theology of History for Which the Cross Is the Hermeneutical Center

Finally, the grand narrative, the story that conditions true historical knowledge, to the extent that historical knowledge would be a Christian knowledge, is a story that has the cross as its end. To the extent that the end is hermeneutically significant for any story, the Christian story can only be told as a story of death and resurrection, but that resurrection is grounded in the same freedom of God that began the world *ex nihilo*. This means that history remains oriented toward death, toward its end, but that the possibility of a future and a hope are grounded in the freedom of God shown in the resurrection of Jesus from the dead. It is the resurrection that grounds any hope for history, but this is a hope that only comes *after* death through the free gracious act of God. Life on this side of death can be free from the constraining logic of death, but only in the reality of the personal and continued life of the resurrected Lord. The implications of this for historiography are significant.

First, historians are limited in the sorts of progressive narratives they can tell. Whether it is a story of the church or a story of a nation, the possibilities that are grounded in human action are bounded at the end in the finality of death. This is so of individuals and is, in the same way, true of the great sweeping narratives of history. There is no room here for any ontologizing of history in any possible way other than as a whole that has for its ending the cross.[106] History arrives at its telos with the death of the

---

[106]I do not mean to deny history a particular kind of reality. On this point I am in complete agreement

Messiah. It is limited and just as transient as the lives of those who make up history.

Second, this means that history is not the sort of thing one can take up and attempt to move in one direction or another. John Howard Yoder writes,

> One way to think about social ethics in our time is to say that Christians in our age are obsessed with the meaning and direction of history. Social ethical concern is moved by a deep desire to make things right and move them in the right direction. Whether a given action is right or not seems to be inseparable from the question of what effects it will cause. Thus part if not all of social concern has to do with looking for the right "handle" by which one can "get a hold on" the course of history and move it in the right direction.[107]

By using this sort of language, Yoder is, among other things, rejecting the assumption that there is a greater meaning to history that has yet to be achieved. The Christian historian that is trying to make sense of the whole, to tell the story that links events to one another through the various forces of cause and effect, always comes up against the cross. It is the Lamb who was slain that holds the key to history.[108] Yoder understands this to mean that it is "the cross and not the sword, suffering and not brute power,"[109] that determine the meaning of history. Yet, rather than ethicizing the meaning of history, giving it over to a principle of nonviolence as if "nonviolence" were an idea that could carry history, the crucial point is that "the obedience of God's people and the triumph of God's cause is not a relationship of cause and effect, but one of cross and resurrection."[110] Cross and resurrection, again, are not stand-ins for an ethical principle, reproducible in varying situations, but rather the reality of the meaning of history. That resurrection is the movement beyond the cross means that the history that moves forward for which there is a future and a hope is the history of Jesus Christ, in actuality. Here, a theologian like Bonhoeffer would point to the church as the body of Christ as his actual presence in the world. But if this

---

with Wright and reject the notion of history as nonexistent or some sort of vacuum. Cf. Michael Bentley, "Past and 'Presence': Revisiting Historical Ontology," *History and Theory* 45 (2006): 349-61.
[107]John Howard Yoder, *The Politics of Jesus: Vicit Agnus Noster*, 2nd ed. (Grand Rapids: Eerdmans, 1994), 228.
[108]Ibid., 231-32.
[109]Ibid., 232.
[110]Ibid.

is so, it is not a *competitive* presence in history, but rather an excessive presence, a presence grounded in the resurrection and mediated by the Spirit. World history stands judged. There is no moving it one way or another. There is only resurrection, God's act in freedom, that, because of his ontological noncompetitiveness with the world, and the nature of his presence in history as the Lamb who was slain, does not move history according to a progressive teleology, but peacefully transforms the lives of disciples freed from the logic of death. This does not rule out human action for justice or liberation in history, but rather qualifies such action within a baptismal logic of death and resurrection.

Finally, this challenges the faithfulness of metaphors that would depict a Christian understanding of history—the Christian story—in terms of the dramatic. This Christian story functions in Wright's work as the normative grounding for the Christian subject's orientation to the good; it is definitive for the Christian's worldview. The normative function of the Christian story is imaginatively appropriated by articulating in word and praxis a biblical view of history according to the model of a five-act drama. Christians find themselves living in the unwritten fifth act of a five-act play. Such a play "would consist in the fact of an as yet unfinished drama, containing its own impetus and forward movement, which demanded to be concluded in an appropriate manner."[111] This corresponds nicely to Charles Taylor's argument in *Sources of the Self*, where he writes, "Since we cannot do without an orientation to the good, and since we cannot be indifferent to our place relative to this good, and since this place is something that must always change and become, the issue of the direction of our lives must arise for us."[112] The biblical narrative, imagined as a drama with an unfinished final act, becomes the story that provides us with the context and norms that determine the direction of our lives within history. The epistemological and hermeneutical concept of worldview provides the theoretical apparatus for this imaginative exercise. Wright's primary concern is to account for the way in which biblical authority functions, yet the implications this has for Christian ethics should be clear, as we take into consideration both the role

---

[111]*NTPG*, 140.
[112]Charles Taylor, *Sources of the Self: The Making of the Modern Identity* (Cambridge, MA: Cambridge University Press, 1992), 47.

of the Bible in moral deliberation and formation, and also the way in which the Christian imagines her own place as an actor in the world.

For Wright, the moral concern that points us to the discipline of history as a theological corrective and as a way to articulate the whole of history is teleologically ordered according to his reading of the moral direction of history: "History and justice belong together, as humans are called to bring the divinely intended order to birth through their speech-acts."[113] In the final chapter of *PFG*, Wright brings together the centrality of the new creation for Paul together with the language of that new creation as a project that Paul's mission was supposed to help realize. Paul "was not just a spectator. He was called to do and say things through which new creation *was happening already*: each personal 'new creation,' through Messiah-faith and baptism, was another signpost to the larger 'new creation' of which the Psalms and the prophets had spoken."[114] After quoting 2 Corinthians 11:2-3, he continues, "Paul could only write like that if he really did believe that his apostolic work was an advance project for the ultimate new creation itself."[115] Earlier in the chapter he writes of Paul, "Since Paul believed that this new creation had already begun in the resurrection of the Messiah, this could not, by definition, remain a mere idea. If it was true, it had to become what we might call a historical reality."[116] If Wright's account of Paul's "project" is to bring about the new creation, I think he oversteps the actual possibilities for human agency in that project. If new creation is what God brings about—in the Messiah through resurrection—then there are implications for human agency with respect to its realization. These are not easy implications to work out in the normal accounts of human agency since they are grounded in Christ and in the gifts he gives in the Spirit. The history that is the new creation is not, therefore, part of the same history that went on before, and that still moves forward toward its judgment, but is something new.

Wright's fear of such a position is that it throws out all the history that has gone before, significantly the history of Israel. This is his critique of the

---

[113]*NTPG*, 136. This is also related to his recent suggestion that Christian are called to "build for the kingdom." See N. T. Wright, *Surprised by Hope* (New York: HarperOne, 2008), 193.
[114]*PFG*, 1489.
[115]Ibid.
[116]Ibid., 1476.

new apocalyptic theology that for him is represented by Martyn's commentary on Galatians, a theology he characterizes as a "present fad for a supposedly . . . 'apocalyptic' of sheer negativity towards the past."[117] I hope that the arguments in this book do not present such a negativity, but rather that they put forward a new reading of the relationship between the new creation and the old way of thinking of historical continuity. The resurrection does not simply lead to a "new creation mode of knowing" that is a "deeper, truer, richer mode of knowing *about the old creation as well*."[118] Of course, if the "as well" in this statement means that a new creation mode of knowing has the *added benefit* of giving us a truer knowledge of the old creation, then this implies that the primary benefit of this new epistemology is located elsewhere. But this would mean that, as our earlier discussion suggested, the resurrection really would change the way we see the history of Jesus and God's revelation in his word and deeds in history, through the history of Israel, in the covenants with his people. The point is that this new mode of knowing goes through death and resurrection, and finds itself located outside of us in the knowing of the one—the only one, so far—to be resurrected.

The point that needs to be made here is that history, with the cross as its telos, is not continued except as it moves toward that end. It is not a project to be improvised nor a drama to be acted. Rather it is a tragic tale that *has been* told, one that has been ended at the cross. All that is now to be done (and here is the crucial point) is done according to the life that comes to us in Christ. Because history is now located in Jesus Christ and his ongoing historicity, it is from Christ in his *enhypostatic, enhistoric* reality that we find the validation of a historical trajectory, and, indeed, it is a story of God's covenant faithfulness to his people, Israel. Yet this story of covenant faithfulness is conditioned, determined and revealed in the apocalypse of Jesus Christ. This apocalypse has, as its center, the death and resurrection of Jesus. God's covenant faithfulness is alive, but only in and through his action in the judgment of history, its end, and its resurrection in the Messiah: death and resurrection, the end of history and new creation.

[117]Ibid., 1478.
[118]Ibid., 1491.

CONCLUSION

The three theses I have presented above still leave many questions regarding the historian's task. Whatever is left to be said surely must not be a new method. How does one go about studying and learning history in light of the apocalypse of Jesus Christ, an epistemological commitment that is grounded not in the center of human intellect, but, eccentrically, in the very mind of Christ? *Method* would be the wrong word. *Hearing* and *proclamation* might be better. *Prayer* and *doxology* come to mind as well. Whatever language we use to describe this preeminently theological task, we can find conceptual help in the task by adopting Christopher Morse's helpful distinction between the kingdom understood as being "at-hand" as opposed to being "in hand."[119] New creation is never in hand, just as the gospel proclamation as good "news" is not history. "News is not history."[120]

---

[119]Christopher Morse, *The Difference Heaven Makes: Rehearing the Gospel as News* (London: T&T Clark, 2010), 7.

[120]Ibid.

6

An Apocalyptic
Reappraisal of Apocalyptic

ON THE ISLAND OF PATMOS, whether there in exile or for reasons related to his prophetic role in the church in Asia Minor, the Christian elder, John, hears a voice and is told to write what he sees in a book. John's vision in written form, far from being a unique literary event, is in fact part of a long tradition that scholars have come to call by the name *apocalyptic*. It is the first line of the book of Revelation—Ἀποκάλυψις Ἰησοῦ Χριστοῦ—that lends this genre its contemporary designation, the first book in its own day, perhaps, to be labeled such.[1] Yet before Revelation there was 1 Enoch and Daniel, and by the end of the first century CE 2 and 3 Baruch bear the label of apocalypse, with many more to follow.[2] Once scholars identified this genre classification it became clear that there were apocalyptic texts spread throughout the Jewish and Christian canons, chapters embedded here and there, and that there was an identifiably apocalyptic worldview to be found, attributable to ancient authors and signaled by certain clues within a text. Whether *apocalyptic* is a technical term at the early date of John's revelation is unclear, but, as John J. Collins reports, there is a general consensus within the guild today regarding what books ought to be discussed when discussing apocalyptic texts, although precisely defining apocalyptic literature, or an apocalyptic worldview, has

---

[1]John J. Collins, *The Apocalyptic Imagination: An Introduction to Jewish Apocalyptic Literature*, 2nd ed. (Grand Rapids: Eerdmans, 1998), 3.

[2]For a helpful account the interrelationship between John's apocalypse and both older and contemporary apocalypses, see "The Use of Apocalyptic Traditions," in Richard Bauckham, *The Climax of Prophecy: Studies on the Book of Revelation* (London: T&T Clark, 1993), 38-91.

been much more difficult.³ The importance of identifying the apocalyptic worldview through an examination of apocalypses emerged as theologians and biblical scholars discovered anew the importance of eschatology and an apocalyptic thought world for the imagination of the early church and for the apostle Paul in particular. Ernst Käsemann is the most important figure in this rediscovery, not because he "discovered" apocalyptic—he did not—but because he is perhaps the first to see in the apocalyptic background of Paul and the first Christian theologians something that was to be appropriated positively for biblical interpretation. J. Christiaan Beker brought the conversation into the English-speaking world with his book, *Paul the Apostle: The Triumph of God in Life and Thought.*⁴ Both were reacting against the negative portrayals of apocalyptic by such eminent scholars as Julius Wellhausen and Klaus Koch.⁵ In the German theological scene, Jürgen Moltmann and Wolfhart Panenberg, in different ways, appropriated apocalyptic in their eschatological projects, utilizing it as a way of opening up the future for theological work given the horrors of the twentieth century.

Christopher Rowland, assessing the value of this discovery, observes that "the contribution of apocalyptic literature to the debate about the Christian hope has been immense, precisely because it appears to be the repository of those ideas in late Judaism which gave meaning and purpose to history as a whole."⁶ If the question is the shape of history, and the way in which people in the first century CE or the Second Temple era imagined the interrelationship of events and the meaning of those events, then apocalyptic is an indispensable source. Apocalypses functioned as literary events within a given community by imaginatively expanding both the temporal and spatial dimensions through "received" revelations about those things that cannot otherwise be seen;⁷ apocalyptic literature revealed the divine will to people who were in need of clarity,

---

³Ibid. See Christopher Rowland's list of apocalyptic writings in his book on the subject, *The Open Heaven: A Study of Apocalyptic in Judaism and Early Christianity* (1982: SPCK, London), 15.

⁴J. Christiaan Beker, *Paul the Apostle: The Triumph of God in Life and Thought* (Philadelphia: Fortress Press, 1980).

⁵This is a very truncated form of the introduction that Wright gives to this history in *Paul and His Recent Interpreters* (Minneapolis: Fortress Press, 2015), 2:4-14. Wright's overall approach to the question of apocalyptic is remarkably similar to Koch's. Cf. Klaus Koch, *The Rediscovery of Apocalyptic*, trans. Margaret Kohl, Studies in Biblical Theology, Second Series, vol. 22 (London: SCM Press LTD, 1972).

⁶Rowland, *Open Heaven*, 1.

⁷See Collins's definition of an apocalypse in *Apocalyptic Imagination*, 5.

not exegetical argument, who needed to see "the true nature of reality so that they may organise their lives accordingly."[8] Those who needed such clarity were often those who were oppressed or whose convictions and worldview were challenged in such a way that they were called by a seer to resist the overt domination or hegemonic influence of empire.[9] It is most likely that the apocalyptic form of literature "would be chosen by those who found themselves on the wrong side of history."[10] If the biblical writers shared such a need for clarity, and if apocalyptic forms of thought contributed to the worldview of the apostles and those overseeing the early church, and if these thought forms are the background, the landscape, in which the New Testament writers operated, then it should be clear that understanding this genre is a key to faithful exegesis and theological interpretation of Scripture.

The thesis that I want to argue in this chapter is in no way intended to undermine the important study of apocalyptic literature undertaken by the many eminent scholars working in this field of research, including Collins, Rowland, Portier-Young and, indeed, Wright himself. Rather, I want to begin by showing how the apocalyptic theology I have articulated thus far interacts with Wright's own account of apocalyptic literature and, perhaps more importantly, the way in which apocalyptic theology works itself out in dialogue with apocalyptic as part of a worldview-focused reading of Paul. This means bringing into the conversation the theology of history assumed in Wright's account, specifically the way in which that theology interacts with apocalyptic, resulting in Wright's move to position the literary genre as the primary framework in which to understand what apocalyptic means. This will show that Wright's methodological commitments in *NTPG* are carried through to his comments in *PFG* and the *Interpreters* volume, and will show with some precision how the theological arguments presented in the previous chapters challenge Wright's account, offering an alternative theological structuring of the relationship between history and whatever it is we mean by *apocalyptic*. By bringing this into the conversation with Wright my intention is to take his

---

[8]Ibid., 11.
[9]"The paired concepts of domination and hegemony illuminate the ways in which the early Jewish apocalypses and related forms could function as a literature of resistance to empire, especially in the face of persecution." Anathea E. Portier-Young, *Apocalypse Against Empire: Theologies of Resistance in Early Judaism* (Grand Rapids: Eerdmans, 2011), 44.
[10]*NTPG*, 287.

arguments seriously but show in as clear a way as possible why apocalyptic theologians will differ from him, and by arguing for this difference this chapter will serve as a sort of apologetic for this direction of study. Furthermore, this will function something like a response to the question, "So what?" that inevitably emerges at the end of a project like this. How might actual exegetical decisions be changed by the theological account of history that I have provided, grounded in the epistemological priority of revelation and the centrality of the cross as a rupture within the very fabric of the way in which we tell and interpret history? In concrete terms, this will be shown in the way we interpret covenant and the place of Israel vis-à-vis the church, both in light of the singular apocalyptic event, the apocalypse of Jesus Christ.

In nuce my argument is this: Wright's commitment to historical method, laid out in his account of critical realism, limits his methodological willingness to consider the claims of apocalyptic theologians, particularly the reality and freedom of God and what this means for historical and theological knowledge. This means he misses the critical relationship between the definitive apocalyptic event, the apocalypse of Jesus Christ, and his own methodological commitments. The task of this chapter, then, is to show how this works out in the way he relates covenant and apocalyptic in his account of Pauline theology.

The chapter will be structured as follows. First, because the reception of *PFG* is, as of this writing, an ongoing conversation, I will begin with a brief look at the state of the controversy, which will help to clarify the need for the approach I am taking. Second, we will need to take a closer look at the way in which covenant and apocalyptic are related in the study of apocalyptic literature. Particularly we will affirm, with Wright, that apocalypses typically engage history as the arena of God's active faithfulness to his covenant, even if present circumstances look otherwise. Third, an engagement with Wright's account of Paul's epistemology must pay attention to the interaction between the new way of knowing introduced by the gospel and the history of God's covenant faithfulness to the people of Israel. As we will see, Wright subjects the disruptive element in Paul's epistemology to the continuity necessary for the coherence of his commitment to a worldview epistemology. The fourth section engages this account from the apocalyptic logic developed in the previous chapters and argues that, in fact, Paul's apocalyptic epistemology conditions the way in which he receives and appropriates an apocalyptic worldview. More significantly, the apocalyptic logic conditions the way in which Christian theology understands the relationship between the present history and the history of the new creation. This develops further the idea that the cross is the end of history. It is only in this way that we can approach the fifth area of concern and articulate the way in which covenant is subsumed in the determinative apocalyptic event, the parousia of the Messiah. Sixth, and finally, the covenant reconfigured according to an apocalyptic theology, rather than superseding history and Israel, recenters history around the Messiah and describes new creation in such a way that it is not competitive with the history of Israel but is excessive to that history, located in the *enhistorical* identity of Jesus Christ. History, finally, is located as that which occurs before the death of Christ and the "death" of baptism; new creation is located as resurrected life, proleptically found in the resurrected Jesus.

THE CONTROVERSY

Reading Wright's *Paul and the Faithfulness of God* with an ear toward his conversation with contemporary apocalyptic readings of Paul, it becomes abundantly clear (if one did not know it already) that he sees this particular school of interpretation to be especially problematic for his project—and for a faithful interpretation of Paul. Following Douglas Campbell's suggestion, I have argued that we should define apocalyptic theology in continuity with a particular trajectory of interpretation that largely follows the concerns of J. Louis Martyn and others.[11] This coincides with Wright's understanding of the movement but also positions the current project directly in the line of fire. In a particularly lucid moment of critique against this trajectory, Wright points to the way in which the apocalyptic reading presented by Campbell, which is, to a large extent, an epistemological reading, is dependent upon the literary reading of apocalyptic by de Boer and Martyn.[12] If all of this attention to apocalyptic is grounded in literary readings of apocalyptic, reconstructed by historians, then the epistemological arguments are grounded in historical arguments and are, therefore, self-contradictory—or are bound to Wright's hermeneutical account of critical realism. Wright concludes that

---

[11]See chap. 3 above, pp. 113-14.
[12]Wright, *Interpreters*, 2:65.

"the 'apocalypses' of the second-temple period are simply not discussing the issues which occupy Martyn, Campbell and others. . . . Books like *1 Enoch* and *4 Ezra* were not in debate with one another over the question of *Vordenken* and *Nachdenken* as theological methods."[13]

Given this critique of the apocalyptic theologians, it makes sense that Wright is dismissive of the movement. And indeed, to the extent that this is an accurate description of the way in which de Boer and Martyn construct their commentaries, the epistemological account of apocalyptic will suffer for want of a more helpful articulation rather than highly specialized accounts of apocalyptic literature. This also serves to justify Wright's own program, which is to look for Paul's apocalyptic worldview in the apocalyptic literature of the time. So when Wright calls Paul an apocalyptic thinker he is not referring to an apocalyptic *epistemology*, but to an apocalyptic *worldview* that affirms his understanding of history and covenant. An apocalyptic worldview, thus grounded in a critical realist historiography, subsumes apocalyptic literature within the context of the long history of the covenant. It appears that Wright's methodological commitment to historiography, naturalistically conceived, serves as the gravitational force that pulls his reading of the apocalyptic theologians always back to a consideration of the genre, to "apocalyptic itself, in any meaningful first-century sense."[14]

By asserting the primacy of the historical/literary view of apocalyptic, Wright effectively dismisses those who would let the word be used to designate an epistemological/theological posture as well as a perspective on the cosmic dimensions of Christ's saving work. In *Interpreters*, Wright lays down the ground rules for the apocalyptic language game:

> Whatever the word "apocalyptic" does in Western scholarship, it always appeals implicitly to a historical context within the so-called "history of religions" of the time. That is, it implies that there is a larger worldview and/or religious movement and/or theological perspective for which the label "apocalyptic" is appropriate; and it claims, again at least by implication, that the material under consideration can best be understood as belonging within that worldview, movement or perspective, rather than within some other.[15]

---

[13]Ibid.
[14]*PFG*, 779.
[15]*Interpreters*, 2:7.

Wright then goes on to list some of the books that operate within and define this worldview. These are Daniel, Zechariah, Ezekiel, Isaiah, 1 Enoch, 4 Ezra and Revelation. He continues,

> If the word "apocalyptic," as a label for a mode or type of thought, is intended to carry any implication in terms of the religio-historical context to which appeal is being made, it must be to these books, and the many others like them, that the writer is appealing. Otherwise the word has cut loose from any recognisable historical moorings.[16]

In sum, Wright reiterates,

> When people use the word as a label for a text, theme, idea or entire book, they are saying, in effect, "There: we have located this within an already-known matrix; now we can move forward from that to draw further conclusions about its meaning." It is therefore vital to be sure that the matrix is carefully described.[17]

In a helpful comment, responding to a review of *PFG* in *The Christian Century* by Alexandra Brown, Wright clarifies, "One of my central arguments is that Paul is both an apocalyptic and a covenant theologian, and that these two define and support one another, as they do in ancient Jewish 'apocalypses.'"[18] The second part of this statement, "as they do in ancient Jewish 'apocalypses,'" affirms what Wright has laid out to be the ground rules for the use of the word *apocalyptic*: it is only to be used in reference to a particular cluster of religio-historical worldviews defined and described by a narrow body of unique literature from the Second Temple period of Jewish and Christian history. The standard is historically determined, not theologically determined. This is Wright's position, and it should be clear that his engagement with apocalyptic theology is always couched within the frustration that the use of *apocalyptic* has "cut loose from any recognisable historical moorings."

---

[16]Ibid.

[17]Ibid., 2:13. Here we can note that "matrix" signals the limitations inherent in the language used of the historical/literary view of apocalyptic, as well as the hermeneutical limits of Wright's method. Also, see G. B. Caird, *The Language and Imagery of the Bible* (London: Duckworth, 1980), 260-71. Caird provides a very helpful summary and overview of apocalyptic literature within a wider discussion of biblical eschatology.

[18]Alexandra Brown, review of *Paul and the Faithfulness of God*, by N. T. Wright, *The Christian Century*, October 16, 2014. www.christiancentury.org/reviews/2014-10/paul-and-faithfulness-god-n-t-wright. Wright's comment was posted on November 17, 2014.

It is clear that in the debate immediately following the release of *PFG*, and in the interim between that and the publication of the *Interpreters* volume, Wright's account of apocalyptic remains highly contentious. John M. G. Barclay writes,

> Wright repeatedly lampoons Martyn's "apocalyptic" reading of Pauline theology, which he misrepresents as practically "sweeping away everything Jewish and replacing it with an entirely new construct" (542). Martyn and de Boer may have (unnecessarily) downplayed the Abraham texts in Galatians 3-4, as merely responsive to Paul's opponents, but they are clear that Paul sees Christ as the fulfilment of God's promises to Abraham. Their essential point is that the continuity of divine purpose typically cuts against the grain of human history and is independent of human processes of development or descent. Wright partly grants that point, and wishes to dub his own reading "apocalyptic" as well. Both sides in fact agree that the load-bearing narrative's in Paul's theology concern God's purposes, gifts, and interventions, but the polemics of this book do not further discussion of this point or of its theological ramifications.[19]

In response to various critics, Wright affirms again and again that the vision he is giving of Paul is one that is both apocalyptic and covenantal, rooted in Paul's new way of knowing that is also, at once, consistent with the long historical narrative of God's covenant faithfulness to his people, Israel. The question of epistemology that in part drives critiques such as those by Beverly Gaventa, Martinus de Boer,[20] Barclay and Douglas Campbell has been met by Wright with a certain exasperation at the way this particular focus of attention has distracted from some of the larger, narratival accounts he provides in *PFG* that are the real focus of his work on Paul; these are the hermeneutical clues (e.g., the themes of exodus and exile) that change the way one sees the world in light of what Paul is saying. According to Wright, in a helpful, clarifying response to his critics that addresses the epistemological question, "The whole book was about Paul's vision of a new, gospel-initiated way of 'knowing' that he believed necessary if the new community was to be true to

---

[19]John M. G. Barclay, review of *Paul and the Faithfulness of God*, by N. T. Wright, *Scottish Journal of Theology* 68, no. 2 (May 2015): 237-38.

[20]For Gaventa's and de Boer's reviews, see Beverly Roberts Gaventa, "The Character of God's Faithfulness: A Response to N. T. Wright," *Journal for the Study of Paul and His Letters* 4, no. 1 (2014): 71-79, and Martinus C. de Boer, "N. T. Wright's Great Story and Its Relationship to Paul's Gospel," *Journal for the Study of Paul and His Letters* 4, no. 1 (2014): 49-57.

its gospel-initiated vocation."[21] Nevertheless, Wright's account of Paul's epistemological encounter with the Messiah is given in terms that continue to
circle back to Wright's historiographical point of departure, his method
grounded in natural ways of knowing, and his commitment to the worldview
epistemological apparatus. In his professed agreement with Gaventa, that the
epistemological point is significant for Paul, and is, indeed, central to his account of Paul's thinking, he characterizes Paul as "eager to promote a new
world view."[22] Such a new worldview involves a certain *Nachdenken,* but it
does so in fundamental continuity with the story of Israel. What Gaventa had
written in review of *PFG* was that "it is not enough to say that Paul thinks
differently about God, the Messiah, and Israel; for Paul, the death and resurrection involves Jesus' followers in thinking differently. Period."[23] While
Gaventa may not have stated the difference as strongly as it could have been
stated, her point cannot be equivalent to what Wright is claiming regarding
Paul's ideas about what one might need for this new worldview. In *Our Mother
Saint Paul,* Gaventa identified a Pauline apocalyptic theology with the

> conviction that in the death and resurrection of Jesus Christ, God had in-
> vaded the world as it is, thereby revealing the world's utter distortion and
> foolishness, reclaiming the world, and inaugurating a battle that will doubtless
> culminate in the triumph of God over all God's enemies (including the captors
> Sin and Death). This means that the gospel is first, last, and always about
> God's powerful and gracious initiative.[24]

The language Gaventa uses is the language of apocalyptic literature, but
the theology is that of the primacy of God's initiative and act in Paul's
knowing, one that is not simply a new worldview, but a new encounter that
implies a new theological epistemology. That is precisely what I have tried
to add to the argument regarding apocalyptic. The biblical scholars writing
on apocalyptic have used the language of apocalyptic literature, found
throughout the New Testament and especially in Pauline corpus, but the
interpretive force of their collective work has shown the contours of an epis-

---

[21]N. T. Wright, "Right Standing, Right Understanding, and Wright Misunderstanding: A Response,"
Journal for the Study of Paul and His Letters 4, no. 1 (2014): 93.
[22]Ibid.
[23]Gaventa, "Character of God's Faithfulness," 76.
[24]Beverly Roberts Gaventa, *Our Mother Saint Paul* (Louisville: Westminster John Knox Press,
2007), 81.

temological piece in the apocalyptic puzzle that has needed to be explicitly shown. By drawing attention to this piece we can see how Wright misses what Gaventa is saying and how Gaventa might need to say what she is saying with more force directed against Wright's methodological assumptions. The problem and the controversy is not in the interpretation of Paul's use of apocalyptic themes, but in the relationship between worldview criticism and the force of the epistemological crisis that the cross and resurrection, the apocalypse of Jesus Christ, exerts on Paul's entire noetic structure.

If there is to be a rapprochement between Wright and the apocalyptic theologians, then I propose that the way forward must be through the account of epistemology that Wright attributes to Paul, and through this account, back to the relationship that exists between the apocalypse of Jesus Christ and the literary apocalypses that determine the apocalyptic worldview. In this way it can been seen how the apocalyptic event that determines Paul's epistemology in turn shapes the sort of apocalyptic theology that emerges, both in terms of his epistemological commitments, and the way he understands history. As this entire project has made clear, this is not for the sake of finding Paul's worldview, but for the sake of articulating in our time a theology that can be faithful to the revelation of God in and as Jesus Christ, the Messiah of Israel.

Apocalypses and the Covenant: Reading Irruption in the Context of a Long Story

In chapter four above, I briefly touched upon the way in which Wright holds together apocalyptic and covenant. It will be helpful at this point to examine this relationship in more depth in order to show the way apocalypses work in Wright's theology to support his theology of history, and how this relationship is challenged by an emphasis on the apocalyptic event at the heart of the apocalypse of Jesus Christ. In the published version of his Hulsean Lectures at Cambridge, he writes, and I quote this again because of its clarity,

> We cannot expound Paul's covenant theology in such a way as to make it a smooth, steady progress of historical fulfilment; but nor can we propose a kind of "apocalyptic" view in which nothing that happened before Jesus is of any value even as preparation. In the messianic events of Jesus' death and resurrection Paul believes both that the covenant promises were at last ful-

filled and that this constituted a massive and dramatic irruption into the process of world history unlike anything before or since.[25]

We can see that by confining the conversation to the literary context of apocalyptic, the relationship between covenant and apocalyptic is essentially supportive, grounded in a covenantal (and political) reading of apocalyptic literature. If history provides the interpretive matrix, then the actual impact of the irruption of God is minimized, even if acknowledged.

> Rather, when we put Paul into his historical context within first-century Judaism itself, not least the writings loosely grouped under the label "apocalyptic," we find all kinds of features which the modern revival of so-called "apocalyptic" has screened out: not only justification (and all the accompanying questions of human sin, atonement, and so on), but also, and more importantly, the divine covenant with Israel, and the constant sense of a long, dark story which finally reaches its goal in the shocking, fresh, but also long-promised and long-awaited new revelation.[26]

To be perfectly clear, there is nothing that I can see that is necessarily wrong with Wright's account of apocalyptic, nor is there a reason for me to weigh in on the correct interpretation of this multifaceted, multidimensional literary phenomenon. I am content to let Wright, Rowland, Collins, Campbell, de Boer, Gaventa and others debate the merits of their respective interpretations. Wright's observation that apocalyptic literature is both political and covenantal seems exactly right and is an important point that needs to be made, especially when interpreting the book of Revelation. John's apocalypse is anything but ahistorical and apolitical. It is clearly about God's faithfulness to history, the faithfulness of Christian witness in the midst of a powerful, idolatrous empire, and in its vast imagery and allusions it relies heavily on Old Testament apocalyptic themes and texts. When Wright critiques Martyn's reading of Galatians based on Martyn's account of apocalyptic literature, his critique, cutting as it is, seems to be an important contribution to the conversation. In *Interpreters* he points out that the "apocalyptic world to which Martyn appeals" is full of "retellings of the story of Israel." These retellings characterize Second Temple apocalyptic literature, a

---

[25]N. T. Wright, *Paul: In Fresh Perspective* (Minneapolis: Fortress Press, 2009), 54.
[26]Wright, *Interpreters*, 91.

literary genre distinguished in part by the presence of "a long narrative in search of a resolution, a conclusion."[27]

The problem here, based on what I have argued, is that when Wright moves from concluding what apocalyptic literature does with respect to "long narratives in search of a resolution" to what Paul must mean, or must be doing with apocalyptic themes and language, he collapses the meaning of apocalyptic into something determined beforehand, something confined within the limited field of worldviews. Even if the worldview has been invaded, it still remains, in Wright's view, a comprehensible apocalyptic worldview in the first-century sense. Wright is explicit about this as he continues his critique of Martyn: "If, however, I read Galatians as 'apocalyptic,' *using that word to place the document within a historical matrix*, I will *expect* the kind of narrative, running from Abraham to the present, which Paul really does seem to be offering—offering, that is, as his own proposal."[28] The question I am posing is not whether or not apocalyptic literature actually invokes such a running narrative—I see no reason to think that it does not—but rather whether or not Paul's experience of the singular apocalypse of Jesus Christ is knowable in these terms. If the epistemological account of the apocalypse of Jesus Christ I have provided, grounded in the reality and freedom of God, is in the realm of being accurate, then there is more "data" to be considered in the actual exegetical decision made with respect to the interpretation of, in this case, Galatians.

Covenant functions in Wright's theology as a shorthand way to designate the gospel as the fulfillment of the promises made to Abraham within which the church is a community formed as a "kind of extension or radical development of the covenantal life of Israel."[29] Articulated as such, the covenant, seen in light of the gospel, is a way of holding in narrative continuity the history of Israel together with the past and present history of the church. There is one history, one drama, that reaches its covenantal climax with the arrival of the Messiah, and continues toward the day of eschatological conclusion. The event of Jesus the Messiah, to be sure, requires a radical revision of the covenant, but it is not a rejection or entirely other thing than what Israel had hoped. It is a "radically new state of affairs, albeit one which had

---

[27]Wright, *Interpreters*, 2:52.
[28]Ibid., 2:53. Italics in original.
[29]*PFG*, 782.

always been promised in Torah, prophets and Psalms."[30] This articulation is pitched against an apocalyptic reading in which, in Wright's characterization, "there is no sense of 'continuity' with Abraham at all, but rather instead a radical inbreaking, an 'invasion' of the world, an entire overthrowing of existing categories, not least the long narrative of Abraham and his family."[31] Barclay's response to *PFG* quoted in the previous section is a helpful response to this claim, although there is certainly room to debate the extent to which Martyn and others really do throw out the long narrative. Whatever one makes of the argument, the conclusion is generally accepted that throwing out Abraham and Israel is a bad thing, that supersessionism is not warranted and that whatever account of apocalyptic we embrace must in some way deal with continuity in terms of God's faithfulness to his covenant.

In Wright's theology, covenant and apocalyptic go hand in hand because apocalyptic literature assumes the problem of the covenant: Will God be faithful to his people given the oppression that they are suffering? Apocalyptic serves as a theodicy of sorts when events seem to pile up and conspire to nullify the covenant God made with Abraham. The question that can be raised in light of this discussion is that of the relationship between covenant, apocalypses and the apocalypse of Jesus Christ. What does the singular apocalypse of Jesus Christ have to say regarding the covenant and the apocalyptic worldview that articulates God's covenant faithfulness on a cosmic, heavenly scope? By addressing Wright's account of Paul's epistemology, we can move closer to addressing the way in which the apocalypse of Jesus Christ might play in to this interpretative morass.

PAUL'S EPISTEMOLOGY

We have already looked closely at Wright's own epistemology as it has been carefully articulated in the methodological and programmatic arguments made at the outset of his larger project, Christian Origins and the Question of God. From the beginning with *NTPG* and through each successive volume, up until his latest contribution in *PFG*, Wright has remained remarkably consistent to his critical realist method. This methodological consistency is not only on display in how he goes about historical research and interpre-

---

[30]Ibid., 783.
[31]Ibid., 784.

tation, but it is also there to be seen in his description of Paul's own epistemology. In other words, the account Wright provides of Paul's epistemology
is remarkably consistent with Wright's account of his own epistemology. On
purely historiographical grounds this might be problematic, suggesting a
break in the attempted objectivity and detachment of the historian. Yet CRw
admits the worldview of the historian and, given that Wright is writing from
a position of faith, taking Paul as an authoritative and normative voice in the
theological task is to be expected. Nevertheless, the question needs to be
raised, Does Wright's own epistemology stand to be critiqued from the
Pauline epistemology he describes? And is there enough integrity in his own
interpretation that we can see the room for a Pauline critique of what Wright
has presented in *NTPG*? Where there is an opportunity for Paul's understanding of a particular gospel way of knowing, an apocalyptic way of
knowing, to influence Wright, we find that Wright incorporates the apocalyptic element into the covenantal/historical matrix, thereby effectively nul-
lifying the irruptive element, even while attempting to include it.

In his Hulsean Lectures, Wright deepened his polemics against the apocalyptic readings of Pauline theology, pushing back against those readings, as
we have already seen, by affirming the importance of covenant within the
overall discussion.[32] The apocalyptic crowd had, by his estimation, rejected
everything that came before the apocalypse of Jesus Christ: the history of
Israel, the covenants, Torah; and, in what he took to be a Barthian move,[33] the
apocalyptic theologians had subjected everything worthy of historical study
to a new, fresh revelation. "God is doing a new thing. Jesus bursts onto the
scene in a shocking, unexpected, unimaginable fashion, the crucified Christ
offers a slap in the face to Israel and the world, folly to Gentiles and a scandal
to Jews."[34] Fideism reared its ugly head, and the popularity of this new reading
of Paul threatened, in a new way, the careful historical and exegetical work
he and others had been faithfully doing.[35] By the time Wright gets to Paul's

---

[32]Wright, *Paul*, 40-58.

[33]While he does not mention Barth in his Hulsean Lectures, he does so at many other places. See,
e.g., N. T. Wright, "Paul in Current Anglophone Scholarship," *The Expository Times* 123, no. 8
(2012): 367-81.

[34]Wright, *Paul*, 51.

[35]Not only had the scholarly commitment to history been challenged, in Wright's perspective,
but Wright himself had been accused of supersessionism by one of the theologians who was
responsible for making apocalyptic part of the vocabulary of the postliberal conversation, Doug-

epistemology in *PFG*, he has developed this critique, nuanced it and is able to show with additional subtlety how we might read Paul as an apocalyptic thinker without giving up the necessary commitment to the historical covenant God made with Israel. In fact, it turns out that Paul's apocalyptic worldview, rather than challenging a covenantal commitment or pulling him away from history itself (the time and space of the created world considered in temporal continuity), affirmed both of these through a historical account of apocalyptic literature. Turning our attention to the account of *Paul's* epistemology in *PFG* to see how it deepens his earlier account of his own theory of knowledge, we can see how this historicizing of apocalyptic takes shape.

Wright's account of apocalyptic in his Hulsean Lectures is tied to his developed account of worldviews,[36] but the apocalyptic epistemology for which I have been arguing is not significantly far off from what Wright would want to affirm regarding an epistemology in Pauline terms. "There is, then, an *epistemological* revolution at the heart of Paul's worldview and theology. It isn't just that he now knows things he did not before; it is, rather, that *the act of knowing* has itself been transformed."[37] If I were to rewrite this statement to reflect more accurately the arguments I have made in previous chapters, the only change I would make is to say that the epistemological revolution is not at the *heart* of Paul's worldview, but rather the epistemological revolution has *determined* Paul's worldview and continues to unsettle it, making it less of a worldview and more of a dialectical engagement with the living and personal God.[38] I suspect that this is at least something of what Wright must mean when he speaks of an epistemology of love.[39] "But now that you've come to know God—or, better, to be known

---

las Harink. See Harink, *Paul Among the Postliberals: Pauline Theology Beyond Christendom and Modernity* (Grand Rapids: Brazos Press, 2003), 198-207.

[36]See above, chap. 4, p. 167.

[37]*PFG*, 1356.

[38]Any "dialectical engagement with the living God" is going to be heavily weighted, if not absolutely determined, by the living God! Nevertheless, in good Kierkegaardian fashion we can affirm that this is still a dialectic if we see it in terms of the equality achieved by the incarnation through which an "understanding" can be had, an understanding gained by the God who comes to us incognito.

[39]In a footnote, Wright mentions others who have worked on an epistemology of love. Among these are Brian J. Walsh and Sylvia C. Keesmat. In their book, an epistemology of love is described in predominantly moral and ecclesial terms, grounded in a theology of truth embodied in Jesus Christ. I think there is some promise in this direction, but I worry that the "plausibility of the gospel" ends up being too closely tied to the ethical performance of the ecclesial community and not to the dynamic presence in the community (and outside it) of the living God. The danger is

by God—how can you turn back again to that weak and poverty-stricken lineup of elements that you want to serve all over again?" Here, citing Galatians 4:8 (his translation), he presents an epistemology of love as a "revision of the *epistemological* order: instead of humans acquiring knowledge of a variety of things within the whole cosmos . . . there is 'One God' who takes initiative. God's 'knowing' creates the context for human 'knowing'; and the result is not a 'knowledge' such as one might have of a detached object (a tree, say, or a distant star). The result, to say it again, is love, *agapē*."[40] To be known by God, and therefore to place the priority of knowing in the knowledge that God has of us, is to be loved by God. It is, we might rightly argue, to be saved; to be known by God, and to be loved in this way by God, is to be in a life-giving relationship that transforms the very noetic structure of one's experience of the world. It is to be given the "condition" and the eyes to see. Theological epistemology, grounded in the priority of the love of God and his saving act of revealing himself, is soteriological through and through. If Wright's Paul is advocating this sort of epistemology, then all the pieces are there for an account that is apocalyptically oriented to the priority of the reality of God, whose being is in the freedom of his saving acts.

"What has happened in and through Jesus the Messiah has resulted in a new sort of *knowledge* commensurate with the new *world* that has now been launched."[41] At this point in Wright's argument, he turns to 2 Corinthians 5:16-17: "From this moment on, therefore, we don't regard anybody from a merely human point of view. Even if we regarded the Messiah that way, we don't do so any longer. Thus, if anyone is in the Messiah there is a new creation! Old things have gone, and look—everything has become new!"[42] This new world or new creation that is launched with the Messiah is a second epistemological shift that Paul identifies. The first was the priority of God's knowledge and the love that characterizes this knowledge. This is the priority of God's act in revealing himself to the one who would know him. The second is this shift from the old world to the new, or from the old creation to the new creation. In Martyn's essay, which Wright cites at certain points

---

when "truth" becomes a project of the church. Brian J. and Sylvia C. Keesmaat Walsh, *Colossians Remixed: Subverting the Empire* (Downers Grove, IL: InterVarsity Press, 2004), 115-31.

[40]*PFG*, 1361.

[41]Ibid.

[42]Ibid., Wright's translation.

here in *PFG* (although not appreciatively), this is the turning of the ages, an apocalyptic motif that provides the interpretive framework for understanding a series of references in 2 Corinthians.[43]

> [Paul] is saying that there are two ways of knowing, and that what separates the two is the turn of the ages, the apocalyptic event of Christ's death/resurrection. There is a way of knowing which is characteristic of the old age. In the past Paul himself knew in that way. And, since Paul now knows Christ (Phil 3.8), there must be a new way of knowing that is proper either to the new age or to that point at which the ages meet.[44]

In similar apocalyptic fashion, Wright claims that

> Paul would want to say to philosophers that wisdom is not simply a matter of learning to see, like owls, in ordinary darkness. It is a matter of the one God piercing the darkness and bringing new light, the light of new creation, and at the same time opening the eyes that have been blinded by "the god" of this world so that they can see that light.[45]

Yet just when you thought Wright would make a genuine apocalyptic turn, he qualifies this epistemological event of new creation as an "eschatological renewal."[46] What emerges in the developing discussion of Paul's epistemology in light of new creation is consistent with the way in which we have already seen him articulate the resurrection as an affirmation of the created order.[47] The new epistemological position from which Paul begins to articulate the gospel is not in any significant way newer than simply a new premise, a new starting point. From this new vantage he sees the world, the world that is and was, as it truly is. This new way of seeing "did not cancel out ordinary knowledge of the world but rather took it up within itself,"[48] employing the normal tools of logic and rhetoric to make persuasive arguments.[49]

---

[43]2 Cor 2:4-17; 3:1-8; 4:1-15; 4:1–5:10; 4:16–5.5; 5:6-10; 5:11-15; 5:16-21; 6:1-10. J. Louis Martyn, *Theological Issues in the Letters of Paul*, Studies of the New Testament and Its World (Edinburgh: T&T Clark, 1997), 92-94.
[44]Ibid., 95.
[45]*PFG*, 1363.
[46]Ibid., 1364.
[47]See above, chap. 4, 154.
[48]*PFG*, 1365.
[49]Ibid., 1366.

New creation, for Wright's Paul, is not a radically new state of affairs, a new ontological existence, but rather a "long-awaited new phase"[50] of history. "The new world, already launched with Jesus' resurrection, reaffirms the essential goodness of the old one even as it relativizes its ultimate significance." What motivates Wright's interpretive choices—beyond, of course, the exegetical insights—is the commitment to see Paul as a theologian within a particular worldview. Paul's worldview, while undergoing on the road to Damascus a "cataclysmic revelation that the crucified Jesus had been raised from the dead," nevertheless "remained, in his own mind at least, firmly on the Jewish map."[51] The new creation, if it were something ontologically other, a new *creatio ex nihilo*,[52] would introduce a discontinuity into the very fabric of history that would, if taken seriously, effectively deny and disrupt the covenant between God and his people that gave a sense of continuity to history and that was the very continuity between Paul's worldview before his conversion and his worldview after. The way that Wright chooses to describe the changes that occur with this "cataclysmic revelation" as he lays out the second volume of *PFG* reflect both the transformation and also the continuity in Paul's worldview occasioned by his apocalyptic experience as he traveled to Damascus to kill the new messianic sect. He titles the chapters in part three as follows: "The One God of Israel, Freshly Revealed," "The People of God, Freshly Reworked," and "God's Future for the World, Freshly Imagined."[53] That the new thing that God is doing can be described as "fresh" and "reworked" clearly points to the continuity that Wright is preserving in his account of Paul's theology. How this all works out and its relationship to history are clearly stated in the following lengthy section from *PFG*:

> Paul believed that *the world had been renewed in the Messiah*; that those who were themselves "in the Messiah" had also been renewed as image-bearing human beings; and that the task of such people was to live in accordance with the *new* world, rather than against *its* grain. Since for Paul, as we saw, this renewal did not mean the abolition of the good creation but rather its transformation and fulfilment (that, of course, is part of the meaning of the resur-

---

[50]Ibid., 1368.
[51]Ibid., 611-12. Cf. N. T. Wright, *What Saint Paul Really Said: Was Paul of Tarsus the Real Founder of Christianity?* (Grand Rapids: Eerdmans, 1997), 37.
[52]See Wright's comments in *Paul*, 51.
[53]*PFG*, chaps. 9, 10 and 11 respectively.

rection), and since the renewal had been *inaugurated within the ongoing flow of history* rather than arriving complete all at once, there is a natural and considerable overlap between what Paul saw as living in accordance with the new creation and what his contemporaries saw as living in accordance with the world as they knew it. For Paul, the renewal of *the existing creation* was just as important as *the renewal* of the existing creation. Without the second, one would be trapped in a world of inevitable entropy. Without the first, the idea of new creation would collapse into some kind of Gnosticism.[54]

The theological account of apocalyptic I have advocated, one that is bound by the cruciform nature of the gospel itself to rupture and, in light of the resurrection, to the newness of the new creation, is clearly at odds with Wright's account of this second shift in Paul's epistemology. For Wright's Paul, this is simply a new layer, a new phase, a new way of seeing what has always been there, and a reinterpretation of that in light of new information given through an apocalyptic event. The new creation turns out to be the same as the old. History, as the interpretation of meaningful events, gains a new premise, a "fresh hermeneutical perspective,"[55] that makes sense in a new, fresh way, of what has always been the case. The same story that has been told continues, except that now it is reworked according to a new event that happens within its grand arc. Wright may have been misread by Harink to have been advocating a progressive view of history when he described the point of view that the apocalyptic readers of Paul were particularly against as the "idea that God was quietly and steadily working his purposes out as year succeeded to year";[56] nevertheless, while there is no slow and steady arc to history, the purposes of God and his covenant faithfulness are narrated on one timeline that begins with creation and ends with the final reconciliation of heaven and earth.[57] Whatever apocalyptic event changes Paul's mind does not disrupt this timeline. Thus, when Wright refers to Paul as having an apocalyptic worldview, he means that it affirms this linear cove-

---

[54]Ibid., 1372. Italics in original.
[55]Ibid., 611.
[56]Wright, *Paul*, 51. See Harink's argument in "Time and Politics in Four Commentaries on Romans," in *Paul, Philosophy, and the Theopolitical Vision: Critical Engagements with Agamben, Badiou, Zizek, and Others*, ed. Douglas Harink (Eugene, OR: Cascade Books, 2010), 289-96. See also Harink, "The Wright Way to Read Paul," *The Christian Century*, December 1, 2009, 31-34.
[57]Cf. N. T. Wright, *Surprised by Hope* (New York: HarperOne, 2008).

nantal narrative. This is affirmed by Wright's reading of apocalyptic literature, to which we will momentarily turn.

To sum up Paul's epistemology, as articulated by Wright, Paul undergoes two shifts in his knowing that comes with the revelation of Jesus the Messiah. The first is noetic; his mind is transformed by God, who knows us, and in this "being known" Paul is loved and knows according to this new epistemology of *agapē*. The second shift is in the way Paul perceives the world. There is no ontological change here, just new information, a new premise and hermeneutic centered around the crucifixion and resurrection of the Messiah. History as a narrative changes or readjusts to this new information, but it is the same history, the same continuous narrative in which God, to be sure, does a new thing. But the new thing belongs in *this* history. To anticipate where my argument will lead, this new thing "competes" for historical space. That is, it claims the story as its own and, from a particular point on that time line, reinterprets and refigures the story so that the one trajectory is freshly reworked into a new history, a new interpretation of the old story. The new creation is a new phase, a new act in the one drama. What I have been arguing, and will do so again, is that this new creation is indeed a new history, a history *alongside* the old history. History as it is and was moves ever on toward its end, toward death. The cross is that end as the judgment on history, even history now, that moves toward the cross. History, in Christ, is history begun anew after the defeat of death, but because we still die, it is begun anew in Christ.

APOCALYPSE AND THE APOCALYPTIC LOGIC OF THE SINGULAR APOCALYPSE

We have seen that Wright calls Paul an apocalyptic thinker while affirming the strong historical continuity that I have repeatedly called into question. He does this by grounding his historical method in an account of worldviews limited to the twin hermeneutical horizons of interpreter and interpreted. By limiting his perspective in this way he forces us to see that apocalyptic refers to a genre of literature, and only to such a genre. Apocalyptic literature, upon careful examination and historical study, is not covenant defying or rejecting; it does not turn one away from history, but rather apocalyptic is precisely about history and the big question of God's faithfulness within history to his covenant. Wright argues this in *NTPG*, in *Paul* and in *Interpreters*. From the perspective that sees apocalyptic in terms of a historical rupture, a *novum* and a new creation in terms of *creatio ex nihilo*, this can be confusing. The confusion works in the other direction too. Wright does not seem to be able to understand the nuanced perspective of apocalyptic that Martyn, Beker, Gaventa, de Boer and others are advocating. And, as I have pointed out, this is often confused because the apocalyptic perspective that is being advocated by these scholars is tied to the literary concept of apocalyptic. How can we sort out this mess? The task in this section is to revisit the apocalyptic logic sketched in earlier chapters in order to move toward an account of apocalyptic theology that is theologically robust, critically engaged with the concerns of Wright and conversant with the literary genre of apocalyptic. This apocalyptic logic moves from the revelational, and so soteriological, starting point to the christological; from the christological it moves to consider creation and then the implications for a theory of history.

Revelation/Soteriology

First, the apocalyptic event, as I have already argued, is apocalyptic in terms of it being revelational. This does not stake a claim for an epistemological position except as that position is claimed by God in his gift of self-revelation, free from human methodological constraints. It is always and only a response. The only way that this can be is if the apocalyptic event is an encounter with the living God. The usual human ways of knowing remain, of course, but the apocalypse of Jesus Christ is more than knowledge *about* God; it is knowledge *of* God that is relational and salvific. In this sense we can agree fully with Wright that knowledge of God is first to be known by God, which is to be loved by God. Being loved by God is to be reconciled and made alive in relation to God. The apocalypse of Jesus Christ implies nothing other than an epistemology of love that is, in the full sense of the word, soteriological: to know God is to be saved by God. The event of the coming of Jesus the Messiah of Israel is, in this way, uniquely revelational. This means that it is not to be subsumed in an apocalyptic worldview that, through any construal of historical method, makes sense out of it, but rather this particular parousia brings its own new epistemological moorings. With respect to ancient apocalypses, the actual event of the coming of the Messiah is an apocalypse that is unlike any apocalypse that came before. Whether or not Paul knew of a body of literature called *apocalyptic* and whether or not he had an apocalyptic worldview is, at this level, irrelevant. Why? Because what was revealed in the coming of the Messiah was an actual revelation in a way that the book of 1 Enoch was not. This was God with us, the Word become flesh. This meant more than a new hermeneutical principle. If we are to call this an apocalypse—and I think we should—before moving in our interpretation to other Second Temple apocalypses, we must pause at the unique event that *this* apocalypse was and is.

Rather than enter into a tradition of apocalypses, a literary and semantic field that will capture within a worldview the events surrounding the birth, life, death, resurrection and ascension of Jesus of Nazareth, we must first see *with Paul* the surprise that this apocalypse was really present in time and space. Paul's apocalypse on the road to Damascus was an event that conditioned every other event of his life. Its totality is so striking that Paul must relate the transformation that occurs in the believer's life to that of death and resurrection, specifically the crucifixion death of Jesus himself: "I have been crucified with Christ; and it is no longer I who live, but it is Christ who lives in me" (Gal 2:19b-20a). Beverly Gaventa, writing about the singularity of the gospel, particularly as Paul articulates it in his letter to the Galatians, writes that "here the gospel's singularity comes to expression in a form that is frightening: the gospel gives life by taking it away,"[58] and that its "singularity involves the all-consuming character of the gospel."[59] Paul's life is more than reversed, Gaventa argues, but it is "actually totalized by the gospel."[60] If we take Wright's position that this text is grounded in the identification of believing Israel with the Messiah, so that the *I* "explains, vividly and dramatically, what has happened not just to Paul, not just to Peter, but to all Jews who believe in Jesus as Messiah,"[61] we still come up against the totality of the claim on Paul's identity ("and not only Paul, but all those Jews who have come to

---

[58]Beverly Roberts Gaventa, "The Singularity of the Gospel Revisited," in *Galatians and Christian Theology: Justification, the Gospel, and Ethics in Paul's Letter*, ed. Scott J. Hafemann, Mark W. Elliot, N. T. Wright and John Frederick (Grand Rapids: Baker Academic, 2014), 195.
[59]Ibid.
[60]Ibid. Cf. N. T. Wright, *Justification: God's Plan and Paul's Vision* (Downers Grove, IL: IVP Academic, 2009), 119-20, and *PFG*, 857-59.
[61]Wright, *Justification*, 120-21.

be 'in Christ'")[62] that has been reconstituted through the death and resurrection of the Messiah "into the new world which God himself is making."[63] For Paul the apocalypse of Jesus Christ is not just a paradigm changing event, but it is a transposition of the life of the believer from a position of death, identified in a saving way with Christ's crucifixion, to life, but a life located in and with the living Jesus. "And the life I now live in the flesh I live by faith in the Son of God" (Gal 2:20b). The significance of the singularity of the gospel, or the apocalypse of Jesus Christ, is grounded in its totality and relocation of the active subject "in Christ." Against a premature realized eschatology, J. Christiaan Beker helps clarify what Paul's hermeneutical intent might be with the phrases *in Christ* and *with Christ*. They "express for him both the ground of our new life in and through the death and resurrection of Christ and our continued participation in his lordship until the day of our eternal communion 'with Christ' in God's glory. Sacramental realism does not mean an ontological usurpation of premature blessedness."[64] If there is an ontological usurpation, the usurpation is Christ's alone as the firstborn of the new creation in whose life we participate through baptism.

The apocalypse of Jesus Christ was, for Paul, an event that did not simply reveal another historical event, or a new worldview, but it revealed a person: the Jesus whom Paul was persecuting addressed him personally. The particularity of this apocalypse, its singularity, requires a theological engagement that is deeper and more penetrating than form-critical analysis and worldview reconstruction. It requires the fullness of transformation that is implied by the death and resurrection of the Messiah and the ontological relocation of our identities onto the one person of the Son of God. It requires a consideration of Christology as an apocalyptic actuality.

Christology

For Christian theology, the apocalypse, that which is revealed or unveiled, is a person, the divine subject who is God with us. In the prologue of the Gospel of John, the divine Logos does the unexpected, becoming flesh and

---

[62]Ibid., 120.
[63]Ibid., 121.
[64]Beker, *Paul the Apostle*, 275.

making a dwelling within the creation among the people. This becoming flesh is the strange and unprecedented transgression of the boundary between the Creator and the created in which what had been known in the abstract, spoken by the prophets, and imagined as *logos*, or truth, or law, or life, or way, had become revealed *as* this man, the man Jesus of Nazareth. History too, like the *logos*, had become flesh. That is, the meaning of history, the story of God with his people and the story of Cain and his children, had become focused in and revealed in the life—and death—of this one man from Galilee. There is in this new becoming a refocusing of theological categories into the personal. We might say that the apocalypse has become flesh, and so when Paul receives his apocalypse, what he sees is the person, the flesh, of Jesus of Nazareth. To make the point even clearer with respect to Wright's reliance on the category of worldviews, we might say that "the worldview has become flesh"; that is, the definitive way of seeing the world has been revealed as a person, but such a personal existence challenges the ability for us to possess such a worldview, just as we cannot possess the *logos* but receive it as we receive the living Christ through the Spirit.

The argument might be returned that Christ was given to history and therefore to historical knowledge. If this is the case, then we know him like we know any other historical figure. But such an argument, while correctly identifying the reality of the incarnation, nevertheless leaves out the confession that Christ remains living; having died once, he now lives. Furthermore, it leaves out the presence of the Spirit, whose very living dynamic is not able to be possessed or contained. If anything, with respect to the historical reality of Jesus Christ, the point is focused in two places: his death and his resurrection. By his death we are reminded that the life he lived in solidarity with humanity is one that occupied this sinful body and enslaved cosmos.[65] It is a life lived as Jewish flesh and lived in faithfulness to the covenant, while oddly but authoritatively interpreting what that faithfulness looks like. But like Paul's in-

---

[65]Cf. Donald MacKinnon, *Borderlands of Theology and Other Essays* (Eugene, OR: Wipf and Stock, 2011), 81: "For the believer knows that the supremely revealing and the supremely authoritative moment in human history (the hour which the Son received from the Father) was that in which he cried upon the Cross: 'My God, my God, why hast thou forsaken me?' Thus it was made plain that in the Son of God's acceptance of the ultimate triviality and failure of human existence, whose deeps at that moment he *finally* plumbed, the whole language of perplexity, uncertainty, bewilderment, hopelessness and pain, even of God-forsakenness, was laid hold of and given a new sense by the very God himself and converted into the way of his reconciling the world unto himself."

structions for the observance of the eucharistic meal, we are to proclaim the Lord's death until he comes (1 Cor 11:26). Such a proclamation—as proclamation—is a strange thing to positively put forth in speech since it announces an absence and a weakness rather than the power of a positive presence. To couple that proclamation with "until he comes" further dispossesses the community of its proclamatory force, with the implication that the presence that fills the vacancy is to come from elsewhere. We are reminded here of the cry in the Apocalypse from the souls under the altar: "O Sovereign Lord, holy and true, how long before thou wilt judge and avenge our blood on those who dwell upon the earth?" (Rev 6:10 RSV). Whatever "until he comes" looks like in the final parousia, it is surely not something "in hand" but is "at hand";[66] the coming of the Lord is the binding of history to the future return of the one who was crucified, dead and buried. Again, like his first parousia, he comes unprecedented and, in sovereignty and freedom, in his own time. History is therefore not simply revealed in the historical events of the life of Jesus, but is revealed to be bound to his living personal existence. That our proclamation of his lordship still proclaims his death implies that this death is somehow still indicative of the direction of our lives. Indeed, as we will all die, so our only hope is that our death will be a death to be found in him, identified with his death and his end. If such is the direction toward which we live—toward the cross—then we can have hope that we will live again, like him, and we know this only in our confession of his resurrection (see Rom 6:5).

The resurrection is that faithful confession that the personal historic reality of Jesus Christ is not given over to historical knowledge but is given over to the faithful confession of his present reality as that which determines life in history. In this way it is the reality of God, the living reality in dynamic transcendent freedom, that confronts our ways of knowing and disrupts any and all final words on theological realities. This is why theology begins and ends in prayer. Any theological historiography must do the same. To not do so would be to deny the unique reality of the object of knowledge and to force the question of god into ways of knowing that are "in hand."

---

[66]Christopher Morse makes use of this distinction with reference to several verses in the New Testament where the Greek ἐγγύς is used to speak of the "at-handedness" of the Lord: Rom 13:12; Phil 4:5; Jas 5:8. Morse, *The Difference Heaven Makes: Rehearing the Gospel as News* (London: T&T Clark, 2010), 6-7.

But to know this and to see this is not a simple matter of persuasion or argument. Even though, as Wright points out, Paul has employed the techniques of rhetoric and logic to present his case, these are subsumed under the priority of God's self-revealing act on the knowing subject. The knowing subject who is reconciled in the gift of knowledge is sustained in this knowledge through the actuality of the person of Jesus Christ. While Wright acknowledges this, the christological center of this apocalypse implies more than a change of worldview; it implies, beyond this, the movement from life, to death, to new life. It is this middle term that is not adequately dealt with in Wright's account of his own or Paul's epistemology. Like von Balthasar's account of the cross as the transitional moment in the course of history that links the past and the future, Wright's account marks a similar transition. But a properly attentive understanding of the christological center of theological epistemology must, it seems, confront the rupture that is the death of Christ and the irruptive parousia that is the resurrection of Christ.

Creation

The apocalypse of Jesus Christ points beyond a new way of seeing to both a new subjectivity for the knower, what we would call salvation, but also to a new reality that is introduced as the objective reality in time and space about which history is the interpretive narration. Creation and history, the new reality of the cosmos and the way of seeing that reality, of telling its story, are both focused on the resurrection of Jesus Christ. Because this is not a resuscitation of a corpse but the resurrection from the dead, a new creation has come into existence that has become the object of theological attention. If Jesus Christ is the apocalypse, if he reveals in himself both the judgment of history and its shape, if he is the *enhistorical* embodiment of the meaning and interpretation of the time span of the cosmos, then the question of apocalyptic is shaped by the life, death, resurrection and ascension of Jesus as well as the mediation of his presence in and through the Spirit. That this is truly apocalyptic, and not something else (e.g., systematic theology), is grounded in its dependence upon the actuality of God, his living and active presence that makes it participate in the irruptive dynamic of God's own self-presentation. This is, of course, second-order reflection on that dynamic,

which is to say that this systematic reflection is simply an attempt to speak
of the apocalypse of Jesus Christ in such a way that the Christian reflection
is opened up to the priority of God's own action in theological knowledge.

Above and beyond the discussion of the new in Christ as a "fresh revelation" or "renewed creation" or "the world, freshly imagined," the apocalypse of Jesus Christ must be understood to be an unveiling of the future of
the creation in the death and resurrection of the one in and through whom
all things were created.

History

We do not need to enter into a discussion of apocalyptic worldviews at this
point precisely because the revelation that Paul received and that he passes
on is not dependent upon another worldview. It is true that the New Testament authors made use of the Old Testament, its images, stories, tropes
and so on, but it is also true that the apocalypse of Jesus Christ was an
anomaly; it was a "fracture" in the course of history that relativized all that
would come before it and all that would come after.[67] We will turn to this
argument in a moment. One does not enter into a communicative act, responding to an apocalyptic event, without borrowing or using the idioms
and language of a tradition. Paul is, as are all people, a historical being. His
identity is a link between past and present, held together by stable contexts
of meaning: language, tradition, story, worldview and so forth.[68] Nevertheless, the event of incarnation and the corresponding revelation of that
event introduces a fracture into Paul's stable identity. To the extent that that
new event can and will be taken up into the tradition and linguistic world
of a stable identity, it will become part of a continual history. Yet to the
extent that an event brings its own truth, its own dynamic of interruption
and irruption, it demands to be taken on its own terms, even if those words
that are its own terms are the words of an older world or worldview. One

---

[67]The language of *fracture* is borrowed from the book of the same name by Roy A. Harrisville:
Fracture: The Cross as Irreconcilable in the Language and Thought of the Biblical Writers (Grand
Rapids: Eerdmans, 2006).

[68]Here I had in mind Gerhard Ebeling's lectures on the problem of historicity and tradition: *The
Problem of Historicity in the Church and Its Proclamation*, trans. Grover Foley (Philadelphia:
Fortress Press, 1967).

cannot call Paul's gospel of the apocalypse of Jesus Christ an apocalypse without attending to the irruptive dynamic, and one cannot attend to this dynamic by simply attending to Second Temple apocalypses. Not only is it a new event, in the full sense of a *novum*, but it is God with us, the living God in hypostatic union with humanity, and it is humanity in a divinely initiated hypostatic union with the living God. This one, singular apocalypse never becomes part of a worldview because it is always irruptive and disruptive to any and every worldview. This is so because it is the apocalypse of the living and free God. The God of Israel, to be sure, but the God of Israel in apocalyptic, electing grace, *once again and like never before!*

Harrisville's *Fracture* takes us back to the biblical account of the crucifixion and its presence in the New Testament to argue that it functions there as a distinct rupture, an impossibility in any of the received or given traditions into which it "arrived":

> Despite the New Testament writer's appropriation of concepts, metaphors, analogies, and comparisons from the world around them, the attempt to derive the New Testament in unilinear fashion from the Old Testament, together with intertestamental Jewish literature, whether enriched by Hellenistic elements or not—or to derive it from oriental, pagan tradition—contradicts the nature of the revolution effected by the "anomaly" of the death of the Messiah, Jesus.[69]

The language of *anomaly* directs us to the account of scientific revolutions in the work of Thomas Kuhn; indeed, Harrisville is borrowing this language from Kuhn.[70] The revolution in thought that comes with the crucifixion of the Messiah upsets the old paradigm and offers a new perspective that, while not derived from the old paradigm, nevertheless incorporates the old data and the troublesome anomaly into a new theory, one that has more and better explanatory power to deal with the anomaly. If this new way of seeing is simply an epistemological revolution, a sudden new way of seeing that, although surprising, nevertheless makes sense of the past and settles hermeneutical issues in a way that was never anticipated until the revolution, it is just a shift in worldviews and remains bound to the immanence that confines the historical method of Wright's epistemology. Transcendence is not

---

[69]Harrisville, *Fracture*, 62.
[70]Thomas S. Kuhn, *The Structure of Scientific Revolutions* (Chicago: University of Chicago Press, 1998).

part of the paradigm. If it were it would bring its own unsettling presence in a way that could never be a resolved anomaly. This sort of unsettling presence is exactly that which Harrisville attributes to the crucifixion by pointing out that there is no "orthodoxy" regarding the crucifixion and the mechanism by which it functions as atonement. Consider the following paragraph from a Kuhnian perspective:

> The biblical authors use no uniform terminology to document their reaction to the total restructuring of their world that results from their encounter with a suffering, dying Christ. There is no "orthodox" view of the meaning of Jesus' death. For example, over against the characteristic narrative style of the Gospels and Acts, the Epistles and Apocalypse "metaphorize" the death of Jesus, offering representations in a profusion that defies attempts to arrive at a univocal meaning.[71]

The anomaly, the death of the Messiah, is not "theorized." Even as trinitarian theology is developed by the church fathers and an "orthodoxy" developed that comes to provide the boundaries of faithful speech about God, no such orthodoxy emerges regarding the atonement or the death of Jesus. This event is not incorporated into a new paradigm with explanatory power. Rather, it remains an enigma and an anomaly even as it is alluded to and upheld as that event around which the Christian faith hinges. The multiplicity of theories (penal substitution, *Christus victor*, moral influence, etc.) "does not involve disorder or self-contradiction; in fact, discomfort arises only when a single idea to which even God is subject is involved."[72]

Therefore, it is important to maintain the faithful disbelief that the revolution that occurs with the apocalypse of Jesus Christ is not simply a new paradigm or, in Wright's terms, a new worldview.[73] It is not simply a new way of seeing what was always the case. It is in a deeper sense a fracture in the continuum of history, a break, a fissure in which the light breaks through, but signals the beginning of a new history, a new way of being in time that is not constrained by the logic and ontological reality of death, but is determined by a logic and ontology of life. From the side of history, the old aeon

---

[71]Harrisville, *Fracture*, 56.
[72]Ibid., 56-57.
[73]The language of *faithful disbelief* is from Christopher Morse, *Not Every Spirit: A Dogmatics of Christian Disbelief*, 2nd ed. (New York: T&T Clark, 2009).

or old creation, this is an apocalyptic logic, for in order for it to do the work of salvation it must break into "this present darkness" (Eph 6:12) and expose the end of history. But in breaking into this darkness, the apocalypse of Jesus opens up the possibility for an alternative history, a history in excess, that is located *en Christo*.[74]

The language of excess as applied to history is clearly expressed by Nathan Kerr, interpreting John Howard Yoder's account of the "dominion of God over history":[75]

> What I would like to emphasise here is the way in which for Yoder the *via crucis* is Christ's victory as precisely a kind of "historical failure." By renouncing the claim to control history, Christ puts himself in the most terrifyingly contingent position of all: as one whose life can only now have "meaning" as an event of God's apocalyptic action from beyond history. And yet, as such, Christ is in the most gloriously free position of all: free to love as God, with utter self-abandon, without concern for historical "effectiveness" or "responsibility," and free to live according to the "more" that God is always doing *in* history as *beyond* what "the historical" as such makes possible.[76]

This history, in this sense, grounded for its interpretive force in the logic of the contingency of Jesus's life and death, does not compete with history for hermeneutical space. The history that is located *en Christo* is a history that does not replace, nor interpret anew, the history in which we find ourselves under the power of sin and death. Or, rather, what interpretation it does provide is that found in the death of the Messiah. The end of history is death. This is the ontological reality of the cosmos in time: death reigns. The cross of Jesus unveils the futility of the forward movement of historical forces under the reign of sin and death. The new life that has been revealed in the resurrection of Jesus is the new life of the new Adam, the firstborn from the dead. Yet this life is not competitive with the lives we live now because it is a life that is given *on the other side of the grave*. That it encroaches upon us now is simply to say that it robs death now of its force to

---

[74]Cf. Beker, *Paul the Apostle*, 272-302.

[75]John Howard Yoder, *The Politics of Jesus: Vicit Agnus Noster*, 2nd ed. (Grand Rapids: Eerdmans, 1994), 236.

[76]Nathan R. Kerr, *Christ, History and Apocalyptic: The Politics of Christian Mission* (Eugene, OR: Cascade Books, 2009), 151-52. Internal quote is from Yoder, *The Politics of Jesus*, 236. Italics in original.

determine the way in which we live our lives; we are "free to live according to the 'more' that God is always doing *in* history as *beyond* what 'the historical' as such makes possible."[77]

Again, interpreting Yoder, Kerr argues that to say

> history itself is a *via crucis*, is to say in some sense that Christ's lordship is yet still—and eternally "is"—a gift to be received from the future, as his own life is yet still to be given—and made present—to us in our very own cruciformity in history with the Lamb who was slain.[78]

All of this is against the notion that history is somehow the same story with just a new gloss that is reinterpreted and reimagined afresh in the light of the worldview gained with the coming of Jesus. History is ontologically limited by the finality of death. There is no historical trajectory that overcomes this limitation except through death itself, so that the history that is determined by the resurrection is not the history that continues on toward its end. To say that this new history is present in this time and space is to affirm that its presence is not anything like a new act in the same drama, but is an excessive history that does not compete for hermeneutical space.

I take it that when Wright talks about history and the apocalyptic theology of Paul he is committed to a certain continuity to that narrative that begins with, at least, the covenant of Abraham, develops in a mostly negative direction, and sees a radical adjustment in the arrival of the Messiah and his proclamation of the kingdom. The articulation of history that I am presenting narrates the same way as Wright, but ends at the cross. The continuing history that characterizes our lives in the present is the same history, moving as it does toward the end of history, the cross. The way that our lives are characterized in history, in Christ, is not ahistorical, but is rather surrendered to the hermeneutical role that death plays in this history, and surrendered to the hermeneutical role that resurrection plays. This latter hermeneutic reads history not as something to be narrated anew but as something given over to the coming of God, as something determined, as it were, apocalyptically.

---

[77]Kerr, *Christ, History and Apocalyptic*, 152.
[78]Ibid., 153.

THE APOCALYPSE OF JESUS CHRIST AS AN APOCALYPSE

Once we have seen that the apocalypse of Jesus Christ is a singular apocalypse that brings its own interpretive context, we can step back and ask in what way this apocalypse is also like other apocalypses. Does it affirm the covenant of Abraham? Does it affirm history as the arena of God's activity? Does it provide an account of the end of history? This topic is, admittedly, huge. The great question regarding apocalyptic and Christian theology is the question of history. Does apocalyptic as a theological theme sweep off the stage all that has come before so that the new that arrives from the transcendent realm of God's heaven is so discontinuous with what has come before that the Christian faith is de-Judaized and dehistoricized? Does apocalyptic theology instead center itself in modern philosophical questioning that molds the biblical material into a form designed to resolve problems that are wholly unrelated to the real problems that the Bible was ever intending to address?[79] The answer is in the singular nature of the apocalypse of Jesus Christ, its absolute uniqueness.

Jesus Christ has, in all senses of the language of history, come to human historical existence, entered its contingency and died. This is the apocalypse of Jesus Christ that has played itself out within time and space, locatable geographically and politically, culturally and religiously, and, most definitely, miss-able. To the extent that apocalyptic literature is concerned with the political and historic, and not a retreat from them into a fanciful heavenly realm, the apocalypse of Jesus Christ is clearly apocalyptic. "From each apocalyptic discourse emerged a program of radical, embodied resistance rooted in covenant theology and shaped by models from Israel's scriptures as well as new revelatory paradigms."[80] If Portier-Young is right, then the apocalypse of Jesus Christ can be understood in a similar way, as an embodied revelation of God himself that presented an alternative kingdom to the kingdom of Caesar, one that is not particularly competitive with Caesar's except as a kingdom that undermines, fundamentally, the assumptions upon which it is built.[81] Again, if the apocalypse of Jesus Christ is grounded in the freedom of

---

[79]This is, perhaps, a blending together of the concerns of Wright and, before him, Klaus Koch.

[80]Portier-Young, *Apocalypse Against Empire*, xxiii. Here Portier-Young is specifically referencing Daniel, the Apocalypse of Weeks and the Book of Dreams.

[81]Cf. Wright's account of Onesimus and Philemon at the beginning of *PFG*.

God to elect, the same God who has elected Israel, making a covenant with Abraham, then there is no reason to dismiss the covenant of Abraham or covenant theology, but rather to see in the freedom of God that continuity that is required to make sense of Israel's long history. If we look specifically to the apocalypse of Jesus Christ for this covenant theology, as we should, we see that this long history is faithfully fulfilled in the life and death of the Messiah. This covenant history has come to an end—*in the Messiah.* That the Messiah lives, having been raised from the dead, means that the covenant lives too, only this covenant history is a new history, a new creation, found in the life of the Messiah and given to the world in the sending of the Spirit. The only reason to think that the singular apocalypse of Jesus Christ, articulated as I have done so according to the discontinuity of death and resurrection, is a rejection of history, or of the covenant, is if one is committed to a linear account of history that is wed to an equally linear account of time. In such an account the new history would overlap and reinterpret where the old left off, and a new existence would emerge. In this case, then the apocalypse of Jesus Christ as rupture would, indeed, be the breaking off of the history of the covenant. Yet, in the nonlinear account I am offering, the account that sees, in baptism, the death that is before us as the death that is in Christ's crucifixion, the history of Israel continues to move toward her recognition of the Messiah (cf. Rom 11:25-36). Because history is an interpretive exercise and not ontological essence, the end of history *can* be articulated as that which happens at the cross. Were one to object, echoing the words of Bultmann who rightly pointed out that "history did not come to an end, and, as every schoolboy knows, it will continue to run its course,"[82] we might reply, "Yes, it did, only you expected something quite different."

Richard Hays has characterized the connection between the apocalyptic theologians and apocalypses as that of analogy.[83] The theological positions of apocalyptic theology line up with certain key themes in apocalypses, but they don't derive from them. Hays refers to this as a shared DNA.[84] Rather, we might say that the apocalypse of Jesus Christ, in its singularity, lines up

---

[82]Hans Werner Bartsch, ed., *Kerygma and Myth: A Theological Debate* (New York: Harper and Row, 1961), 5.

[83]Richard B. Hays, "Apocalyptic *Poiēsis* in Galatians: Paternity, Passion, and Participation," in Hafemann et al., *Galatians and Christian Theology*, 202-3.

[84]Ibid., 203.

with these themes but reinterprets them around its own singularity. In dialectic fashion, the revelation of God's self makes use of human language and concepts—even worldviews—in order to make known who this God is. Nevertheless, in the unveiling, in the use of apocalyptic images and language, the reality of God remains veiled. The point is that one does not move from the apocalyptic worldview to the apocalypse of Jesus Christ without expecting that worldview to be shown in significant ways to be part of the veiling of God. One cannot dismiss this dialectical theology as too esoteric if one takes seriously the reality of God. Again, it is the reality of God—that this is God revealed in the apocalypse of Jesus Christ—that forces our thinking to stretch to the point of requiring noetic restructuring, a *metanoia*, that is finally given over to God's agency.

THE QUESTION OF ISRAEL

If Jesus is Israel's Messiah, as the church must confess, then the question of unbelieving Israel raises important theological questions. These questions were somewhat sidelined until the horrors of the last century forced the church to confront the murderous ugliness of anti-Semitism. It is as Johann Baptist Metz says: "We find there another 'interruption' of theology's stream of ideas. It is concerned with the name 'Auschwitz.' I am convinced that this makes every Christian theology that does not want to be unveiled as a latter-day platonism or a pure idealism into a 'post-Auschwitz theology.'"[85] Doing theology or biblical studies, especially Pauline studies, "post-Auschwitz" means that the question of Israel is a politically, morally and emotionally charged issue. The accusation of supersessionism lands on this field of study in such a way that it quickly turns into a battlefield because of its close association to the (perhaps) more devastating charge of anti-Semitism. This is the charged theological minefield into which I now take my arguments. I will try and tread carefully.[86]

---

[85]Ekkehard Schuster and Reinhold Boschert-Kimmig, *Hope Against Hope: Johann Baptist Metz and Elie Wiesel Speak Out on the Holocaust*, trans. J. Matthew Ashley (New York: Paulist Press, 1999), 13.

[86]I am especially mindful of the disagreement between Douglas Harink and Wright over this very issue. Harink, in a chapter on Israel in *Paul Among the Postliberals*, wrote that "the supersessionist interpretation of Paul, of which Wright is one of the most able, unapologetic, and forceful contemporary proponents, is not only less than persuasive, but also seriously damaging to a proper and critically important Christian theology of Israel." Harink, *Paul Among the Post-*

The question of Israel is closely bound to the way in which we understand the relationship between history and the apocalypse of Jesus Christ. If the apocalypse of Jesus Christ is subsumed within the category of covenant, as it is in Wright's account, then the history of the Messiah is a history that competes with Israel's own story as long as Israel refuses to believe that Jesus is the Messiah. When Jesus comes, Wright points out, it is as the fulfillment of the promise made to Israel. "It would be extremely odd if, in a group whose whole existence depended on being the people of a promise-making God, nobody was ever allowed to claim that the promises had been fulfilled for fear of being called 'supersessionist.'"[87] Wright acknowledges this interpretation to be a form of supersessionsim, although with enough qualifications that the sting of the term is significantly reduced if not eliminated altogether.[88]

> This is the claim that the creator God has acted at last, in surprising but prophecy-fulfilling ways, to launch his renewed covenant, to call a new people who are emphatically in continuity with Abraham, Isaac and Jacob, to pour out his spirit afresh upon them, to enable them to keep Torah in the new way he had always envisaged and to assure them that he and his angels were present with them in their worship (even though they were not in the Jerusalem temple) and that their united community was to be seen as the real focal point of "Israel."[89]

On the other hand, Wright interprets the implications of the apocalyptic perspective to be a "sweeping supersessionism":

> This is the sweeping claim, in line with a certain style of post-Barthian (and perhaps "postliberal") theology, that what happened in Jesus Christ constituted such radical inbreaking or "invasion" into the world that it rendered redundant anything and everything that had gone before—particularly anything that looked like "religion," not least "covenantal religion." This view is unlike "hard supersessionism" because it denies that there is any historical continuity at all: it isn't that "Israel" has "turned into the church," but rather

---

liberals, 184. Wright, who has generally avoided direct engagement with Harink, nevertheless has described Harink as one who has been "eager to sign up to Martyn's vision of 'apocalyptic' theory," which Wright harshly criticizes as being a "sweeping supersessionism" and noting the irony (Wright, *PFG*, 808n108). See also Douglas Harink, "Paul and Israel: An Apocalyptic Reading," *Pro Ecclesia* 14, no. 4 (Fall 2007): 359-80.

[87]*PFG*, 810.

[88]Ibid., 809-15.

[89]Ibid., 809.

that Israel, and everything else prior to the apocalyptic announcement of the gospel, has been swept aside by the fresh revelation.[90]

Perhaps the sage advice of Richard Hays ought to be heeded at this point: "Pauline interpreters ought to quit lobbing the accusation of 'supersessionsim' at one another."[91] By entering this already contentious discussion I am not trying to make the claim that Wright's theology and his interpretation of Paul are supersessionist in any way that he does not claim for himself; compared to other options out there, I do not think they are particularly troubling in this way. My intent is simply to show in what way the apocalyptic theology that I am advocating is decidedly *not* supersessionist—perhaps even less so than the "Jewish supersessionism" of Wright.[92] Why this is the case I will try to show in series of claims gathered from the previous arguments I have made and focused here to show with some measure of clarity the way this pays off with respect to the question of Israel. I have numbered them as if they were a series of theses to make them easier to follow.

1. An apocalyptic theology is grounded in the confession that the God who, in freedom, elected Israel has been and will be faithful to that election, and in a definitive way has been faithful to that covenant by acting to save Israel.

2. This saving act is unprecedented, new and not in any way grounded in the necessity of historical continuity. The apocalypse of Jesus Christ comes to history, enters it, "takes it up" and ends it. Douglas Harink is correct to say that "the continuity rests in God's action, not in the continuous forward 'movement' of history. God's apocalyptic action cannot contradict God's electing action."[93] So far this is consistent with Wright's emphasis on the promise-fulfilling God of Israel. But that this promise is fulfilled by the cross goes beyond what could be seen as a simple promise-fulfillment sequence. Roy Harrisville has drawn our attention to this aspect of the fulfillment of the promise, and is worth quoting at length:

> What was new in the Christian community was its exclusive reference to the suffering and death of Jesus of Nazareth as the point of hermeneutical

---

[90]Ibid., 807.
[91]Quoted in Gaventa, "Character of God's Faithfulness," 79n15. Original in Hays, "Apocalyptic *Poiēsis* in Galatians," 216.
[92]This is Wright's own term. Wright, *PFG*, 809.
[93]Harink, *Paul Among the Postliberals*, 179n34.

departure. Thus, as Hans Weder says, by virtue of its relationship to the cross, a truth was attached to the biblical word that it did not initially possess. This attachment renders the relationship between cross and scripture more than dialectical; rather, the relationship is *diastatic*. The fulfillment does not automatically follow from the promise; for the premise cannot be what it is, cannot emerge as promise, without first being shattered, or fractured. "Scripture fulfillment" is thus far too facile an expression for New Testament interpretation of the event of Christ. In fact, there would never have been a "scandal" if that event had been seen as making one, two, or even three Old Testament predictions come true. . . . Nothing in Paul's method distanced it from that of his contemporaries. It was the incessant emphasis on the singular occurrence of the crucifixion of one lone victim and the submission to it of all the language and conceptuality adhering to Israel's hope that fixed the gulf.[94]

It is not only the unprecedented nature of the cross that signals the fracture or rupture in history, but, more than that, it is that this Messiah is God with us, and that the cross is the death of God with us. There is no historical continuity that makes sense of this. This is why this is the end of history.

3. That the end of history is not decisively a past event means that the end of history is still before us. That the end of history is still before us is derived from at least three facts. First, the *enhypostatic* movement of Christ to take humanity in and to himself implies the corollary *enhistoric* movement in which human history is given hermeneutical shape by the life and death of Christ. Second, Christian baptism orients the life of the disciple toward her own death and identifies that death with the cross. That death remains before us suggests that the cross remains, in an important sense, before us as well. Third, the Christian community is told by Paul, in his instructions regarding the eucharistic meal, that the church "proclaim[s] the Lord's death until he comes" (1 Cor 11:26b RSV). Given the first two points, this proclamation takes on the added dimension of declaring the shape of history itself. The movement toward the cross only ends when he comes.

4. That the end of history remains before us means that the time lived now, to the extent that is is conditioned by the apocalypse of Jesus Christ, is ex-

---

[94]Harrisville, *Fracture*, 272. Harrisville references Hans Weder, *Das Kreuz Jesu* (Götingen: Vandenhoeck & Ruprecht, 1981), 145.

cessive history, noncompetitive with present historical forces.[95] This points to the tension that exists with those, like Wright, who want to reject a progressive view of history, and yet still maintain a "soft-progressivism" such that our work in history might be seen as "building for the Kingdom" but not "building the Kingdom."[96] Somehow continuity must be maintained, but the commitment to continuity, once it acknowledges the problem with progressivism, must find a way to make human works endure into the future kingdom. The excessive nature of the history of the new creation, in Christ, is positively understood as the cruciform nature of Christian discipleship, freed from the constraining logic of historical forces that attempt, through coercion, to resist the inevitability of death. Christian discipleship on the way to the cross is free from this logic of death because in and through the cross death has been swallowed up. It has been defeated, and Christians join the victory of Christ over death in the identification of their deaths with his death. Our future deaths are therefore located with Christ at the cross; they are there with him in the past but still yet to come. Having been united with him in death, through baptism, "we shall certainly be united with him in a resurrection like his" (Rom 6:5 RSV). Thus, the limiting logic of death has been undone, and we are free to love radically and unconditionally here and now as we move forward in history toward the cross.

5. This life here and now in history is grounded in the present only in and through lives that engage the world through the Spirit in the Son. Having been delivered in this way from the power of history in darkness and death, we are "transferred . . . to the kingdom of his beloved Son, in whom we have redemption, the forgiveness of sins" (Col 1:13-14 RSV). Rather than move us away from this world and even this history, the claim that history is ended at the cross is a claim regarding the quality of the life lived in history and certainly not a claim that might in any way excuse the baptized from a fully embodied life in the world; there is no other world. What there is is the new creation, a new ontological reality in the resurrected life of the Son. It is ontological because in Christ's ongoing life he is free from the ontological

---

[95]By *historical forces* I mean the relationship between the interpretive power of historical narrative and the progressive movement of human history, irrespective of whether or not that progress is morally positive, negative or neutral.

[96]Wright, *Surprised by Hope*, 218-44.

limit of death. We do not share that ontological reality now except as we participate in that identity through the Spirit. Ontologically, our lives are here, before death, before the cross and bound to the history that moves toward death. The new creation, of which Christ is the firstborn from the dead (Col 1:18) and in which we participate being made new in Christ—"for we are his workmanship, created in Christ Jesus for good works" (Eph 2:10 RSV)—is that reality that is always bound to the way in which Christ gives himself to the world.

How does this all pay off for the question of supersessionism? First, the history in which we find ourselves, the history that moves toward the cross, is the history in which Israel remains the definitive people of God. There is no replacement because there is no history that does not end at the death of the Messiah. The church participates in the singular peoplehood of Israel as those who have been grafted into the covenant of Abraham, but not as a natural branch; rather the Gentile church is a foreign, wild branch (Rom 11:17). Gentile membership in this covenant, through the gift of the Spirit, is a gracious membership grounded in the election of Israel, not the replacement of Israel. Second, that Christian life is a life in the Spirit means that it is the Spirit of God who is the life animating our dry bones. Having borne witness to the resurrection, to the life breathed back into one Israelite, the believing and witnessing church looks to Israel as the prophet Ezekiel looked upon the valley of dry bones (Ezek 37:1-14), but we look as ones who have hope that our bones will one day live because we have seen his bones live. We are not those who have been given the flesh already—except in the Spirit. And it is the Spirit who will make these bones—all these bones—live.

But the history of the covenant is the history of this valley of dry bones. The continuity is only a continuity of the word of God and the action of the Spirit. "Israel," Michael Welker writes,

> is not only threatened, lost, and despairing. It is not even present. It has become unrecognisable. It is no longer even capable of a relation with itself. It is beyond sorrow, complaint, and horror. The prophet led by God in the Spirit perceives the dimensions of the catastrophe and the dimensions of the hopelessness. According to the vision, Israel is so lost, so destroyed, that it can no longer even perceive and lament its own downfall. The abyss of death,

chaos, becomes visible. But with this it also becomes possible to recognise that if Israel is still capable of lament, it is still given space for renewal.[97]

This is the history that continues to play itself out. This is the history that matters: the history of Israel as it is still given space for renewal, that "they too may now receive mercy" (Rom 11:31b).

> At God's behest [the prophet] addresses the Spirit directly. He induces the Spirit to become present and active. The Spirit—difficult to grasp, coming from all four winds—becomes manifest by giving life to the Israelites who find themselves between death and life. Led in the Spirit, the prophet can directly address the Spirit, inducing the Spirit to engage in life-creating action and thus to become knowable.[98]

There is something to this picture from Ezekiel that is important for the present understanding of the Gentile relationship to Israel in this history that is a history of dry bones. The Gentiles are grafted into this covenant that locates us, in our death, with this place of death, a place of death that Christ took upon himself. He entered this valley, became one of the dead, and lamented from that place, "My God, my God, why have you forsaken me?" (Mt 27:46b). It is only from the depths of this lament, uttered by God the Son, in the face of the abyss, that the rupture in history opens up to something truly new, even as the old bones continue to rattle in the valley of history. "The Spirit comes upon them from outside in a way that is not at their disposition. Through this process they are returned to spontaneity and to vitality: 'They became alive and stood up.'"[99] Such is the hope of resurrection, a hope that is ever before us, but seen already in the resurrection of the Messiah. History, our history, is a history in the valley of dry bones. And it is Israel's valley.

The importance of this sort of nonsupersessionist reading of history is that it rejects the positive replacement of the people of God, even in the "Jewish supersessionism" of Wright with a cruciform self-emptying movement into the world in the power of the Spirit of God. I want to end this section with a brief illustration of what this might look like in our present time given the long history of colonialism by Western Christendom.

---

[97]Michael Welker, *God the Spirit*, trans. John F. Hoffmeyer (Minneapolis: Fortress Press, 1994), 179.
[98]Ibid., 180.
[99]Ibid.

Willie James Jennings, in his book *The Christian Imagination: Theology and the Origins of Race,* has shown how the supersessionism of the church not only contributed to anti-Semitism in the Christian West, but fueled the colonialist project of multiple Christian empires, as each learned to see themselves in the place of Israel. Returning the church to an understanding of its place in the world as a Gentile place, guests by God's grace in the covenant of Abraham, would, Jennings argues, disarm the colonial impulse and open the way for the (Gentile) church to begin to see itself as having occupied a place that it has no rightful claim to occupy. Essential, therefore, for his argument is the theological centrality of Israel and the covenant God made with Abraham. Within this argument, Jennings articulates an account of the "counterhegemonic reality" that is the coming of the Spirit at Pentecost.[100] The Spirit does not come to the disciple community in any sort of competitive mode whereby the new church finds itself acquiring an identity in conflict with other identities. Rather, as a miracle of tongues, rather than of hearing, the disciples speak the language of the other: "The speaking of another's language signifies a life lived in submersion and in submission to another's cultural realities."[101] While this new event takes place within the land and culture of Israel, it has wider implications that only begin to be known as the disciples are moved by the Spirit in mission toward Gentiles. Jennings argues that Acts 10, 11 and 15 narrate the movement of this communion in the Spirit outward into the cultural lives of the other, which is the enacting of God's "boundary-shattering love between strangers and enemies. The election of Jesus turns Israel's election outward."[102] The significance of Gentile inclusion in the covenant of Abraham is not found in some narrated account of the history of the covenant, but rather in the surprising event that the Gentiles have also received the Spirit of God. "God was also making real the implications of Gentile election: They stood in the presence of Israel and called back to them a sharing in communion with the God of Jesus in the Spirit. The one communion in the Spirit illumines the obvious for Peter: 'Can anyone withhold

---

[100]Willie James Jennings, *The Christian Imagination: Theology and the Origins of Race* (New Haven: Yale University Press, 2010), 266.
[101]Ibid.
[102]Ibid., 267.

the water for baptising these people who have received the Holy Spirit just as we have?' (Acts 10.47)."[103]

Jennings signals the apocalyptic when, commenting on this episode with Peter at Cornelius's house, he writes,

> Now Peter, in accordance with the work of the Spirit, received the invitation from the Gentiles "to stay [with them] for several days" (Acts 10:48). This invitation, this simple gesture, symbolised a trajectory of new belonging enacted by the Spirit. Yet none of this was of Peter's own accord. This event was fundamentally counterhegemonic, holding within itself the potential to reorder the world. If a centurion and his household could be drawn into a new circle of belonging, then its implication for challenging the claims of the Roman state were revolutionary. If Israel could be drawn into a new circle of belonging, then the implications for how it might envision its renewal and restoration were equally revolutionary. If a world caught in the unrelenting exchange system of violence was to be overcome, then here was the very means God would use to overcome violence—by the introduction of a new reality of belonging that drew together different peoples into a way of life that intercepted ancient bonds and redrew them around the body of Jesus and in the power of the Spirit.[104]

Far from being an ahistorical life, the life of the Christian community is fundamentally counterhegemonic. We do not narrate a counterhistory, or counternarrative; rather we enter those histories or narratives as what they are—histories limited by death. In this counterhegemonic historical life, the way is opened up for a positive account of Christian life that lives in the power of the Spirit toward the cross, free from the constraining logic of death. For now it is enough to conclude that the apocalypse of Jesus Christ wipes nothing off the table, least of all the history of the covenant, but Christ enters history only to take history's end and make it his own, thus ending history before its time. Life in the meantime is life in the Spirit, "a trajectory of new belonging enacted by the Spirit."

CONCLUSION

Klaus Koch, at the end of his important book on apocalyptic, *The Rediscovery of Apocalyptic* (*Ratlos ver der Apocalyptic*), writes,

---

[103]Ibid., 268-69.
[104]Ibid., 269.

New Testament exegesis will not be able to avoid the theme [apocalyptic] because the question of the historical Jesus demands a clear and concrete historical answer. We would probably not be wrong in the impression that, if
theology wants still to be taken seriously by contemporary man, its christological statements will have to be more precise. But where is this precision to
come from if not from historical research?[105]

What I have tried to show is that the confidence that Koch, and with him,
Wright, has placed in historical research with respect to the question of Jesus,
by virtue of the singular apocalyptic event that was the parousia of Jesus
Christ, is in need of significant qualification. Historical research into apocalyptic literature permits scholars to understand apocalyptic literature, but
not the singular apocalypse of Jesus Christ. This is because this apocalypse
is absolutely unique with respect to any and all worldviews to which it comes.
This "coming" brings with it the necessary condition for its recognition, a
condition that is, from the human subject's perspective, equivalent of a
death and rebirth. The condition to see this is nothing less than salvation.
But the quality of life once located in Christ is conditioned both by the
movement of historical life toward death, and the freedom of that life from
the logic of death, by the hope that comes in and through the gift of the
Spirit. Because this is a life in Christ, through the Spirit, it does not offer a
history competitive with the history of death; rather it disarms that history
as it lives in the freedom of the life of the resurrected Lord.

---

[105]Koch, *Rediscovery of Apocalyptic*, 130. Italics in original. Wright points out that this title in German
translates as "clueless in the face of apocalyptic." Perhaps "baffled" is a kinder rendering?

7

Conclusion

THE QUESTION OF HISTORY is the question of eschatology. It is not only a question of the past, but a question of the future and the human relationship to the forward movement of history in time. By affirming an account of the end of history, an end that somewhat paradoxically comes in the middle of history, we raise the question of hope: If history is ended at the cross in the sense that the telos of human historical meaning is revealed in the crucifixion of the Son of God, what then are we left to do with respect to the future direction of history? Is there no hope? Does the long arc of history *not* bend in the direction of justice? Is there any reason to work to make things better? Are we left with a pessimism that defunds action for social justice? Is liberation *not* a theological theme?

From the outset the issue has been the reality of God and the theoretical implications of that reality for the work of historiography—historiography, that is, in the service of theology. A theology of historiography, as I have argued, is not divorced from a theology of history because historiography must assume a narrative, a story, in order to make sense of historical "data." Bare facts do not exist outside of the complex webs of human interpretation. The stories that make up history are never metaphysically or theologically neutral. Therefore, it is methodologically dishonest not to begin with a theology of history, even if that theology is informed to a large extent by historical events. There is no way out of this circularity, nor should there be. But there is a way *into* this circularity. This is what is referred to (perhaps ambiguously) as the "apocalyptic event," the breaking-in from outside that both sets anew the agenda for the story and also maintains at all times a transcendent corrective/critique. This somewhat abstract and theoretical way of speaking of the theology of history is only a conceptualization of the concrete reality of the incarnation and the relationship of the Father's action in sending the Son, becoming Jesus of Nazareth, living, bearing witness to the kingdom, dying, rising and ascending. This is the reality of God that is given in history but cannot be contained by any one prior telling of history, except to say that the final meaning of all history is revealed in the life, death and resurrection of this same Jesus of Nazareth.

It is the death of Jesus that ends history. This is not history in the sense that calls to mind concrete "historical" reality: the world of actual happenings in time and space. Time did not stop at the crucifixion. It is history in the sense that history has a direction, a trajectory, a narrative that makes sense of all things; it is history in the sense that history has meaning in the relationship and continuity of human actions and intentions. History is the story that humans tell of the relationship through time of human events, and it is a story that imagines both a past and a future. To the extent that that future is taken up in the incarnation, as the Son *enhypostatically* takes up the life of Jesus of Nazareth as his life and so takes up this particular history as his history, it is a future that necessarily conforms to the singular event that is Jesus' cross and resurrection.

If this is the case—and I have sought to present a coherent case for recognizing that this is indeed so—then the historiographical practice, for the Christian historian, is determined by this end; the historian cannot rule out the question of Jesus' identity as the Son, the second person of the triune Godhead. This is the interpretive key to the whole story. History and theology are thus integrally connected. For Wright to rule out the theological claim until the history has been done is to be disingenuous with respect to this relationship. His attempt to include theology in the conversation as a part of the worldview of both the subject and object of historical investigation—the historian and the historical object—is helpful but neglects the reality of God, the actual personal agency of the one who holds history in his hands. To borrow his analogy of the prodigal son and the older brother, in Wright's account it is the Father who is left out of the picture. Rather, the historian and the theologian are reconciled, peacefully, in the loving embrace of the Father. For the methodological question of the historian, this means that naturalistic accounts will never do. For the theologian, this means that theology is never finished, for theology is always engaged in thoughtful reflection on the continuation of a new history located in the continuing personal existence of Jesus, the risen and ascended Lord. For both, the reality of God means that doxology and prayer are the ground out of which each practice springs. Unsettled from their naturalistic soil, the historian and the theologian find themselves replanted in the living soil of the triune God's new creation, and therefore new history.

Indeed, there is hope. It is a hope of liberation and justice. But it is a hope that is also cruciform and so realistic about the trajectory of history. But in this cruciformity it is open to the reality of God's action in the midst of a fallen and falling world. As history arcs to the cross, the good news is that in the darkest hour that arc will break free—it has broken free—into a world made new, into the new creation that lives according to the life of the Lamb who was slain.

Bibliography

Balthasar, Hans Urs von. *A Theology of History*. San Francisco: Ignatius Press, 1994.

Barber, Daniel Colucciello. *On Diaspora: Christianity, Religion, and Secularity*. Eugene, OR: Cascade Books, 2011.

Barclay, John M. G. "Paul, the Gift and the Battle over Gentile Circumcision: Revisiting the Logic of Galatians." *Australian Biblical Review* 58 (2010): 36-56.

———. Review of *Paul and the Faithfulness of God*, by N. T. Wright. *Scottish Journal of Theology* 68, no. 2 (May 2015).

Barrett, C. K. *The Gospel According to St John: An Introduction with Commentary and Notes on the Greek Text*. London: SPCK, 1962.

Barth, Karl. *Church Dogmatics*. Edited by G. W. Bromiley and T. F. Torrance. Translated by G. W. Bromiley et. al. 14 vols. Edinburgh: T&T Clark, 1969.

———. *The Epistle to the Romans*. Translated by Edwyn C. Hoskyns. 6th ed. London: Oxford University Press, 1968.

———. *The Göttingen Dogmatics: Instruction in the Christian Religion*. Edited by Hannelotte Reiffen. Translated by Geoffrey W. Bromiley. Vol. 1. Grand Rapids: Eerdmans, 1991.

———. *Letters 1961–1968*. Translated by Geoffrey W. Bromiley. Grand Rapids: Eerdmans, 1981.

———. *Der Römerbrief*. 2nd ed. Zürich: TVZ, 2005.

Bartsch, Hans Werner, ed. *Kerygma and Myth: A Theological Debate*. New York: Harper and Row, 1961.

Bauckham, Richard. *The Climax of Prophecy: Studies on the Book of Revelation*. London: T&T Clark, 1993.

Beale, G. K. *The Book of Revelation: A Commentary on the Greek Text*. The New

International Greek Testament Commentary, edited by I. Howard Marshall and Donald A. Hagner. Grand Rapids: Eerdmans, 1999.

Beker, J. Christiaan. *Paul the Apostle: The Triumph of God in Life and Thought.* Philadelphia: Fortress Press, 1980.

Bentley, Michael. "Past and 'Presence': Revisiting Historical Ontology." *History and Theory* 45 (2006): 349-61.

Bockmuehl, Markus. "Compleat History of the Resurrection: A Dialogue With N. T. Wright." *Journal for the Study of the New Testament* 26, no. 4 (2004): 489-504.

Bonhoeffer, Dietrich. *Act and Being: Transcendental Philosophy and Ontology in Systematic Theology.* Edited by Wayne Whitson Floyd Jr. Translated by H. Martin Rumscheidt. Dietrich Bonhoeffer Works, vol. 2. Minneapolis: Fortress Press, 1996.

———. *Creation and Fall: A Theological Exposition of Genesis 1-3.* Edited by John W. deGruchy. Translated by Douglas Stephen Bax. Dietrich Bonhoeffer Works, vol. 3. Minneaopolis: Fortress Press, 2004.

———. *Discipleship.* Edited by Geffrey B. Kelly and John D. Godsey. Dietrich Bonhoeffer Works, vol. 4. Minneapolis: Fortress Press, 2001.

———. *Ethics.* Edited by Clifford J. Green. Translated by Reinhard Krauss, Charles C. West and Douglass W. Scott. Dietrich Bonhoeffer Works, vol. 6. Minneapolis: Fortress Press, 2005.

———. "Lectures on Christology." In *Berlin: 1932-1933,* edited by Larry L. Rasmussen. Dietrich Bonhoeffer Works, vol. 12. Minneapolis: Fortress Press, 2009.

Bromiley, Geoffrey W. *An Introduction to the Theology of Karl Barth.* Grand Rapids: Eerdmans, 1979.

Brown, Alexandra. Review of *Paul and the Faithfulness of God,* by N. T. Wright. *The Christian Century,* October 16, 2014. www.christiancentury.org /reviews/2014-10/paul-and-faithfulness-god-n-t-wright.

Brunner, Emil, and Karl Barth. *Natural Theology: Comprising "Nature and Grace" by Professor Dr. Emil Brunner and the Reply "No!" by Dr. Karl Barth.* Translated by Peter Fraenkel. Eugene, OR: Wipf and Stock, 2002.

Bultmann, Rudolf. *History and Eschatology: The Gifford Lectures.* Edinburgh: Edinburgh University Press, 1975.

———. *Jesus and the Word.* Translated by Louise Pettibone Smith and Erminie Huntress Lantero. London: Charles Scribner's Sons, 1958.

Burrell, David B., CSC. "*Creatio Ex Nihilo* Recovered." *Modern Theology* 29, no. 2 (2013): 5-21.

Caird, G. B. *The Language and Imagery of the Bible.* London: Duckworth, 1980.

Campbell, Douglas A. *The Deliverance of God: An Apocalyptic Rereading of Justification in Paul*. Grand Rapids: Eerdmans, 2009.

——. "Is Tom Right? An Extended Review of N. T. Wright's *Justification: God's Plan and Paul's Vision.*" *Scottish Journal of Theology* 65, no. 3 (2012): 323-45.

Collingwood, R. G. *An Essay on Metaphysics*. Oxford: Clarendon Press, 1940.

——. *The Idea of History with Lectures 1926–1928*. Edited by Jan van der Dussen. Revised ed. Oxford: Oxford University Press, 1994.

Collins, John J. *The Apocalyptic Imagination: An Introduction to Jewish Apocalyptic Literature*. 2nd ed. Grand Rapids: Eerdmans, 1998.

Cone, James H. *God of the Oppressed*. Revised ed. Maryknoll, NY: Orbis Books, 1997.

Crisp, Oliver. *Divinity and Humanity: The Incarnation Reconsidered*. Cambridge: Cambridge University Press, 2007.

Danker, Frederick William, ed. *A Greek-English Lexicon of the New Testament and Other Early Christian Literature*. 3rd ed. Chicago: University of Chicago Press, 2000.

Davidson, Ivor. "Theologizing the Human Jesus: An Ancient (and Modern) Approach to Christology Reassessed." *International Journal of Systematic Theology* 3, no. 2 (2001): 129-53.

Davis, Joshua B., and Douglas Harink, eds. *Apocalyptic and the Future of Theology: With and Beyond J. Louis Martyn*. Eugene, OR: Cascade Books, 2012.

De Boer, Martinus C. *Galatians: A Commentary*. The New Testament Library. Louisville: Westminster John Knox Press, 2011.

——. "N. T. Wright's Great Story and Its Relationship to Paul's Gospel." *Journal for the Study of Paul and His Letters* 4, no. 1 (2014): 49-57.

——. "Paul, Theologian of God's Apocalypse." *Interpretation* 56, no. 1 (2002): 21-33.

DeJonge, Michael P. *Bonhoeffer's Theological Formation: Berlin, Barth, and Protestant Theology*. Oxford: Oxford University Press, 2012.

Denton, Donald L. Jr. *Historiography and Hermeneutics in Jesus Studies: An Examination of the Work of John Dominic Crossan and Ben F. Meyer*. London: T&T Clark, 2004.

Ebeling, Gerhard. *The Problem of Historicity in the Church and Its Proclamation*. Translated by Grover Foley. Philadelphia: Fortress Press, 1967.

Evans, C. Stephen. *The Historical Christ and the Jesus of Faith: The Incarnational Narrative as History*. Oxford: Clarendon Press, 1996.

——. *Kierkegaard's Fragments and Postscript: The Religious Philosophy of Johannes Climacus*. Atlantic Highlands, NJ: Humanities Press International, 1983.

————. *Passionate Reason: Making Sense of Kierkegaard's Philosophical Fragments.* Bloomington, IN: Indiana University Press, 1992.

Fasolt, Constantin. *The Limits of History.* Chicago: University of Chicago Press, 2004.

Ferguson, Everett. *Baptism in the Early Church: History, Theology, and Liturgy in the First Five Centuries.* Grand Rapids: Eerdmans, 2009.

Frei, Hans W. *The Identity of Jesus Christ: The Hermeneutical Bases of Dogmatic Theology.* Eugene, OR: Cascade Books, 2013.

Gaventa, Beverly Roberts, ed. *Apocalyptic Paul: Cosmos and Anthropos in Romans 5–8.* Waco, TX: Baylor University Press, 2013.

Gaventa, Beverly Roberts. "The Character of God's Faithfulness: A Response to N. T. Wright." *Journal for the Study of Paul and His Letters* 4, no. 1 (2014): 71-79.

————. *Our Mother Saint Paul.* Louisville: Westminster John Knox Press, 2007.

————. "The Singularity of the Gospel Revisited." In *Galatians and Christian Theology: Justification, the Gospel, and Ethics in Paul's Letter,* edited by Scott J. Hafemann, Mark W. Elliot, N. T. Wright and John Frederick. Grand Rapids: Baker Academic, 2014.

Gaventa, Beverly Roberts, and Richard B. Hays. "Seeking the Identity of Jesus: A Rejoinder." *Journal for the Study of the New Testament* 32, no. 3 (2010): 363-70.

Godsey, John D., ed. *Karl Barth's Table Talk.* Richmond, VA: John Knox Press, 1963.

Gunton, Colin. *Enlightenment and Alienation: An Essay Toward a Trinitarian Theology.* Eugene, OR: Wipf and Stock, 2006.

Gutiérrez, Gustavo. *A Theology of Liberation: History, Politics, and Salvation.* Translated by Sister Caridad Inda and John Eagleson. 15th anniversary ed. Maryknoll, NY: Orbis Books, 1988.

Hagner, Donald A. *New Testament Exegesis and Research: A Guide for Seminarians.* Pasadena, CA: Fuller Seminary Press, 1999.

Harink, Douglas. *Paul Among the Postliberals: Pauline Theology Beyond Christendom and Modernity.* Grand Rapids: Brazos Press, 2003.

————. "Time and Politics in Four Commentaries on Romans." In *Paul, Philosophy, and the Theopolitical Vision,* edited by Douglas Harink, 282-312. Eugene, OR: Cascade Books, 2010.

Harnack, Adolf von. *Marcion: The Gospel of the Alien God.* Translated by John E. Steely and Lyle D. Bierma. Eugene, OR: Wipf and Stock, 1990.

Harrisville, Roy A. *Fracture: The Cross as Irreconcileable in the Language and Thought of the Biblical Writers.* Grand Rapids: Eerdmans, 2006.

Harvey, Van Austin. *The Historian and the Believer: The Morality of Historical Knowledge and Christian Belief*. London: SCM Press, 1967.

Hays, Richard B. "Apocalyptic *Poiēsis* in Galatians: Paternity, Passion, and Participation." In *Galatians and Christian Theology: Justification, the Gospel, and Ethics in Paul's Letter*, edited by Scott J. Hafemann, Mark W. Elliot, N. T. Wright and John Frederick. Grand Rapids: Baker Academic, 2014.

———. "Story, History and the Question of Truth." In *Jesus, Paul, and the People of God: A Theological Dialogue With N. T. Wright*, edited by Nicholas Perrin and Richard B. Hays, 41-65. London: SPCK, 2011.

Hoskyns, Edwyn C. *The Fourth Gospel*. Edited by Francis Noel Davy. London: Faber and Faber, 1947.

Howland, Jacob. *Kierkegaard and Socrates: A Study in Philosophy and Faith*. Cambridge: Cambridge University Press, 2006.

Hunsinger, George. *Disruptive Grace: Studies in the Theology of Karl Barth*. Grand Rapids: Eerdmans, 2000.

Israel, Jonathan I. *Democratic Enlightenment: Philosophy, Revolution, and Human Rights 1750–1790*. Oxford: Oxford University Press, 2011.

———. *Radical Enlightenment: Philosophy and the Making of Modernity 1650–1750*. Oxford: Oxfor University Press, 2001.

Jennings, Willie James. *The Christian Imagination: Theology and the Origins of Race*. New Haven: Yale University Press, 2010.

Johnson, Roger A. *The Origins of Demythologizing: Philosophy and Historiography in the Theology of Rudolf Bultmann*. Studies in the History of Religions. Leiden: E. J. Brill, 1974.

Jüngel, Eberhard. *God as the Mystery of the World: On the Foundation of the Theology of the Crucified One in the Dispute Between Theism and Atheism*. Translated by Darrell L. Guder. Grand Rapids: Eerdmans, 1983.

———. *God's Being Is in Becoming: The Trinitarian Being of God in the Theology of Karl Barth. A Paraphrase*. Translated by John Webster. Grand Rapids: Eerdmans, 2001.

———. *Karl Barth: A Theological Legacy*. Translated by Garrett E. Paul. Philadelphia: The Westminster Press, 1986.

Kant, Immanuel. *Critique of Pure Reason*. Translated by Paul Guyer and Allen W. Wood. Cambridge: Cambridge University Press, 1998.

Käsemann, Ernst. *Commentary on Romans*. Translated by Geoffrey Bromiley. 4th ed. Grand Rapids: Eerdmans, 1994.

———. *New Testament Questions of Today*. Translated by W. J. Montague and

Wilfred F. Bunge. New Testament Library. London: SCM Press, 1969.

———. *On Being a Disciple of the Crucified Nazarene: Unpublished Lectures and Sermons.* Edited by Rudolf Landau and Wolfgang Kraus. Translated by Roy A. Harrisville. Grand Rapids: Eerdmans, 2010.

Kerr, Nathan R. *Christ, History and Apocalyptic: The Politics of Christian Mission.* Eugene, OR: Cascade Books, 2009.

Kierkegaard, Søren. *Concluding Unscientific Postscript to Philosophical Fragments.* Translated by Howard V. Hong and Edna H. Hong. Kierkegaard's Writings, vol. 12.1. Princeton, NJ: Princeton University Press, 1992.

———. *Kierkegaard's Journals and Notebooks.* Edited by Niels Jørgen Cappelørn et al. Vol. 4. Princeton, NJ: Princeton University Press, 2011.

———. *Philosophical Fragments/Johannes Climacus.* Translated by Howard V. Hong and Edna H. Hong. Kierkegaard's Writings, vol. 7. Princeton, NJ: Princeton University Press, 1985.

———. *Practice in Christianity.* Edited by Howard V. Hong and Edna H. Hong. Translated by Howard V. Hong and Edna H. Hong. Kierkegaard's Writings, vol. 20. Princeton, NJ: Princeton University Press, 1991.

Koch, Klaus. *The Rediscovery of Apocalyptic.* Translated by Margaret Kohl. Studies in Biblical Theology, Second Series, vol. 22. London: SCM Press LTD, 1972.

Kuhn, Thomas S. *The Structure of Scientific Revolutions.* Chicago: University of Chicago Press, 1996.

Le Donne, Anthony. *The Historiographical Jesus: Memory, Typology, and the Son of David.* Waco, TX: Baylor University Press, 2009.

Lessing, Gotthold Ephraim. *Philosophical and Theological Writings.* Translated by H. B. Nisbet. Cambridge Texts in the History of Philosophy. Cambridge: Cambridge University Press, 2005.

Lewis, Alan E. "Apocalypse and Parousia: The Anguish of Theology from Now till Kingdom Come." *Austin Seminary Bulletin* 103, no. 8 (1988): 31-45.

———. "The Burial of God: Rupture and Resumption as the Story of Salvation." *The Scottish Journal of Theology* 40, no. 3 (1987): 335-62.

Lonergan, Bernard. *Insight: A Study of Human Understanding.* London: Longmans, 1968.

———. *Method in Theology.* 2nd ed. London: Longman & Todd, 1973.

Lowe, Walter. "Prospects for a Postmodern Christian Theology: Apocalyptic Without Reserve." *Modern Theology* 15, no. 1 (1999): 17-24.

———. "Why We Need Apocalyptic." *Scottish Journal of Theology* 63, no. 1 (2010): 41-53.

MacKinnon, Donald. *Borderlands of Theology and Other Essays*. Eugene, OR: Wipf and Stock, 2011.

———. *Explorations in Theology 5*. Eugene, OR: Wipf and Stock, 1979.

———. *Philosophy and the Burden of Theological Honesty: A Donald MacKinnon Reader*. Edited by John McDowell. London: T&T Clark, 2011.

Martyn, J. Louis. *Galatians: A New Translation with Introduction and Commentary*. The Anchor Yale Bible, vol. 33A. New Haven: Yale Universty Press, 1997.

———. *Theological Issues in the Letters of Paul*. Edited by John Barclay, Joel Marcus and John Riches. Studies of the New Testament and Its World. Edinburgh: T&T Clark, 1997.

May, Gerhard. *Creatio Ex Nihilo: The Doctrine of "Creation out of Nothing" in Early Christian Thought*. Translated by A. S. Worrall. London: T&T Clark, 2004.

Meyer, Ben F. *The Aims of Jesus*. Edited by Dikran Y. Hadidian. Princeton Theological Monograph Series, vol. 48. Eugene, OR: Pickwick Publications, 2002.

———. *Critical Realism and the New Testament*. Princeton Theological Monograph Series. Eugene, OR: Pickwick Publications, 1989.

———. *Reality and Illusion in New Testament Scholarship: A Primer in Critical Realist Hermeneutics*. Collegeville, MN: The Liturgical Press, 1994.

———. "Resurrection as Humanly Intelligible Destiny." *Ex Auditu* (1993): 13.

Moltmann, Jürgen. *The Coming of God: Christian Eschatology*. Translated by Margaret Kohl. Minneapolis: Fortress Press, 1996.

———. *Theology of Hope: On the Ground and the Implications of a Christian Eschatology*. Translated by James W. Leitch. London: SCM Press, 2002.

Morse, Christopher. *The Difference Heaven Makes: Rehearing the Gospel as News*. London: T&T Clark, 2010.

———. *Not Every Spirit: A Dogmatics of Christian Disbelief*. 2nd ed. New York: T&T Clark, 2009.

Murdock, William R. "History and Revelation in Jewish Apocalypticism." *Interpretation* 21 (1967): 167-87.

Newman, Carey C., ed. *Jesus and the Restoration of Israel: A Critical Assessment of N. T. Wright's* Jesus and the Victory of God. Downers Grove, IL: InterVarsity Press, 1999.

Niiniluoto, Ilkka. *Critical Scientific Realism*. Oxford: Oxford University Press, 1999.

O'Donovan, Oliver. *Resurrection and Moral Order: An Outline for Evangelical Ethics*. 2nd ed. Grand Rapids: Eerdmans, 1994.

Osborn, Eric. *Irenaeus of Lyons*. Cambridge: Cambridge University Press, 2001.

Perrin, Nicholas, and Richard B. Hays, eds. *Jesus, Paul and the People of God: A Theological Dialogue with N. T. Wright*. London: SPCK, 2011.

Portier-Young, Anathea E. *Apocalypse Against Empire: Theologies of Resistance in Early Judaism*. Grand Rapids: Eerdmans, 2011.

Quash, Ben. *Theology and the Drama of History*. Cambridge Studies in Christian Doctrine. Cambridge: Cambridge University Press, 2005.

Rad, Gerhard von. *Old Testament Theology: The Theology of Israel's Historical Traditions*. Translated by D. M. G. Stalker. 2 vols. New York: Harper & Row, 1962–65.

Rae, Murray A. *Kierkegaard's Vision of the Incarnation: By Faith Transformed*. Oxford: Clarendon Press, 1997.

Rahner, Karl. "Immanent and Transcendent Consummation of the World." In *Theological Investigations*, vol. 10. New York: Seabury, 1978.

Roberts, Robert C. *Faith, Reason, and History: Rethinking Kierkegaard's Philosophical Fragments*. Macon, GA: Mercer University Press, 1986.

Robinette, Brian D. "The Difference Nothing Makes: *Creatio Ex Nihilo*, Resurrection, and Divine Gratuity." *Theological Studies* 72 (2011): 525-57.

Robinson, James M. "Hermeneutic Since Barth." In *The New Hermeneutic*, edited by James M. Robinson and John B. Cobb Jr., 1-77. New York: Harper & Row, 1964.

Rowe, C. Kavin. *World Upside Down: Reading Acts in the Graeco-Roman Age*. Oxford: Oxford Unversity Press, 2010.

Rowland, Christopher. *The Open Heaven: A Study of Apocalyptic in Judaism and Early Christianity*. London: SPCK, 1982.

Schaff, Philip, and Henry Wace, eds. *Cyril of Jerusalem, Gregory Nazianzen*. Nicene and Post-Nicene Fathers, vol. 7. Peabody, MA: Hendrickson Publishers, 2012.

Schneiders, Sandra M. "Born Anew." *Theology Today* 44, no. 2 (1987): 189-96.

Schröter, Jens. *From Jesus to the New Testament: Early Christian Theology and the Origin of the New Testament Canon*. Edited by Wayne Coppins and Simon Gathercole. Translated by Wayne Coppins. Baylor-Mohr Siebeck Studies in Early Christianity. Waco, TX: Baylor University Press, 2013.

Schuster, Ekkehard, and Reinhold Boschert-Kimmig. *Hope Against Hope: Johann Baptist Metz and Elie Wiesel Speak Out on the Holocaust*. Translated by J. Matthew Ashley. New York: Paulist Press, 1999.

Scott, Ian W. *Implicit Epistemology in the Letters of Paul: Story, Experience and the Spirit*. Tübingen: Mohr Siebeck, 2006.

Sokolowski, Robert. *The God of Faith and Reason: Foundations of Christian*

Theology. Washington, DC: The Catholic University of America Press, 1995.

Spinoza, Benedict de. *Ethics*. Translated by Edwin Curley. London: Penguin Books, 1996.

Stanley, Timothy. *Protestant Metaphysics After Karl Barth and Martin Heidegger*. Eugene, OR: Cascade Books, 2010.

Stout, Jeffrey. *Ethics After Babel: The Languages of Morals and Their Discontents*. Princeton, NJ: Princeton University Press, 2001.

Taubes, Jacob. *From Cult to Culture: Fragments Toward a Critique of Historical Reason*. Edited by Charlotte Elisheva Fonrobert and Emir Engel. Stanford, CA: Stanford University Press, 2010.

———. *Occidental Eschatology*. Translated by David Ratmoko. Stanford, CA: Stanford University Press, 2009.

———. *The Politcal Theology of Paul*. Edited by Aleida Assmann and Jan Assmann. Translated by Dana Hollander. Stanford, CA: Stanford University Press, 2004.

Taylor, Charles. *Sources of the Self: The Making of the Modern Identity*. Cambridge, MA: Cambridge University Press, 1992.

Thielman, Frank. *From Plight to Solution: A Jewish Framework for Understanding Paul's View of the Law in Galatians and Romans*. Supplements to Novum Testamentum, vol. 61. Leiden: E. J. Brill, 1989.

Thistelton, Anthony C. *The Two Horizons: New Testament Hermeneutics and Philosophical Description with Special Reference to Heidegger, Bultmann, Gadamer, and Wittgenstein*. Grand Rapids: Eerdmans, 1980.

Thompson, Marianne Meye. "Word of God, Messiah of Israel, Savior of the World: Learning the Identity of Jesus from the Gospel of John." In *Seeking the Identity of Jesus: A Pilgrimage*, edited by Beverly Roberts Gaventa and Richard B. Hays, 166-79. Grand Rapids: Eerdmans, 2008.

Torrance, Alan J. "Analytic Theology and the Reconciled Mind: The Significance of History." *Journal of Analytic Theology* 1, no. 1 (2013): 30-44.

———. "*Creatio Ex Nihilo* and the Spatio-Temporal Dimensions, with Special Reference to Jürgen Moltmann and D. C. Williams." In *The Doctrine of Creation: Essays in Dogmatics, History and Philosophy*, edited by Colin E. Gunton, 83-103. London: T&T Clark, 2004.

Torrance, T. F. *The Christian Doctrine of God: One Being Three Persons*. London: T&T Clark, 1996.

———. *God and Rationality*. Edinburgh: T&T Clark, 1997.

———. *Incarnation: The Person and Life of Christ*. Edited by Robert T. Walker. Downers Grove, IL: IVP Academic, 2008.

————. *Karl Barth: An Introduction to His Early Theology, 1910–1931*. London: SCM Press, 1962.

————. *Theological Science*. London: Oxford University Press, 1969.

————. *Theology in Reconstruction*. London: SCM Press, 1965.

————. *Transformation and Convergence in the Frame of Knowledge: Explorations in the Interrelations of Scientific and Theological Enterprise*. Belfast: Christian Journals Limited, 1984.

Troeltsch, Ernst. "Historiography." In *Encyclopedia of Religion and Ethics*, edited by James Hastings, 716-23. New York: Charles Scribner's Sons, 1914.

Walsh, Brian J., and Sylvia C. Keesmaat. *Colossians Remixed: Subverting the Empire*. Downers Grove, IL: InterVarsity Press, 2004.

Walsh, Sylvia. "Echoes of Absurdity: The Offended Consciousness and the Absolute Paradox in Kierkegaard's Philosophical Fragents." In *International Kierkegaard Commentary: Philosophical Fragments and Johannes Climacus*, edited by Robert L. Perkins. Macon, GA: Mercer University Press, 1994.

Webster, John. *Holy Scripture: A Dogmatic Sketch*. Current Issues in Theology. Edited by Iain Torrance. Cambridge: Cambridge University Press, 2003.

Weder, Hans. *Das Kreuz Jesu*. Götingen: Vandenhoeck & Ruprecht, 1981.

Welker, Michael. *God the Spirit*. Translated by John F. Hoffmeyer. Minneapolis: Fortress Press, 1994.

Wells, Samuel. *Improvisation: The Drama of Christian Ethics*. Grand Rapids: Brazos Press, 2004.

Wright, N. T. *The Climax of the Covenant: Christ and the Law in Pauline Theology*. Minneapolis: Fortress Press, 1993.

————. *How God Became King: The Forgotten Story of the Gospels*. New York: HarperOne, 2012.

————. "In Grateful Dialogue: A Response." In *Jesus and the Restoration of Israel: A Critical Assessment of N. T. Wright's* Jesus and the Victory of God, edited by Carey C. Newman, 244-77. Downers Grove: InterVarsity Press, 1999.

————. *Jesus and the Victory of God*. Christian Origins and the Question of God, vol. 2. Minneapolis: Fortress Press, 1996.

————. *Justification: God's Plan and Paul's Vision*. Downers Grove, IL: IVP Academic, 2009.

————. *The Kingdom New Testament: A Contemporary Translation*. New York: HarperOne, 2011.

————. *The New Testament and the People of God*. Christian Origins and the Question of God, vol 1. London: SPCK, 1992.

———. *Paul and His Recent Interpreters*. Minneapolis: Fortress Press, 2015.

———. *Paul and the Faithfulness of God*. Christian Origins and the Question of God, vol. 4. Minneapolis: Fortress Press, 2013.

———. "Paul in Current Anglophone Scholarship." *The Expository Times* 123, no. 8 (2012): 367-81.

———. *Paul: In Fresh Perspective*. Minneapolis: Fortress Press, 2009.

———. "Resurrection: From Theology to Music and Back Again." In *Sounding the Depths: Theology Through the Arts*, edited by Jeremy Begbie, 193-202. London: SCM Press, 2002.

———. *The Resurrection of the Son of God*. Christian Origins and the Question of God, vol. 3. Minneapolis: Fortress Press, 2003.

———. "Right Standing, Right Understanding, and Wright Misunderstanding: A Response." *Journal for the Study of Paul and His Letters* 4, no. 1 (2014): 87-103.

———. *Scripture and the Authority of God: How to Read the Bible Today*. New York: HarperOne, 2011.

———. *Surprised by Hope*. New York: HarperOne, 2008.

———. *What Saint Paul Really Said: Was Paul of Tarsus the Real Founder of Christianity?* Grand Rapids: Eerdmans, 1997.

Yoder, John Howard. *The Original Revolution: Essays on Christian Pacifism*. Scottdale, PA: Herald Press, 2003.

———. *The Politics of Jesus: Vicit Agnus Noster*. 2nd ed. Grand Rapids: Eerdmans, 1994.

Ziegler, Philip G. "Dietrich Bonhoeffer—an Ethics of God's Apocalypse?" *Modern Theology* 23, no. 4 (2007): 579-94.

Zimany, Roland Daniel. *Vehicle for God: The Metaphorical Theology of Eberhard Jüngel*. Macon, GA: Mercer University Press, 1994.

Author and Subject Index

abstraction, problem of, 60

actualism, 106

anachronism, 177-78

anhypostasia, anhypostatic, 141, 142, 143-46

apocalypse, 157, 169
  of Jesus Christ, 19, 112, 118-19, 120-23, 126-28, 136, 142, 155, 169, 215, 226-27, 231, 237, 239, 240-41, 248, 250-51, 253-56, 259-64, 269-70
  as literary genre, 191, 194, 203, 228, 228n2, 229-31, 233-34, 237-38, 240, 248-49, 255, 259-60
  as revelation, 119-21, 165, 168-69, 215, 226, 249-51

apocalyptic, 157, 168, 236, 247, 253, 255, 259
  as describing Karl Barth's theology, 138
  event, 122, 127, 132, 168, 201, 231-32, 237, 244, 246, 248, 254, 270-71
  as literary genre, 18n7, 19, 113, 119n29, 120, 183, 207, 228-30, 238-39, 247, 270
  logic, 108, 140-42, 152-53, 194, 257
  as movement, 142, 144, 146, 165, 241
  Pauline, 157, 193, 229, 236-37, 245, 258
  theologians, 120, 156, 231, 237, 241, 260
  theology, 18, 18n7, 19, 108, 112-29, 132, 141, 152-53, 155-56, 166, 171, 182-83, 189, 196, 207, 226, 230, 260, 263
  worldview, 102n125, 134, 228-29, 236, 242, 246, 248-49, 254, 261
  N. T. Wright's account of, 166-71, 192, 225-26, 231-48, 258

apocalypticism, 192-93

Aquinas, Thomas, 218

Aristotle, 97

ascension, 127, 165, 249, 253

Athanasius, 198

atonement, 128, 130-31, 133, 135, 146, 171, 238, 256

authority, 25, 28, 124, 216, 224

Balthasar, Hans Urs von, 179-80, 186, 188-90, 204, 253

baptism, 103, 109, 148-53, 155, 168, 172, 194-96, 198, 202, 224-25, 232, 250, 260, 265

Barclay, John M. G., 117n21, 218n102, 235, 240

Barrett, C. K., 100

Barth, Karl, 18, 29, 32n37, 65, 68, 77, 95-96, 116-17, 120, 122-24, 128, 130, 134-39, 143-46, 150, 159, 165, 170, 175, 185-86, 189, 212, 241, 262

Beale, G. K., 203

Beker, J. Christiaan, 229, 248, 250, 257n74

Bentley, Michael, 223n106

Boer, Martinus de, 114, 120, 127, 157, 192, 232-33, 235, 238, 248

Bonhoeffer, Dietrich, 18, 133, 139-40, 143n4, 153, 160-61, 189-98, 203, 214, 221, 223

Borg, Marcus, 59, 75

Bristow, William, 39

Brown, Alexandra, 234

Brown, Colin, 27

Brown, James, 71-72

Brunner, Emil, 95, 120

Bultmann, Rudolf, 24n11, 26n17, 27, 29, 52, 167-68, 176, 206n72, 260

Burrell, David B., 161

Caird, G. B., 234n17

Campbell, Douglas A., 113, 114n14, 120, 232-33, 235, 238

Christology, 18, 24, 39, 57-59, 80, 108-9, 128, 141-42, 149, 160, 164, 171, 186n27, 198, 250 church, 21, 23-24, 31, 59, 61, 74, 103, 109, 151, 158, 176, 182, 194, 212, 214-15, 222, 224, 228-31, 239, 243, 261-62, 264, 266, 268

Climacus, Johannes, 67, 83-94, 97-98, 101, 105-6, 134n72, 166, 186, 209

Collingwood, R. G., 47, 173-75, 183, 205-8

Collins, John J., 113n8, 118, 228-30, 238

condition, the, 85-108, 115, 119, 133, 135, 184, 186, 202, 270

contextualization, 119, 121-22

creatio ex nihilo, 145, 153, 159-67, 196, 248

creation, 41, 105, 126, 139, 152-56, 196, 251, 253-54, 257
    doctrine of, 109, 128, 141-72
    new, 221-22, 225-57, 232, 243-48, 254, 260, 265-66, 273
    order, 153-56, 217, 219n102

creator-creature distinction, 97, 99

Crisp, Oliver, 144n9, 145n17

critical realism (CRw). *See* epistemology
    defined, 42

cross, 103, 142, 151-52, 157, 168-69, 185, 188-91, 194-97, 202, 204, 206, 212, 216, 220, 222-23, 226, 231-32, 237, 251-54, 257-58, 260, 263-66, 269, 271-73

death, 149-52, 190, 194-95, 197, 202-3, 252-53, 258, 260, 264-67
    history of, 190-91, 196, 223, 247, 269-70
    of Jesus, 24, 126, 150-52, 157, 185, 190, 195, 220, 223, 232, 249, 251-53, 255-57, 260, 263, 265
    logic of, 150, 152, 197, 222, 224, 269-70
    and resurrection, 103, 109, 149, 151, 155, 165, 168-69, 184, 193, 216, 224, 226, 236-37, 244, 249-51, 253-54, 260, 272

Denton, Donald L., 34

Descartes, Renee, 40

discipleship, 133, 150, 168, 214, 265

ditch, ugly, broad, 16-17, 28, 30, 71, 181

doctrine, 23-25, 27, 30-31, 38-39, 60-62, 83, 180

le Donne, Anthony, 175-76n8

Dorrien, Gary, 26

drama, 224, 226, 239, 247, 258

dualism, 35, 41, 47, 56, 71-74, 82, 153, 191, 193, 196

eisegesis, 61

election, 116, 138-40, 153, 159, 170, 189, 200, 263, 266, 268

Emmanuel, 59, 142, 184, 186

empiricism, 25-26, 43, 72

enhistoric, 200-202, 226, 232, 253, 264

enhypostasia, enhypostatic, 109, 141-49, 165, 199, 201-2, 218-20, 226, 264, 272

Enlightenment, 21-27, 29-43, 181, 205, 209

epistemology, 53, 62, 67-68, 71-72, 82, 85, 88, 109-10, 113, 126, 205, 217, 235
    apocalyptic, 233
    coherentist, coherence theory of, 46, 54
    of contact, 42-47, 49, 74, 112, 131, 210
    critical realist, 43, 46
    and humility, 33
    of love (*agape*), 45, 61n151, 247-48
    Paul's, 114, 117-18, 120n32, 211, 231, 233, 237, 240-47, 253
    realist, 38, 40, 44, 46
    relational, 35, 42
    theological, 78, 80, 87, 103, 106-7, 109, 117, 119, 131, 156-57, 181-83, 206, 210, 213, 215, 219, 221-22, 236
    N. T. Wright's, 40-60, 65, 66n1, 74-77, 103-4, 141, 154, 213, 216, 255

eschatology, 229, 234n17, 250, 271

eschaton, 193

Evans, C. Stephen, 86, 91, 207-8, 211-12

exegesis, 60n150, 61-63, 108n1, 123-24, 190, 212, 230, 270

existentialism, 27

fall, the, 83, 190n42

Fasolt, Constantin, 176-79

fideism, 117, 241

Gaventa, Beverly, 63, 120, 235-38, 248-49, 263n91

Geschichte, 175-76n8, 191

Hagner, Donald A., 124

Harink, Douglas, 114, 120, 123-24, 126, 137n77, 242, 246, 261n86, 263

Harrisville, Roy A., 254-56, 263, 264n94

Harvey, Anthony, 58

Harvey, Van Austin, 207n75

Hays, Richard, 63, 130n57, 219n103, 260, 263

Hegel, Georg Willhelm Friedrich, 26-27, 84n61, 86, 88, 196, 199

Heidegger, Martin, 27

hermeneutic, hermeneutics, 24, 66n1, 108-12, 115-20, 122, 124-25, 134, 141, 167, 175n8, 180, 184, 222, 224, 247, 249

historian, 20-22, 31-32, 34n44, 35, 47-50, 52, 60-61, 66, 68, 148, 175-85, 195, 202, 204-9, 218, 221-23, 241, 272-73

    biblical, 41, 62

    positivist, 36

historical criticism, 30, 47, 123

historical Jesus, 23, 24

    quest for, 22, 27, 30, 38, 186, 270

    Third Quest, 57

Historie, 175-76n8

historiography, 19, 35-36, 65, 69n8, 122, 129, 173-74, 176-79, 181-83, 185, 188, 204-6, 210, 212, 214, 222, 233, 252, 271

history

    contingent truths of, 16, 28-29

    end of, 185, 190, 193-94, 197-98, 203, 226, 232, 257, 258-60, 264, 271

    of Israel, 119, 134, 137-38, 158, 167, 200-201, 220, 225, 226, 232, 239, 241, 260, 267

    rupture in, 28, 190, 264, 267

Holy Spirit, 81n54, 101-3, 106, 109, 131, 133, 146-49, 152, 168, 172, 182-83, 186, 189, 202, 210, 212-14

homoousion, 147, 215

humanity, 44, 82, 94, 96-98, 105, 107, 109, 126, 130-32, 138, 140, 145, 157-58, 165, 196, 198-203, 215, 219, 251

    of Christ, 39, 60-61, 138, 143-44, 146-51, 172, 181, 186, 190, 197, 220, 255, 264

Hume, David, 71

Howland, Jacob, 91-92

Hoskyns, Edwyn C., 101

hypostatic union, 138, 142-45, 147, 150, 181, 196, 255

hypothesis and verification, 44-45, 47, 50, 55, 63, 178, 181

idealism, 25-43, 73, 79, 84n61, 86, 88, 181, 261

immanence, 30, 98, 130, 145, 163, 197, 208, 209, 255

incarnation, 54, 81, 91, 93-94, 98, 105, 137, 142-44, 147-48, 152, 162, 165-66, 184-85, 188-89, 197, 200-201, 215-16, 242, 251, 254, 272

invasion, 127, 142, 156-58, 240, 162

Irenaeus, 163

Israel, 74, 119, 126, 134, 137-38, 158, 161n46, 167, 169-71, 201, 231-32, 235-36, 238-39, 242, 249, 259-64, 266-69

Jennings, Willie James, 201, 268-69

Jüngel, Eberhard, 110n3, 116-17, 143n3, 145n15, 164-65

Kant, Immanuel, 26, 29, 37-40, 71-73

Käsemann, Ernst, 120n32, 127, 167-68, 171, 229

Keesmat, Sylvia C., 242n39

Kerr, Nathan R., 114n12, 115, 129, 131n63, 139n86, 257-58

Kierkegaard, Søren, 17-18, 66-67, 76, 83-84, 86, 89-90, 92, 95-99, 102n127, 105, 109, 125, 137, 149, 166, 184, 186, 187n29, 189, 196, 200, 209, 211, 214, 242

kingdom of God, 39, 265

knowledge

    actuality of, 78

    as contact, 42-47, 185

    objectivity of, 78-79

    possibility of, 80

    See also epistemology

Koch, Klaus, 269

Koopman, Colin, 69n8

Kuhn, Thomas S., 36, 255

Lessing, Goothold Ephraim, 16-17, 26n17, 27-30, 166, 180-81

Lewis, Alan E., 125, 189-90, 197

Logos, 144, 147, 186, 188, 215, 250-51

Lonergan, Bernard, 43, 66, 115

Lowe, Walter, 121

MacKinnon, Donald, 121, 124, 152-53, 251

MacMurray, John, 72, 74, 76

Marcionite, 134, 156

Martyn, J. Louis, 18, 113-16, 118, 120, 123-25, 137, 157, 158, 168-69, 171, 192, 194, 226, 232-33, 235-36, 238-40, 243, 248, 262

Melanchthon, Philip, 24, 28-29, 38

Messiah, 39, 58, 101, 103, 105, 138, 167, 168, 170-71, 183, 185, 191, 202, 215, 220, 223, 225-26, 232, 236, 239, 245, 249-50, 255-58, 260, 262, 264, 266-67

metaphysics, 68-69, 71, 83, 85n64, 125, 153, 166

methodological naturalism, 206-13

Meyer, Ben F., 43, 48-49, 52, 66, 115, 208

Miller, Alexander, 49

Murdock, William R., 192-93

Nachdenken, 233, 236

Nazianzus, Gregory, 144

Niiniluoto, Ilkka, 68

novum, 129, 132, 134-40, 196, 248, 255

objectivity, 15, 21, 33, 35, 38, 67, 73, 78-81, 85-86, 106, 117, 119, 126, 128, 241

   of God, 67, 79, 83-85, 99, 105, 107, 110, 116, 126, 166, 173

   in Kierkegaard (Climacus), 88-89, 93, 98-99, 105

   of knowledge, 78-80, 87, 105, 122

O'Donovan, Oliver, 154-56, 160, 217

Osborn, Eric, 161, 163n55

Pannenberg, Wolfhart, 229

paradox, 91-94, 102n127, 215

parousia, 132, 145, 157, 232, 248, 252-53, 270

Paul, 18-19, 101-3, 113-14, 116-18, 120-21, 123-26, 134, 137n77, 139, 149-51, 168-70, 192-94, 198, 209, 221, 225, 229-30, 232, 235-39, 243-47, 249-51, 253-55, 263-64

   See also epistemology; theology

Pauline theology. See theology: Pauline

phenomenalism, 37-38, 40-41

Piper, John, 60n150

Plato, 90

Polanyi, Michael, 36, 42-43

Portier-Young, Anathea E., 118, 192, 230, 259

positivism, 36-37, 38, 40-41

postmodernity/ism, 15, 21, 32-33, 38

pragmatism, 69

praxis, 44, 51, 59, 224

predestination, 188

pro me, 23-24, 38, 40

prodigal son, 32, 272

Protestant Reformation, 22-25, 29, 33, 35, 38, 41, 80, 176, 199

Rae, Murray, 30, 91

Rahner, Karl, 163

Räisänen, Heikki, 26n17

recapitulation, 188

Reimarus, Hermann Samuel, 16, 27-31

resurrection, 75n29, 103, 109, 126, 139, 149-52, 154-56, 159-61, 163, 165, 168-69, 184, 189-90, 193-97, 216-26, 236-37, 244-47, 249-58, 265-67

revelation, 29, 51-53, 55, 63, 65-66, 81, 83-84, 91-93, 95, 103, 105-6, 108-9, 111-12, 114-20, 122, 125-29, 132, 134, 138, 140-42, 145, 149, 153-55, 160, 164, 168, 170-71, 183, 191, 193, 210-15, 220, 226, 229, 231, 237-38, 241, 245, 247-49, 254, 259, 261, 263

Revelation (book of), 203, 228, 234, 238

Robbins, J. Wesley, 69n9

Robinette, Brian D., 163

Rowe, C. Kavin, 151

Rowland, Christopher, 113, 118, 229-30, 238

Rudd, Anthony, 91

rupture, 19, 24, 28, 30, 100, 131-32, 136, 139, 141, 151, 155, 171, 188-90, 201, 231, 246, 248, 253, 255, 260, 264, 267

Schillebeeckx, Edward, 58n141

Schleiermacher, Friedrich D. E., 184
Schweitzer, Albert, 30
scientific method, 36, 44
sin, 82-84, 90, 96-97, 99, 105, 116, 137,
    139-40, 145, 150-51, 158, 166, 171, 188, 191,
    195-96, 236, 238, 257
    See also fall
Sokolowski, Robert, 66
sola scriptura, 25
soteriology, 18, 24, 60n150, 80, 105, 108-9,
    126-29, 156-57, 162, 164, 171, 248
de Spinoza, Benedict, 27, 30
spirit, 111
    See also Holy Spirit
stories, 23-24, 34-35, 42, 45-47, 49-55,
    60-61, 167, 175, 254, 269, 271
Stout, Jeffrey, 15
Strauss, David Friedrich, 27, 29
subject-object distinction, 72-74
subjectivism, 26, 31, 38-40, 46, 48
subjectivity, 33, 37, 40, 67, 82, 84, 86-89, 93,
    99, 105, 106-8, 110, 115, 119, 125, 127-29,
    131, 132n68, 140-41, 147-49, 166, 178-79,
    253
    truth is, 86-89
supersessionism, 114, 240-41, 261-63,
    266-68
Taylor, Charles, 224
theology
    apocalyptic (*see* apocalyptic:
        theology)
    German, 29, 175n8

New Testament, 39
    Pauline, 62n153, 114, 157, 180, 198, 201,
        210, 231, 234, 236-37, 241, 245, 258
    Protestant, 27, 38, 168
    scientific, 76-83
Thielman, Frank, 116
Thompson, Marianne Meye, 100-101
Torrance, Alan J., 56n134, 60n149, 125,
    161n52
Torrance, T. F., 66-67, 72, 74, 76-86, 88-92,
    96, 98-99, 104-6, 108-9, 128, 142-46, 149,
    161, 181, 198, 213-16, 219-20
transcendence, 51-52, 98, 115, 145, 163, 208,
    255
Troeltsch, Ernst, 16
Walsh, Brian J., 242n39
Webster, John, 110-11, 122, 143
Welker, Michael, 266-67
Witherington, Ben, III, 58n143
worldview, 20, 33-35, 44-57, 59, 61-63, 67,
    69, 74, 78, 111-13, 115, 118-21, 125, 129-30,
    135, 153, 167, 169, 175, 178-81, 206-9, 211,
    213-14, 216, 218, 224, 228-34, 236-37,
    239-42, 245-51, 253-56, 258, 261, 270, 272
    apocalyptic (*see* apocalyptic:
        worldview)
    biblical, 62-63
    Paul's, 167, 169, 211, 233, 237, 242, 245
Wrede, William, 26n17
Yoder, John Howard, 139, 223, 257-58
Ziegler, Philip G., 114, 127

Scripture Index

OLD TESTAMENT

Genesis
4:1-16, 191

Psalms
73, 192n47

Isaiah
55:10-11, 111

Jeremiah
31:31-34, 170

Ezekiel
37:1-14, 266

Daniel
2:31-45, 191

NEW TESTAMENT

Matthew
16:13-17, 214
27:46b, 267
28:20b, 182

Mark
1:17, 214

Luke
1:23, 142

John
1, 52
1:3, 162
1:5, 8-9, 101
1:14a, 145
1:31, 33, 102
1:33-34, 102
1:45b, 171
1:50-51, 171
3:1-21, 99-103
3:2-3, 100
3:3, 101, 131
3:5, 101, 103
3:6, 102
3:16, 164
3:19, 101
3:19-21, 101
3:20, 101
12:35, 101
18:36, 101
21:22, 214

Acts
1:8a, 182
10, 11, 15, 268
10:47, 269

Romans
4:17, 161
5:12-21, 146
6:1-11, 149
6:3-4, 149
6:4, 99

6:5, 150, 252, 265
6:6, 150
6:7, 150
6:9, 150
6:12, 151
8:17, 155
8:18-25, 155
9–11, 200n63
11:17-24, 200n63
11:31b, 267

1 Corinthians
11:25, 170
11:26, 252
11:26b, 264
15:20-23, 45-49, 146

2 Corinthians
5:1-5, 155
5:16-17, 243
5:16-18a, 139
5:17, 102
11:2-3, 225

Galatians
1:1, 123
1:4, 102
1:12, 112, 123
2:19-20, 170
2:19b-20a, 249
2:20b, 250
3:22, 158
4:3-5, 157

4:4, 157
6:14, 193

Ephesians
2:6, 100
2:10, 266

Philippians
3:8, 244

Colossians
1:13-24, 265
1:15-18, 161
1:15-20, 162
1:18, 266
3:1, 99-100
3:2, 195

Hebrews
4:12, 111

1 Peter
1:3-5, 155
1:3b, 103

Revelation
1:1, 112
5:1-3, 6-10, 203
6:9, 203
6:10, 252
8, 203

New Explorations in Theology

Theology is flourishing in dynamic and unexpected ways in the twenty-first century. Scholars are increasingly recognizing the global character of the church, freely crossing old academic boundaries and challenging previously entrenched interpretations. Despite living in a culture of uncertainty, both young and senior scholars today are engaged in hopeful and creative work in the areas of systematic, historical, practical and philosophical theology. New Explorations in Theology provides a platform for cutting-edge research in these fields.

In an age of media proliferation and academic oversaturation, there is a need to single out the best new monographs. IVP Academic is committed to publishing constructive works that advance key theological conversations. We look for projects that investigate new areas of research, stimulate fruitful dialogue, and attend to the diverse array of contexts and audiences in our increasingly pluralistic world. IVP Academic is excited to make this work available to scholars, students and general readers who are seeking fresh new insights for the future of Christian theology.

DISTINCTIVES OF NEW EXPLORATIONS IN THEOLOGY:

- Best new monographs from young and senior scholars
- Volumes explore systematic, historical, practical and philosophical theology

FUTURE VOLUMES INCLUDE:

- *Karl Barth's Infralapsarian Theology: Origins and Development, 1920–1953*, Shao Kai Tseng
- *A Shared Mercy: Karl Barth on Forgiveness and the Church*, Jon Coutts

Finding the Textbook You Need

The IVP Academic Textbook Selector
is an online tool for instantly finding the IVP books
suitable for over 250 courses across 24 disciplines.

ivpacademic.com